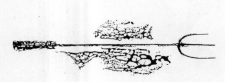 *Sunset*
BARBECUE
COOK BOOK

Happy Cooking John.
Pleasant Eating Anne.

Muriel & alwyn.

June 26th. 1965

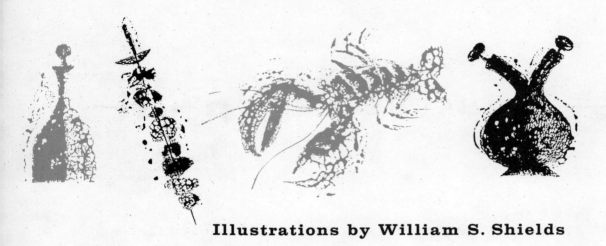

Illustrations by William S. Shields

Sunset BARBECUE COOK BOOK

By the editors of Sunset Books and Sunset Magazine

LANE BOOK COMPANY • **Menlo Park, California**

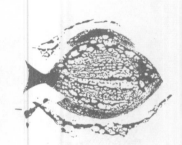

Library of Congress Catalog Card 62-11827

Fourth Printing July 1964

Copyright © 1962
Lane Book Company, Menlo Park, California

Designed by Adrian Wilson

Composition by Griffin Brothers Inc.
Types: Linotype Granjon and handset Craw Clarendon

Paper: Antique offset book paper by Northwest Paper Company

Lithographed in the United States of America by Phillips & Van Orden Company

Binding by Phillips & Van Orden Company and Cardoza Bookbinding Company

CONTENTS

THE ART OF BARBECUING

◆ The Art of Barbecuing

It takes just one or two good whiffs of the aroma of meat sizzling on an open grill and just one or two good mouthfuls of juicy barbecued steak to make a man want to try his own hand at barbecue cookery. And once he dons cap and apron, he is on his way to becoming a master chef.

The beginning barbecuer will be generously loaded down with instructions by his experienced friends; but he has no need to be discouraged by their apparent expertness, for the techniques are easily learned. The novice should have no trouble in mastering this deft art once he has learned how to control his fire, how to make the most out of his equipment, how to cook which kinds of meat, and how to plan a meal.

◆ Firemanship

At least half of barbecuing is not cooking at all. It comes under the general heading of "firemanship"—which means getting the fire to start in the first place, keeping it going neither too fast nor too slow, maneuvering the meat so the fire—or the smoke—gives it just the right treatment, testing its temperature, making adjustments, keeping fuel and all equipment in working order for the next time.

◆ The Right Kind of Fire

The beginner often makes the mistake of trying to cook over open flame instead of waiting for coals to form. Only coals that have been allowed to burn to a gray color, shot with a ruddy glow, give the even, constant heat needed for barbecuing.

The distinctive flavor of barbecued meat comes less from the smoke of the burning fuel (some charcoal briquets give off no scent) than from the singeing of the meat's surface and from the smoke that rises from the smouldering meat drippings.

If a wood-smoke flavor is desired, there are several ways of obtaining it. Liquid smoke may be included in the marinade or basting sauce. With skill, the meat may be grilled before the bed of coals has fully formed and while the fuel is still giving off some smoke; or wood that is slightly damp or green may be used. Favorite method is to toss a few chips of aromatic wood or leaves on the coals just before the meat is removed from the barbecue. Favorite aromatic varieties are oak, hickory, bay, alder, myrtle, and the orchard woods such as apple, lemon, orange, and cherry. Some kinds are too zestful—eucalyptus gives meat a medicinal flavor, pine imparts a turpentine taste.

◆ Charcoal as a Barbecue Fuel

Charcoal is obtainable in either lump or briquet form. Briquets produce uniform heat, yield long-lasting coals, and burn without sparking. However, the lump style is cheaper and gives off a truer wood aroma than briquets.

Charcoal briquets may look alike, but different brands perform in different ways. As shown in rough temperature tests made by our staff (see page 10), some brands start up promptly, reach cooking heat in record time, and then die down quickly; others follow an opposite pattern. Of course, knowledge about these variations is useful to the barbecuer. Where he has the choice, he can select a quick-heat type for steaks or hamburgers, and a slow-burning kind for spit roasting. It may pay you to experiment with the heat output of the various brands obtainable in your locality. (A grill thermometer with a range of 0° to 500° or 700° will do.)

How much charcoal? Most beginners make the mistake of using far more charcoal than they need. You don't need to cover the entire firebed with briquets unless you expect to use the whole grill. Just make the charcoal layer a little wider all around than the area of food to be cooked. Small, efficient barbecues, such as the hibachi, will perform capably with a handful of charcoal.

◆ Fire Control

The following recommendations apply principally to charcoal briquets, but may be adjusted to chunk charcoal or wood embers.

PREPARING THE FIREBED: Briquets burn from the bottom to the top, hence require draft from below. If your barbecue unit is designed with an open-work grate, the draft is taken care of. But if you are broiling on a barbecue with a solid metal firebox—such as a brazier bowl—cover it with a level layer of sand or gravel.

This partly protects the metal from the intense heat of the charcoal; and it facilitates cleaning the unit, because the sand rather than the metal collects the grease and ashes. Gravel provides better bottom draft than sand, and it may be washed in hot water and re-used after it has been spread and dried in the sun (dry it thoroughly—wet gravel will pop).

If you don't like the messiness of a barbecue fire, line the firebox with heavy aluminum foil. It will increase the radiant heat. Afterwards, lift out the whole thing—ashes, meat drippings, and all—and discard it in the garbage can.

STARTING THE FIRE: Charcoal is regarded as a stubborn fuel, but there are several proven ways of coaxing it into flame:

1. Kindling will often start it burning. Build a paper and kindling fire tepee fashion and when it is burning drop charcoal on it. Or, arrange charcoal around the kindling pile before lighting paper. Or, build the fire on top of charcoal. All these methods are slow, and you will probably need to encourage the coals with blowing, a fireplace bellows, an air mattress or bicycle pump, or, for heroic measures, the blower on your vacuum cleaner.

2. Electric starters work quickly on most types of charcoal. You merely set the hot coil on top of the briquets and they will begin to glow in a few minutes. A small electric starter is available, specifically for hibachis.

3. Liquid starters, sold specifically for starting barbecue fires, are simple and effective to use. However, they should be used with caution and according to the directions given by

the manufacturer. Use the liquid starter to *start* a fire, but never squirt it on a lighted fire. The fire will seem to die down after the initial blaze, but do not add any more starter.

Liquid starters may be applied in two ways: (1) You can pour ½ cup on the briquets, arranged in a pyramid, wait a few minutes, then throw a lighted match onto the dampened charcoal. (2) Or you can pre-soak a few briquets, arrange them at the base of a pyramid, and light them. To pre-soak, immerse briquets in a coffee can until they stop bubbling. Some barbecuers keep a dozen or so "marinated" briquets in a sealed can or jar, so they can start a fire without delay.

Another method is to soak a brick with starter fluid, stack briquets around it, and light it. Remove it after the fire is going.

4. Pre-ignition can sometimes be used to advantage, particularly with a kitchen barbecue. Place a few briquets in a wire basket or frame and set over an open gas flame until they are ignited, then transfer to the barbecue firebed.

5. A "kindle can" will give you quick results. This is simply a tin chimney in which you can efficiently start charcoal burning. You can buy them ready-made or you can easily make one from an empty 2-pound coffee can. Remove the bottom, and with a beer can opener, punch 4 legs around the bottom by bending the tabs

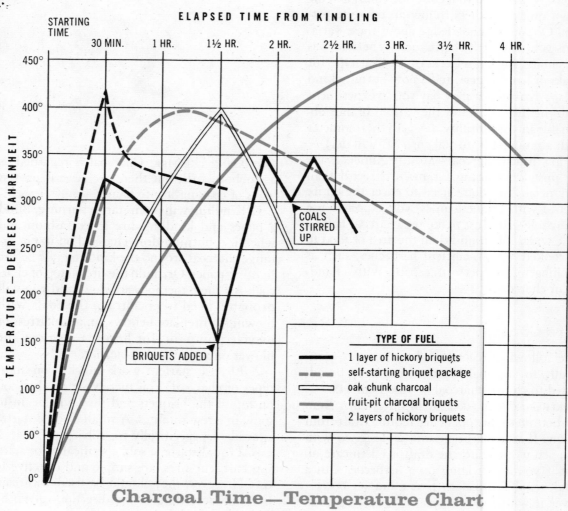

Charcoal Time—Temperature Chart

of metal in and all the way down. Between the legs, punch 4 air vents—leaving the metal tabs sticking straight in.

Set the can on your barbecue firebed, put in it 4 or 5 marinated briquets or a crushed milk carton, and fill the can with briquets. Light the carton or the starter briquets, and wait about 15 minutes, or until coals are glowing. Then remove can with tongs or pliers (you can use it over and over again), spread the coals on the firebed, or add fresh coals around the edge of the pilot fire if you need large coverage.

TEMPERATURE MEASUREMENT: A grill thermometer (obtainable in patio shops) is the most accurate way to tell when the fire is at the cooking temperature. Veteran barbecuers recommend 350-375° for steaks, hamburgers, lamb chops, kebabs, and fish; 300-325° for pork and poultry.

You can also be your own thermometer. Just hold your hand at "meat level" (grill or spit height) and count seconds until the heat makes you remove your hand. Use a watch with a sweep-second hand or one of the many photographers' methods for counting seconds ("one sub-one, two sub-two, etc."). As a general rule, if you can hold your hand over the heat for less than 3 seconds, the fire is ready for barbecuing.

FIRE CONTROL: If you want low heat, use tongs to space out the coals so they won't touch, in a kind of checkerboard pattern. Fire control on a hibachi is simply a matter of closing or opening the draft door. On other miniature barbecues, the quickest way to reduce heat is to remove some of the glowing coals. You will find metal tongs or chopsticks almost indispensable.

To eliminate those annoying flareups from fat drippings, arrange your fire in a ring, on sand. Put your meat on the spit or grill so the drippings will fall on the bare sand inside the circle of fire. The heat of such a fire will be

just about as even as that of the usual bed of coals, and it is likely to do a better-than-usual job of cooking the outside edges of meat.

If you need more heat, flick the white ashes off the tops of the coals and you nearly double their heat for the next 5 minutes or so. To add fuel, introduce it from the edge of the fire; don't put fresh briquets on top of those that are already burning.

DOUSING FLAMES: You often have to act fast if you don't want your meat charred. A sprinkler bottle is effective in quenching flame, but it tends to kick up ash and it may put on too much water and steam the meat. A water pistol has some of the disadvantages of the sprinkler, but it is more fun to use and more accurate. A spray attachment such as that sold for bottles of insecticides and glass cleaners gives a finer spray than you get from a sprinkler bottle or a water pistol. You can also use a water soaked rag on a stick, if your fire is accessible. A unique method is to lay a lettuce leaf over the flame—the flame subsides and the lettuce disintegrates.

DOUSING THE COALS: Many times, after you are through cooking, there is plenty of fuel value left in the charcoal. It is easily saved. Either toss with tongs into a water-filled bucket or into an old, riddled bucket or paint can and run water through. Let charcoal dry out thoroughly before re-using.

The answer to the old question, "What can we barbecue?" is not as simple as it might seem. Spareribs, steak, chicken, and hamburgers may be the time-tested favorites of many barbecuers, but the list of meats that can be deliciously cooked over a fire of glowing coals is much longer. Actually, you can barbecue literally anything that can be pan-fried or broiled or oven roasted indoors.

Since some barbecue "naturals" may be strangers to your indoor range, here is a description of old-time favorites and the many tempting alternates.

◆ Beef

Of all the major cuts of beef, the loin is by far the most tender and the most expensive. From it are taken the five standard steaks pictured on pages 130-131: sirloin, pinbone, porterhouse, T-bone, and club.

If the loin is boned before it is cut into steaks, there are two other choices: the fillet and the New York cut. The portion of the meat above the bone is called the New York strip; the meat below the bone is the fillet or tenderloin. The rest of the meat on the loin goes into ground beef or stewing meat.

All of these steaks, with two exceptions, are about equally tender. The first of the sirloin steaks (the one that is next to the round) is a little "rough" because part of it is cut with the grain of the meat instead of against it. This steak isn't quite so tender as the sirloin next to it. The other exception is the fillet, the most tender steak of all.

Steaks up to about 2½ inches in thickness can be grilled over coals, and any thicker cut

from the loin can be roasted on a spit or in a smoke oven.

The grade of beef determines the tenderness and juiciness of your steaks. Steak that is cut from choice grade beef is well marbled (tiny lines of fat running all through the meat), and the outside fat is white. Such beef has been scientifically fed so there will be an even distribution of fat all over the animal. In addition, today's beef is much plumper and stockier than the steers that used to go to market. As a result, there is a much larger percentage of edible meat in relation to bone in all top quality beef.

When you ask for choice beef, you can expect to be shown steaks (or roasts) that have a large amount of fat on the outside and in the meat. If the fat isn't there, the steak isn't choice grade, and it will be dry, less flavorful, and less tender. Actually, much of the fat on choice beef goes to salvage and isn't passed on to you. The waste on this grade of beef will run from 35 to 40 per cent of the total weight. Naturally, part of this waste is figured into the cost of the steak.

Before the steak is weighed, it is also trimmed. Not only is the fat evened up, but part of the "tail" is usually cut off. This piece of less tender meat goes into ground beef or stew meat. The price difference between ground meat and top quality meat is also figured into the total cost of your steak.

Next to loin, the rib is the most useful major cut of beef for the barbecuer. The standing rib can be roasted or cut into steaks for broiling, but that isn't the limit to the rib's versatility. The photos of Rib Roast Plans 1 and 2 on page 136 show two ways of cutting the rib into a variety of cuts, most of which are suitable for outdoor cooking.

Steak hungry? Take a look at Rib Roast Plan Number 1. You can have choice market steaks, 2 pot roasts, short ribs, and soup bones.

Roast beef a rarity on your table lately? Check Rib Roast Plan Number 2. You can dine on rare spit-roasted beef, put away enough cube steaks and short ribs for several meals, and have meaty bones for soup.

Starting point for both plans is the full length (10-inch) 2-rib roast. Whichever rib roast plan you choose, you'll save money because the full 10-inch cut is always less expensive than the standard, shorter 7-inch cut. Once you try either of these plans, chances are you'll graduate from the 2-rib roast to a 3-rib, because you'll get even more meat at the same lower price per pound. For instance, a 3-rib, 10-inch roast will cut into 9 or possibly 10 market steaks plus two large-sized pot roasts and enough short ribs to serve six in a generous fashion.

An extra dividend of these two meat plans is that the tender meat is separated from the less tender. Market steaks and cut-down roasts are equally tender throughout because they come from the "eye" of the meat. The tougher outside parts are "cubed" to tenderize the fibers or rolled together for pot roasting.

The standing rib roast used in either plan must be cut off the heavy end of a whole standing rib. The smaller end has too much bone and too little meat to work with. Should you decide to buy a whole standing rib (7 or 8 ribs) to put in your freezer, ask to have the heavy end cut according to either of the plans, and then use the smaller end for rib steaks and a 7-inch standing roast with all the bone left in. You'll still have all the short ribs left for barbecuing.

Naturally, you can't expect to walk into your meat market and ask to have a rib roast cut up following either plan with the same casualness you use when buying a pound of ground chuck. Your meat cutter needs some advance notice because it takes time to cut, saw, slice, tie, and wrap the meat.

When you wrap the various cuts for freezing, don't forget the unexpected guest. Put away a few single servings.

◆ Lamb

For some barbecuers, the tender meat of young lamb has no peer when it comes to outdoor cooking. Whether it is lean chunks cut from the leg and skewered with green pepper and onion in the centuries-old tradition of Armenian cookery, or a boned loin roast, or chops, or spareribs, if the meat is good lamb, almost any cut can be cooked over the coals. Only the neck, the square-cut shoulder, and the shank are too tough for barbecuing without special preparation.

The less tender cuts of lamb come from the forequarter, and the picture on page 141 shows the variety of cuts that can be taken from this section. All but the shoulder cut in the upper right hand corner are ready for the barbecue. Actually, the meat from the shoulder will make acceptable shish kebab if taken from a choice lamb and well marinated before skewering.

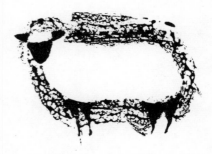

The choicest cuts of lamb come from the hindquarter—the leg and both the large and small loin. Since meat from the hindquarter is preferred by most, it costs more per pound than cuts from the forequarter. Cuts from the hindquarter are pictured on page 140.

If you have a freezer, you might consider buying a whole hind or forequarter of lamb. The meat costs you less per pound than if you buy the separate cuts, and lamb gives you a wide range of barbecue choices.

Lamb is defined as meat from animals less than a year old; mutton is from animals 1½ years old or more. However, one rarely finds mutton or lamb older than a year in markets today. Although it was once considered seasonal meat, improved breeding and feeding have now made a supply of lamb available the year around.

When you think of lamb for the barbecue, don't forget the liver and the kidneys. Both are easily and temptingly prepared over the coals.

◆ Pork

Pork spareribs rank as one of the all-time favorites with the barbecuing fraternity. The ribs can be grilled, spitted, or hung in a smoke oven, and after frequent basting with a spicy basting sauce, they reach a crisp, glazed brown stage—good enough to turn the head of any gourmet.

Many fresh cuts of pork other than the spareribs deserve consideration when you shop for barbecue meat. Any fresh roast or broiling cut can be cooked on an outdoor grill or in a barbecue oven. Though it takes longer to cook a piece of pork thoroughly than it does to cook a piece of beef or lamb of the same weight, the end product may well be more than worth the extra effort.

◆ Fowl

Any fowl, except tough stewing birds, can be deliciously broiled or roasted over coals. Remember that fowl tends to be dry and requires frequent basting. To avoid scorching, cook over relatively low coals.

◆ Fish and Shellfish

You'll find a wide range of seafoods at your market that can be easily cooked on your barbecue. Any steak or boneless cut may be broiled if you use a toasting rack or hardware cloth tray to prevent the meat from sticking to the grill. Whole fish also need special care to prevent the meat from falling apart.

Fish, like fowl, are usually short on fat and need frequent basting to protect the meat from excessive drying.

BROILING ON THE GRILL

◆ Broiling on the Grill

The barbecue grill is a versatile cooking device. Any of the meats—steaks, chops, bacon, frankfurters, half chicken, ham slices—that can be broiled or fried on a kitchen range, can be cooked on a grill.

STEAKS: The proper way to grill steaks is a matter of personal preference. Many cooks like to broil them quickly, searing them over a hot fire or even slapping them on the coals. Other barbecuers prefer to broil slowly over a coolish fire. You will probably wish to try both techniques before choosing sides.

About turning, salting, and basting meat—most barbecuers prefer to turn the meat only once during broiling and to salt at the end of the cooking. Do not puncture the meat when you turn it, for this lets the rich juices sizzle into the fire. Flip it over gently with a pair of cooking tongs or a spatula. If you must use a fork, jab it into the fat rather than the lean portion of the meat.

Steaks can be served with only salt, pepper, and butter for seasoning—and many barbecuers feel this way is best—but some like to sharpen the flavor by soaking the meat ahead of time in a marinade or by basting on the grill with a favorite barbecue sauce. You will find sauce recipes that span the full taste spectrum, but you are well advised to start off with the gentler ones and graduate to the hair-raising mixtures.

FISH, FOWL: Fish can be deliciously broiled, but they are tricky to handle because they tend to stick to the hot grid, even when it has been well greased. To overcome this, wrap fish in foil, or place in a hinged broiler.

Chickens sold now are much younger, more tender, and more lean than formerly. For grilling, choose halves (if birds are under 2 pounds), quarters, or thighs and drumsticks. You can also grill breasts if you follow the special directions on page 40. Chicken cooks so quickly that it can easily be overcooked and become dry. To adjust most old recipes for the new broiler-fryers, reduce total cooking time 5 to 10 minutes. Frequent basting is usually recommended.

IN GENERAL: Before cooking on the grill, grease it with a piece of suet or a rag dipped in cooking oil. This prevents meat from "freezing" to the hot metal. Many experts recommend that you let the grill stay dirty after using —next time, heat it up, brush the grease loose, and wipe clean with paper towels.

BEEF

◆ Steak with Garlic Oil

    Steak (12 oz. to 1 lb. per person)
    2 cloves garlic
    1 cup olive oil
    Salt and pepper to taste

Have meat cut from ¾ to 1 inch thick and gashed around the edge about every 4 inches so it won't curl during grilling. Put the garlic to soak in oil the night before the barbecue. Pour the oil into a shallow pan, remove the garlic and dip the steak in the oil, coating both sides. Then place the steak on the grill. When it is about done, season it with salt and pepper.

◆ Top o' the Morning Steak

    Steak, medium thick
    Olive oil
    Salt
    Onion salt
    Garlic salt
    Pepper, freshly ground
    Bay leaves

Paint the steak on both sides with olive oil. Sprinkle liberally with seasonings, place on the grill, and cook as desired. Just before removing the meat, quickly burn a spray of bay leaves under one side and then the other.

◆ Salt-Broiled Steak

This steak must be boneless, lean meat, from 2 to 3 inches thick. Use a large double grill, or toaster, with long handles that loop together. Place the steak on the grill and cover the top with about half an inch of thoroughly dampened coarse salt (not rock salt). Then put a paper napkin over it. Turn the grill over and cover the other side of the steak in exactly the same way. Close the toaster and put it over a very hot charcoal or wood fire, allowing from 15 to 20 minutes for each side.

Melt 1 or 2 pounds of butter in a large roasting pan and have ready sliced bread (preferably French).

When the steak is done, remove the salt, now

a hardened cake. Lift the steak into the hot butter and slice. The meat juices will run into the butter—the salt flavor will not go into the meat. With a fork, dip a slice of bread into the melted butter and meat juices. Place a slice of beef on each piece of bread. Serve immediately.

◆ Grilled Steak Sandwich

    Chives
    Butter
    Small fillet steaks, ¼ inch thick
    Hamburger buns

Chop chives fine and mix in melted butter. Place steaks on grill and brush frequently with butter-chives mixture. A few minutes before the steaks are done, toast bun halves on the grill. Butter buns and serve steaks between the halves.

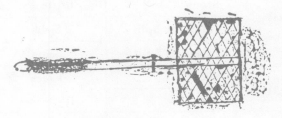

◆ Snoqualmie Steak

    ¼ cup butter (4 tablespoons)
    1 clove garlic, chopped fine
    1 teaspoon seasoned salt
      Paprika
    ¼ teaspoon Worcestershire
      Top sirloin steak, 1½ inches thick
    6 or 8 frankfurter rolls

Melt butter. Mash garlic and salt together; add to butter with paprika and Worcestershire. As mixture boils, swab the upper side of the steak with it. Turn the steak about four times during the cooking; and swab each time with the butter mixture.

While the steak is cooking, slice 6 or 8 frankfurter rolls in half. Serve up the steak with potatoes that have been cubed raw, unpeeled, and fried with onions in salad oil. Then, paint the rolls with the remaining sauce and toast them over the coals. Enough sauce for 4 servings. Figure on ⅓ pound steak per person.

Variety of Meat	Cut of Meat	Size or Weight	Warm-up Time for Frozen Meat		Recommended Heat of Fire*
			In Refrigerator to 40°	In Room 40° to 70°	
Beef	Steak	1 Inch	8 Hrs.	4 Hrs.	Hot
	Steak	1½ Inches	9½ Hrs.	5 Hrs.	Hot
	Steak	2 Inches	10½ Hrs.	7 Hrs.	Medium to Hot
	Steak	2½ Inches	12 Hrs.	10 Hrs.	Medium to Hot
	Flank Steak	Whole	8 Hrs.	2½ Hrs.	Hot
	Hamburger	1 Inch	8 Hrs.	3 Hrs.	Medium to Hot
	Tenderloin	Whole	12 Hrs.	10 Hrs.	Medium
Fish	Steak	1 Inch	If frozen, do not thaw.		Medium
	Steak	1½ Inches	"		Medium
	Fillets or Split	Small	"		Medium
	Fillets or Split	Large	8 Hrs.	4 Hrs.	Medium
Ham	Slice	1 Inch	8 Hrs.	4 Hrs.	Low to Medium
	Slice	1½ Inches	9½ Hrs.	5 Hrs.	Low to Medium
Lamb	Chops or Steaks	1 Inch	8 Hrs.	4 Hrs.	Medium
	Chops or Steaks	1½ Inches	9½ Hrs.	5 Hrs.	Medium
	Chops or Steaks	2 Inches	10½ Hrs.	7 Hrs.	Medium
Lobster	Split	1 to 2½ Pounds	If frozen, do not thaw.		Medium to Hot
Pork	Chops or Steaks	1 Inch	8 Hrs.	4 Hrs.	Low to Medium
	Chops or Steaks	1½ Inches	9½ Hrs.	5 Hrs.	Low to Medium
	Chops or Steaks	2 Inches	10½ Hrs.	4 Hrs.	Low to Medium
	Spareribs	Whole	7 Hrs.	3 Hrs.	Very Low
Poultry	Chicken	Split	10 to 12 Hrs.	6 Hrs.	Medium
	Cornish Hen	Split	8 to 11 Hrs.	2 to 3 Hrs.	Medium
	Duck	Split	11 to 12 Hrs.	6½ Hrs.	Medium to Low
	Squab	Split	8 to 11 Hrs.	2 to 3 Hrs.	Medium
	Turkey	Split (3½ to 6 lbs.)	12 to 16 Hrs.	8 Hrs.	Medium
Veal	Steaks or Chops	1 Inch	8 Hrs.	4 Hrs.	Medium
	Steaks or Chops	1½ Inches	9½ Hrs.	5 Hrs.	Medium
Venison	Steaks or Chops	1 Inch	8 Hrs.	4 Hrs.	Hot
	Steaks or Chops	1½ Inches	9½ Hrs.	5 Hrs.	Hot
	Steaks or Chops	2 Inches	10½ Hrs.	7 Hrs.	Medium to Hot

* Hot fire, 375° and over; medium, 325°; slow, 200 to 275°. Check with thermometer.

TEMPERATURE CHART

Very Rare	Rare	Med.-rare	Medium	Well-done		Comments
			Approximate Time for Cooking (each side)			
4 Min.	5 to 6 Min.	7 Min.	7 to 8 Min.	10 Min. or More	1	1. May be cooked frozen if desired medium or well done.
5 Min.	6 to 7 Min.	8 to 9 Min.	10 Min.	12 to 15 Min.	1	To ascertain degree of doneness, cut steak near center with sharp knife.
7 to 8 Min.	8 to 10 Min.	10 to 15 Min.	15 to 18 Min.	20 Min. or More	1	
10 to 12 Min.	12 to 15 Min.	15 to 17 Min.	18 to 23 Min.	25 Min. or More	1	
3 to 4 Min.	4 to 5 Min.	5 to 6 Min.	———	———	2	2. Will not be tender unless very rare or rare.
3 Min.	4 Min.	5 Min.	6 Min.	7 Min. or More		
10 to 12 Min.	12 to 15 Min.	15 to 17 Min.	18 to 23 Min.	———	3	3. Should be served rare.
———	———	———	———	3 to 5 Min.	4	4. Do not overcook lest fish become dry. When fish flakes easily with a fork it is done. Internal temperature 135° to 150°.
———	———	———	———	4 to 6 Min.	4	
———	———	———	———	3 to 6 Min.	4	
———	———	———	———	6 to 9 Min.	4	
———	———	———	———	15 to 18 Min.		
———	———	———	———	18 to 23 Min.		
———	4 to 5 Min.	6 Min.	6 to 7 Min.	8 Min. or More	5	5. Lamb may be cooked rare to med.-rare. However, it is a matter of taste.
———	5 to 6 Min.	7 Min.	8 to 9 Min.	10 Min. or More	5	
———	6 to 7 Min.	8 Min.	9 to 10 Min.	12 Min. or More	5	
———	———	———	———	12 to 16 Min. in All	6	6. Cook 4 minutes meat side down, then turn. If frozen, cook longer.
———	———	———	———	13 to 18 Min.	7	7. Pork should be well done but juicy. Cooked to 180° to 185° internal temperature.
———	———	———	———	15 to 23 Min.	7	
———	———	———	———	20 to 30 Min.	7	
———	———	———	———	1 to 1½ Hrs. in All	8	8. Turn every few minutes.
———	———	———	———	15 to 30 Min.	9	9. Do NOT overcook.
———	———	———	———	15 to 20 Min.		10. For wild duck have very hot fire and cook rare.
———	4 to 6 Min.	6 to 8 Min.	9 to 10 Min.	15 to 25 Min.	10	
———	———	———	———	12 to 18 Min.		
———	———	———	———	20 to 30 Min.		
———	———	———	———	9 to 10 Min.	11	11. Veal should be well done but never dry.
———	———	———	———	12 to 15 Min.	11	12. Some hunters prefer venison rare rather than well done.
4 Min.	5 to 6 Min.	6 to 7 Min.	7 to 8 Min.	10 Min. or More	12	
5 Min.	6 to 7 Min.	8 to 9 Min.	10 Min.	12 to 15 Min. or More	12	
7 to 8 Min.	8 to 10 Min.	10 to 15 Min.	15 to 18 Min.	20 Min. or More	12	

◆ Steak Marchand de Vins

2 tablespoons chopped shallots
1 cup dry red wine
¼ pound butter
1 teaspoon chopped parsley
3 tablespoons very thick soup stock
A few drops of lemon juice
Salt and pepper
Beef marrow
4 porterhouse steaks, 1½ inches thick

Put the chopped shallots and the wine in a wide saucepan and cook until the total volume has been reduced by more than half; let cool. Then cream this wine and shallot mixture into the butter, along with the parsley, soup stock, lemon juice, salt, and pepper. The marrow should be poked from 2-inch sections of beef leg bone and poached in salted water for 1 minute before slicing.

Grill the steaks over a wood fire (use dried grape shoots if possible). At the moment of serving, strew small pieces of beef marrow over the steak and pour the sauce over all. Enough sauce for 4 good-sized steaks.

This is a true Bordelaise sauce. It's also excellent on broiled lamb or mutton chops, grilled mushrooms, or liver.

◆ Steak Wohlford

6 to 8 cloves garlic
½ cup salt
Juice of 3 or 4 lemons
⅛ cup pepper (or more)
Good sized pinch of thyme
Small pinch of oregano
½ cup olive oil or salad oil
3 or 4 large sirloin steaks, 1½ inches thick
Bay leaves

Mash garlic in a pestle with salt, or put in a blender with some of the oil. Blend lemon juice, salt, pepper, garlic, thyme, oregano, and olive oil. The finished mixture should be about the consistency of library paste, thicker than the usual marinade. Spread on steaks at least 4 to 8 hours ahead of cooking time.

Use all the marinade mixture, pile one steak on top of the other, and let them stand—the longer the better. Do not forget to coat both sides of the bottom steak.

Make a strong tea of bay leaves, letting the leaves steep in hot water half an hour.

Start a fire of lemon wood and let it burn until practically no flame remains. Just before putting steak on the grill, scrape off practically all vestiges of marinade. Grease the grill well with chunks of beef suet. Coat the steaks lightly with melted beef suet, if you have it, otherwise bacon grease.

Sear steak on both sides and then allow to cook slowly on one side without turning until cooked halfway through, then turn and complete cooking to guests' preference. Continue to baste with melted suet to keep from drying.

Whenever the fat dripping from the meat causes the fire to flame, sprinkle the flame lightly with the bay leaf mixture, using a spray of white sage as a brush. Also, at intervals, place several sprays of white sage on the coals.

NOTE: While almost all the marinade should be scraped off, a little left on makes a thin delicious crust.

◆ Poor Man's Filet Mignon

2 pounds flank or top round steak
1 tablespoon meat tenderizer
1 cup red table wine
2 cloves garlic, finely chopped
½ teaspoon freshly ground pepper

Using a large hunting knife or similar blade, score both sides of the steak with a light chopping motion. Sprinkle the tenderizer evenly on both sides and let steak stand at room temperature for the time specified in the tenderizer package directions. Then pour over the wine, add chopped garlic, and sprinkle on the pepper (no salt). Place in refrigerator until ready to cook.

Grill, brushing with marinade as steak cooks, or pan fry to desired rareness over a quick fire. Serve with French-fried onion rings, hot garlic bread, a green salad, and chilled red wine. Makes 4 servings.

◆ Marinated Beef Short Ribs

Two days before the barbecue purchase 6 pounds of beef short ribs cut about 3 inches long. Marinate the meat for 48 hours in the following mixture:

2½ cups tomato juice
1 tablespoon sugar
1 teaspoon Worcestershire
¼ teaspoon each ginger and allspice
1 teaspoon celery salt
½ cup vinegar

Place in the refrigerator and turn the meat frequently. For the last 4 hours, remove from the refrigerator and add 1 finely chopped onion and 1 cut clove of garlic.

Remove the meat from the marinade, and pot-roast it in a Dutch oven on top of the stove or in a covered roasting pan in the oven. Use a minimum of water, and keep the heat low. When almost tender, take out and complete cooking on the grill. Baste with basting sauce described below until brown and slightly crisp. Serve with sauce.

BASTING SAUCE

While meat is cooking, strain marinade; discard onion and garlic. Mix ½ cup of marinade with ¼ cup of olive oil or drippings. Baste the meat with this mixture while barbecuing.

SAUCE FOR SERVING

Use the rest of the marinade to make the following sauce to serve with the meat. Sauté a finely chopped onion until brown; add the marinade and 1 teaspoon each of powdered oregano and cumin. (If these are not available, substitute 2 teaspoons of chili powder.) Boil the sauce down until it is about half the original volume. Makes 8 servings.

◆ Brandy-Broiled Steaks

About 15 minutes before you get ready to barbecue steaks, sprinkle both sides of the steaks generously with brandy. Then let them stand in a crock or an enamel plate. Broil over coals. When nearly done, salt both sides to taste.

◆ Boolkoki

This Korean dish, pronounced "Bullgogi," is usually served with plain boiled rice, a cabbage salad, and fruit dessert.

3 pounds lean beef (chuck, sirloin tips, or steak)
1 cup salad oil
¼ cup sugar
2 tablespoons soy
4 tablespoons finely chopped green onion
2 cloves garlic, minced
½ teaspoon salt
½ teaspoon pepper
4 tablespoons sesame seed

Cut beef in rather thin slices or strips. Mix remaining ingredients and pour over meat. Be sure that meat is well covered with sauce. Let stand overnight in refrigerator.

Remove from refrigerator and bring to room temperature. When ready to broil over hot coals, drain off surplus sauce. Cook on narrow-mesh grill or thread on skewers. Baste with sauce as necessary during broiling. Makes 6 servings.

◆ Sliced Sirloin

Instead of individual steaks, try serving your guests ½-inch slices of sirloin, cut from a 2½-inch steak broiled over the coals. Serve with melted butter.

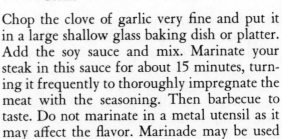

◆ Steak Hawaiian

1 clove garlic
½ to 1 cup soy
Steak

Chop the clove of garlic very fine and put it in a large shallow glass baking dish or platter. Add the soy sauce and mix. Marinate your steak in this sauce for about 15 minutes, turning it frequently to thoroughly impregnate the meat with the seasoning. Then barbecue to taste. Do not marinate in a metal utensil as it may affect the flavor. Marinade may be used for other meats.

◆ Steakburgers

Steakburgers, served open face on toasted French bread, are a nice change from the customary hamburgers.

To make 6 steak sandwiches, you need 3 slices of top round steak, cut ¼ inch thick (approximately 1 pound of meat); 1 small loaf of sour dough French bread; and the usual relishes for burgers.

Cook the meat over the charcoal; season with salt and pepper; then cut each piece in half, crosswise.

While the meat cooks, slice the French bread in half, lengthwise; spread each half with butter, and toast until golden brown. Cut each half in thirds, making good-sized pieces to fit the meat. (Or you can use sour dough French rolls, split and toasted.) Place barbecued steak on the bread and garnish with condiments.

◆ Barbecue Steak Western

Try this on costly or economical cuts. If the cut needs tenderizing, use packaged meat tenderizer as directed.

1 cup bacon drippings
½ cup finely chopped onions
⅓ cup lemon juice
2 tablespoons catsup
1 tablespoon each Worcestershire and prepared horse-radish
1 teaspoon paprika
½ teaspoon salt
⅛ teaspoon pepper
1 large clove garlic, minced or mashed
2 bay leaves
Steaks at least 1 inch thick for broiling (weight should total about 4 pounds)

Melt bacon drippings in a saucepan. Add chopped onions, lemon juice, catsup, Worcestershire, horse-radish, paprika, salt, pepper, garlic, and bay leaves. Stir thoroughly. Place steaks in a single layer in a shallow pan. Pour sauce over meat. Allow to stand 30 minutes at room temperature. Turn steaks once during marinating time to be sure sauce reaches all surfaces of meat. Lightly grease barbecue grill or oven broiler rack. Drain excess marinade from steaks. Place on grill over hot barbecue coals. Broil on each side to your liking, basting with remaining marinade during grilling. Makes 6 generous servings.

◆ Steak on the Coals

There's a good parlor trick that can be worked with this formula for Steak on the Coals. All you have to do is to persuade your guests that you are really throwing the meat away. The directions are simplicity itself (see the picture sequence on page 132):

Use any good steak cut 1 to 1½ inches thick. Build up your fire until you have about 2 to 3 inches of coals. Have steak at room temperature and throw it directly on the coals. Turn it when the juices show on top and place on an area of coals not previously covered by steak. The cooking process should take about 10 to 15 minutes. Season to taste and serve from the fireplace.

In our testing we found it advisable to use a hard charcoal or hard wood that gives off a very fine ash after it burns. Also, it's a good idea to whisk any surplus ash off the top of the coals with a fireplace broom or blow it off with a bellows. Actually, the steak doesn't burn; it damps down the fire a bit, unless you get your bed of coals too thick and too hot.

However, this method of cooking steak cannot be done altogether satisfactorily by rote. You have to practice it a time or two before you can count on reasonably consistent results. It's so much fun, though, that you'll probably consider it worth the risk.

◆ Skirt Steak Fillets

    1 skirt steak (1 to 1½ pounds) scored
    ¼ cup soy
    2 teaspoons Worcestershire
    2 tablespoons water
    ¼ pound salt pork, cut in 3 or 4 very thin
         strips about 1 inch wide

Marinate skirt steak in a mixture of the soy, Worcestershire, and water—about 30 minutes if you heat the marinade, several hours or overnight if the marinade is not heated.

Roll up skirt steak and wrap pieces of salt pork tightly around it, securing each one with a skewer. Then cut through the roll, between the skewers, to form individual fillets. Broil over charcoal (fairly close to the fire) for about 30 minutes, or under the oven broiler for 15 minutes at 450° and then 20 minutes at 200°. Makes 3 or 4 servings.

◆ Rib Steaks

When barbecuing rib steaks, pound finely minced or crushed garlic into the steaks. Cover with wine vinegar; let stand for several hours at room temperature. Drain and grill.

◆ Garlic Steak in a Crust

Cut boned chuck steaks, 1 inch thick, into 6 pieces about 3 by 4 inches each. Follow directions with unseasoned meat tenderizer to prepare steaks for cooking. Rub all sides of meat with salad oil; sprinkle generously with garlic salt.

Make pastry using 4 cups sifted flour, 2 teaspoons salt, 1 cup shortening, and cold water (about ¾ cup) to make a soft dough. On lightly floured board, roll out dough about ⅛ inch thick. Cut into 6 ovals, each about 6 inches wide, 8 inches long. Place a piece of steak on one half of a pastry circle; fold over pastry, moisten and seal edges together (see photo, page 134). Prick crust several times with a fork. Place steak turnovers on grill above low coals. Cook about 45 minutes, turning to brown crust on all sides. Makes 6 servings.

◆ Barbecued Flank Steak

This, we think, is a superior variation of London Broil. You marinate the steak in teriyaki sauce before cooking.

    ¼ cup soy
    3 tablespoons honey
    2 tablespoons vinegar
    1½ teaspoons each garlic powder and
         ground ginger
    ¾ cup salad oil
    1 green onion, finely chopped
    1 flank steak, approximately 1½ pounds

Mix together soy, honey, and vinegar, and blend in garlic powder and ginger. Add oil and chopped green onion. Place meat in a small pan and pour over the marinade; let stand 4 hours or longer. Barbecue over glowing coals, about 5 minutes on each side for medium rare, or until done to your liking. Baste occasionally with the marinade. Slice on the diagonal to serve. Makes 4 servings.

◆ Charcoal-Broiled Short Ribs

Have beef short ribs separated but left long. Marinate for 24 to 48 hours in a mixture of ½ cup salad oil, ½ cup soy, 2 cloves crushed garlic, 2 teaspoons sugar, and 3 tablespoons crushed sesame seeds. Broil the ribs slowly until crisp and brown and tender to the fork; this will take from 30 to 60 minutes.

◆ Easy Beef Short Ribs

    3 pounds short ribs of beef
    2 tablespoons prepared mustard
    ¼ cup vinegar
    ¼ teaspoon black pepper
    1 cup tomato juice
    1 teaspoon salt
    ½ tablespoon sugar

The day before meat is to be served, pack into a bowl. Beat the other ingredients together and pour over the meat. Cover and let stand overnight. Drain meat and place on grill. Cook slowly, turning meat about every 15 minutes. Makes 4 servings.

◆ Cube Steaks, Pizza Style

Brush cube steaks (6 ounces each, about ½ inch thick) with a mixture of half salad oil, half lemon juice. Broil quickly on one side, very close to hot coals. Turn and sprinkle browned side with dill weed, oregano, rosemary, or a favorite herb blend. Top each steak with a thin slice of natural jack cheese and a slice of tomato. When brown on under side, lift steak to a hot, crusty buttered bun or slice of French bread to serve.

◆ Barbecued Whole Fillet

The fillet can be barbecued right on the grill or on the spit. If you do it on the grill, turn it quite often, exposing all sides to the heat. It's a lean cut, so brush frequently with a mixture of half melted butter, half oil. Or you may choose to have your meat man lard the fillet, wrapping a layer of fat around the meat so it self-bastes as it grills; this costs more, of course. It will take about 30 minutes to grill a whole fillet if you like it rare. Timing will be about the same when you spit roast.

For the most dramatic serving, place the charcoal-browned whole tenderloin on a handsome platter or board, surround with brimming relish-filled "tomato box" garnishes (see below), sprigs of water cress, and a log of blue-cheese butter (also below). Then carve generous, thick slices and serve as individual steaks. Place a pat of the butter on each steak serving and let it melt.

TOMATO BOX GARNISH

Select large, firm tomatoes with stems, if possible Cut off tops to use for lids. Hollow out inside of tomato, leaving a shell. Heap full of favorite relishes—small radish roses, carrot curls, tiny onions and pickles, ripe and green stuffed olives. Set lids on top of tomatoes so relishes show.

BLUE-CHEESE BUTTER ROLL

Blend ½ pound soft butter and ¼ pound blue cheese with 1 tablespoon finely chopped green onions, fresh rosemary, or basil. Place on a sheet of waxed paper, shape into a log, and roll in finely chopped parsley. Wrap with waxed paper; refrigerate until firm. Serve on water cress.

◆ Beef Teriyaki

The most popular barbecue meat in Hawaii is *teriyaki*. This Japanese word means to charcoal *(teri)* broil *(yaki)*. Meats are first marinated in a mixture that is chiefly soy, sweetened with sugar, but it is often varied with other seasonings. The meat is usually beef, but it would be difficult to think of a meat, fish, or fowl that doesn't take well to the teriyaki treatment.

Any good beef steak can be used for teriyaki. These are recommended: sirloin tip, eye of the rib (also called market steak), New York strip, club, top sirloin, T-bone, and top round. If you choose a boneless cut, or bone the meat into serving-sized sections before you broil it, you can serve it in Oriental fashion—sliced in finger-sized pieces to be eaten with chopsticks (see photo, page 134). It can be sliced for fork eating, too.

If your meat is a less tender cut, first tenderize it, following directions on the package of a meat tenderizer. Or cut the meat into thin strips or cubes before you marinate and broil it.

    2 pounds boneless beef steak
 1¾ cups soy
  ½ cup sugar
  ½ teaspoon crushed garlic
    1 tablespoon grated fresh ginger or 2
        tablespoons minced preserved or
        candied ginger
  ½ teaspoon monosodium glutamate
        (optional)

Cut meat into 4 pieces and place in a bowl. In a pan combine the soy, sugar, garlic, ginger, and monosodium glutamate, if used. Heat just until sugar is dissolved; cool. Pour mixture over meat and marinate for 1 hour or longer. Remove meat from marinade and grill over glowing coals until done to your liking. (Leftover marinade keeps well in the refrigerator

for several weeks.) Slice each steak into finger-sized pieces and serve one steak to a customer. Makes 4 servings.

FLAVOR VARIATIONS FOR BEEF TERIYAKI

Add to the marinade given above any one of these: 1 tablespoon sake (Japanese rice wine) or sauterne, or 1 tablespoon chili sauce, or 1 tablespoon catsup.

SESAME BEEF TERIYAKI

Prepare a marinade of ½ cup soy, ½ cup sesame oil, ⅓ cup minced onion, and 1 clove garlic, crushed. Marinate 2 pounds beef steak, cut into serving-sized pieces, for 1 hour. Grill until almost done. About 2 minutes before removing from heat, spread with ½ cup toasted and ground sesame seeds. (You'll need about 4¼ ounces of sesame seeds.) Grill 2 minutes. Serve as you would plain beef teriyaki. Makes 4 servings.

PORK TERIYAKI

Buy a 2-pound boneless pork steak; cut it into serving-sized pieces. Marinate for 1 hour in a mixture of 1 cup soy, ¼ cup sherry, 1 clove garlic, crushed, and 1 teaspoon sugar. Grill slowly, basting with the marinade during grilling. After grilling, slice as for beef teriyaki. Makes 4 servings.

VEAL TERIYAKI WITH PEANUT SAUCE

Buy 2 pounds veal round. Marinate for 1 hour in ¼ cup *each* salad oil, lemon juice, and soy. Meanwhile, prepare peanut butter sauce: Mash into a paste 1 small green pepper, 4 almonds, ½ teaspoon minced onion, and a dash salt. Add 2 tablespoons of this mixture to ½ cup peanut butter. Add ¼ cup of the marinade; blend thoroughly. Grill veal steaks until done; spread with peanut butter sauce, and put back on grill until sauce melts and glazes the meat. Makes 4 servings.

◆ Chef's Chuck Roast

- 2 cloves garlic, finely minced
- 2 tablespoons olive oil
- ¼ teaspoon dry mustard
- 1 teaspoon soy
- ½ teaspoon rosemary, crushed, or 1 sprig of the fresh herb
- 2 tablespoons wine vinegar
- 4 tablespoons sauterne
   Chuck roast, 2½ to 3 inches thick
- 2 tablespoons catsup
- ½ teaspoon Worcestershire
- 1½ teaspoons A-1 sauce

Sauté garlic gently in olive oil, add mustard, soy, and rosemary. Remove from fire and stir in vinegar and wine. Place roast in a bowl and pour sauce over it. During the next 24 hours, turn the meat frequently in the sauce.

Prior to barbecuing, remove the meat and to the remaining sauce add the catsup, Worcestershire, and A-1 sauce. Stir well and apply some of mixture to meat before barbecuing; continue using as a basting sauce during cooking. If the sauce appears too thick, add more olive oil.

The meat should be turned frequently and basted often. A piece of meat 2½ inches thick should be cooked over hot coals for 40 minutes. When served it will be charred outside, rare in the middle. Makes 4 to 6 servings.

◆ Charcoal Roast

   4-pound rolled beef roast

MARINADE
- 5 tablespoons Worcestershire
- 2 tablespoons Kitchen Bouquet
- 1 clove garlic, crushed
- 4 tablespoons soy
- 1 cup olive oil

The rolled roast must be cut so it is flat on each end.

Mix together the Worcestershire, Kitchen Bouquet, garlic, and soy in a bowl to make the marinade. Stir well; put roast into the bowl; then rub marinade into the roast with your hands. Cover bowl, place in refrigerator, and let stand for at least 4 hours—overnight is even better.

When you are ready to barbecue, remove cover from bowl containing meat and marinade and pour olive oil over the roast. Again using your hands, rub meat well with the marinade and the olive oil.

Place the roast on the grill so that it is standing on one end. Cook for about 1 hour, basting frequently with the remaining marinade and oil mixture. After a short while, it will turn black; but fear not. At the end of the hour, stand it on the other end and let it continue to cook for a second hour. Makes 8 to 10 servings.

◆ Savory Chuck Roast

 5 pounds chuck roast, about
 2 inches thick
 Meat tenderizer

SAUCE

 1 onion
 4 tablespoons olive oil
 1 clove garlic
 ½ cup finely sliced celery
 ¾ cup chili sauce
 ¾ cup catsup
 ½ cup water
 2 tablespoons Worcestershire
 2 tablespoons wine vinegar
 1 teaspoon horse-radish
 1 teaspoon prepared mustard
 2 tablespoons lemon juice
 2 teaspoons hickory smoked salt
 Tabasco to taste
 ½ teaspoon freshly ground black pepper
 3 tablespoons brown sugar,
 firmly packed
 ½ cup sherry or white or dry red wine

Treat meat with tenderizer according to manufacturer's directions. Slice onion finely and break into rings. Put olive oil in skillet; add chopped garlic and the onion; sauté until onions are golden brown. Thoroughly mix all remaining ingredients except wine and add to onions when they are brown. Bring to a very

slow simmer and continue simmering for 20 minutes. Add wine, increasing amount if necessary so the mixture will have a moderately thick consistency and will be just right for applying with a brush. Simmer for an additional 10 minutes.

With the sauce, thoroughly baste the tenderized chuck roast. Place roast on grill close to a hot barbecue fire and brown on both sides. Then raise the grill so the roast will get only moderate heat; cover it with the top of a roasting pan, and, turning once, cook until done (2 hours or more depending on heat of fire and degree of rareness you wish). Baste *very* frequently. Cut in thin slices across the grain. Makes 4 to 6 servings.

The sauce may be used either hot or cold. It keeps well in the refrigerator and may also be frozen in freezer cartons for use several weeks later.

◆ Barbecued Chuck with Mushroom Stuffing

The beef chuck roast is one of the most flavorful meat cuts, yet still relatively thrifty to barbecue. Here is an excellent way to grill a chuck roast over coals. It is split into steaks, stuffed with a sautéed mushroom mixture, then tied and barbecued. You can slice it into tender strips, as you might carve a thick Porterhouse.

 3 to 4-pound chuck roast, sliced through
 the center
 ⅔ cup dry red table wine
 ⅓ cup salad oil
 3 cloves garlic, minced or mashed
 ⅛ teaspoon each rosemary, marjoram,
 and thyme
 Freshly ground pepper to taste
 ½ pound fresh mushrooms, sliced, or 2
 cans (4 oz. each) sliced mushrooms
 6 tablespoons butter or margarine
 3 green onions, finely chopped
 ¼ cup finely chopped parsley

Ask your meat man to saw a 2-inch-thick chuck roast through the center to make 2 chuck steaks, each 1 inch thick. (If possible, have it cut from the chuck steak section—close to the rib end—so the bones will be smaller and the meat more tender.) Or you can start with 2 chuck steaks of the same size.

With a sharp knife, cut out the long, slender blade bone in each steak, but leave the other large bone that is on the side of each steak.

For the marinade, mix together wine, oil, garlic, rosemary, marjoram, thyme, and pepper to taste. Turn into a large, shallow baking dish, add meat, and let marinate overnight, turning occasionally.

For the stuffing, sauté mushrooms in butter until golden brown, or drain canned mushrooms. Mix in chopped green onions and chopped parsley. Spoon mushroom mixture over 1 chuck steak and arrange the second steak on top. Tie securely with string. Barbecue over medium coals about 45 minutes, allowing 20 to 25 minutes on each side for medium rare. To serve, cut away string and slice slightly on the diagonal into strips about ⅛ inch thick. Serve mushroom stuffing on the side. A 3½ pound roast makes 4 servings.

◆ Chuck Western

  5-pound chuck roast, 2 to 2½ inches thick
2½ teaspoons meat tenderizer
½ teaspoon garlic salt
2 teaspoons salt
½ to 1 teaspoon coarse ground pepper (depending on your taste)
4 tablespoons olive oil (more if desired)

First sprinkle the chuck with meat tenderizer on both sides and rub it into the meat. Do the same thing, successively, with the garlic salt, salt, pepper, and olive oil. Allow the meat to marinate for at least 6 hours, turning several times. Place on a charcoal broiler with the grate

set close to the coals, and sear meat for about 10 minutes on each side. Then raise the grate a few inches and broil for another 10 minutes to a side. This will give the chuck a nice rare center.

To carve the chuck, cut lengthwise between the blade bones, remove all bones, push meat together. Then slice against the grain as you would a large sirloin. Makes 10 servings.

SAUCE

  1 can (4 oz.) mushroom stems and pieces, including liquid
 ⅓ cup catsup
 ¼ cup wine vinegar
  4 tablespoons sherry
  5 medium-sized green onions, finely chopped
  1 ring of bell pepper ½ inch thick, finely chopped
  1 small clove garlic, finely chopped
  1 tablespoon Worcestershire
  4 drops Tabasco
  2 tablespoons sugar
  1 teaspoon Kitchen Bouquet, or other gravy concentrate
  2 teaspoons salt
   Coarsely ground black pepper to taste
  1 teaspoon chili powder
  3 tablespoons butter

Combine all ingredients in a small heavy saucepan and simmer slowly for approximately 2 hours. Spoon the sauce over servings of broiled chuck.

This barbecue sauce may also be used for other purposes (try it out as a filling for Spanish omelet).

◆ Chuck Roast Teriyaki

    7 to 8 pounds chuck roast, about 2 inches
        thick
    Meat tenderizer

TERIYAKI SAUCE

    1 cup soy
    ¼ cup sherry
    2 tablespoons ginger root or 1 tablespoon
        powdered ginger
    2 cloves garlic
    2 teaspoons sugar (optional)

Cut all bone and fat from meat and then tie up the lean pieces (see photos, page 137). Don't throw away the cuttings; they will help make a good rich soup stock.

Sprinkle meat liberally with tenderizer and let it stand—follow the manufacturer's directions. Then marinate for about 1 hour in teriyaki sauce.

Finally, broil the meat slowly over a charcoal fire for about 1½ hours, turning only once during the cooking. Makes 8 servings.

GROUND BEEF

◆ Hamburger Steak in the Round

    1 round loaf French bread
    ¼ pound soft butter
    ½ teaspoon prepared mustard
    ½ teaspoon chili powder
    3 pounds ground chuck
    2 teaspoons seasoned salt
    ½ cup finely chopped green onions with
        tops
    2 tablespoons chili sauce
    1 tablespoon soy sauce or Worcestershire
        Cucumber and tomato half-slices for
        garnish

Cut bread in half, horizontally, and spread cut surfaces with seasoned barbecue butter made by blending soft butter, mustard, and chili powder. Lightly combine ground chuck with seasoned salt, chopped green onions, chili sauce, and soy sauce or Worcestershire. Shape into 2 round patties each a little larger than the bread (the meat shrinks slightly when cooked). Place bread, crust side down, at back of grill (away from hottest coals) to heat slowly. Barbecue meat patties on one side until browned and partially done. Turn patties, and place bread, buttered side down, on top of them. Continue grilling patties unitl under sides are browned and meat is cooked to degree desired.

To serve, turn meat and bread onto serving platter with bread on bottom, meat on top. Garnish with alternating thin cucumber and small tomato half-slices on top of meat patties, marking individual portions. Cut each round into wedges to serve 10 to 12.

◆ Hamburger Doughnuts

Pat out seasoned meat and cut rounds with a doughnut cutter. Grill over coals in usual manner. Serve on buns, filling the center hole with relish or melted cheese.

◆ Potato Hamburger

    1½ pounds ground beef
    3 medium-sized unpeeled raw potatoes,
        diced
    1 small onion, chopped
    2 tablespoons chopped parsley
        Salt and pepper

Mix together the meat and the unpeeled potatoes; run through the food grinder. Add the chopped onion and parsley; salt and pepper to taste. Shape into medium-sized patties and broil. Serve without sauce. Makes 8 servings.

For variety, fry in skillet. Brown flour in the pan juices after frying the patties, add milk, and season with salt and pepper, making a thick milk gravy. Pour the gravy over the patties and serve. A delicious quick gravy can be made by emptying a can of condensed mushroom soup in the cooking pan and thinning slightly with milk.

◆ Hamburger with Milk

 2 pounds ground beef
 1 egg
 ¾ cup milk
   Chopped onion
   Pinch each of marjoram and mace
   Salt and freshly ground pepper

SAUCE

 3 parts olive oil
 1 part red wine or wine vinegar
   Trace of thyme and garlic
   Pinch each of sugar, dried marjoram,
     and rosemary

Break the egg on the meat, add the milk, onion, and seasonings, and mix and knead well before forming into balls or one large hamburger.

Mix together ingredients for sauce. Baste with sauce during broiling. Makes 8 servings.

◆ Burgers for a Crowd

Form 10 pounds of ground beef into patties. Salt and pepper the hamburgers as they are placed on the grill and brush with the following sauce as they broil:

 4 tablespoons olive oil
   Chopped onion to taste
 1 cup chili sauce
 1 cup catsup
 2 tablespoons dry mustard
 2 tablespoons Worcestershire
 1 cup wine vinegar
 6 tablespoons brown sugar
 1 cup water
   Savor salt

Put oil in a skillet, add chopped onion to taste, and brown. Add chili sauce, catsup, mustard, Worcestershire, vinegar, brown sugar, and water. Sprinkle with savor salt and let simmer for 15 minutes. Makes 40 servings.

◆ Sweet-Sour Hamburger

For a change try this: Place slice of raw sweet onion on top of grilled hamburger and cover with sugar.

◆ Beef and Grass

 1 pound ground beef
 1 egg
 1 handful each of finely chopped
     spinach and watercress
 1 tablespoon chopped onion
 ½ teaspoon paprika
   Salt and freshly ground pepper

Break the egg over the meat, add the spinach and watercress, chopped onion, and seasonings, and work together until well blended. Then broil on the grill. (Chopped oysters can also be added to the formula, parsley substituted for watercress.) Makes 6 servings.

◆ Frenchman's Loaf

Split large heated French roll lengthwise. Spread with garlic butter. Place overlapping small, thin, broiled hamburger patties on bottom half of roll; cover with cheese, onion, tomato, and pickle slices. Sprinkle with salt and chili sauce. Add a little finely chopped crisp lettuce and cover with top of roll. Press down firmly. French bread may be used in the same way, cutting the loaf in 4 or 5 pieces.

◆ Hamburger on the Lean Side

 1 pound of beef
   Salt and freshly ground pepper
   A dash of meat sauce
 ½ teaspoon curry powder
 ½ jigger cognac
 1 egg
 1 small can chopped mushrooms
   Chopped onions
   Olive oil

Have most of fat trimmed from meat before it is ground, or buy lean ground round. Season with salt, pepper, meat sauce, curry powder, and cognac. Add the egg, mushrooms, and the chopped onions that have been fried to a delicate golden brown in olive oil. Form meat into generous cakes and broil. Makes 4 servings.

Smoky Hamburgers

Broil hamburger patties on each side. Place on lightly toasted buns spread with smoke butter, made by blending ¼ cup of soft butter or margarine with ⅛ teaspoon liquid smoke. Top with thin slices of tomato and onion, and a few mushrooms that have been sliced and sautéed in butter.

VARIATION

  1 pound ground beef
  ½ teaspoon liquid smoke
  1 egg
    Salt and freshly ground pepper

Add the liquid smoke and the egg, beaten, to the meat; season, and mix thoroughly. Form into cakes and broil.

Hamburger Hot Dogs

Form ground meat into shape of frankfurters. Barbecue as usual. Serve in frankfurter rolls with relishes.

Ground Round and Marrow

Have a pound of top round steak passed through the grinder three times with a quarter pound of marrow. Shape meat into cylindrical form. When ready to cook, just cut a thick, liberal slice and place it upon the grill. The marrow will give it a natural flavor and will practically eliminate the necessity for condiments and sauces. Makes 4 servings.

Hamburger De Luxe

Press ground beef into very thin, flat cakes between waxed paper. Put two cakes together with a filling made from finely chopped raw onion mixed with steak sauce; crimp the edges of the cakes firmly together. Broil over the coals and serve in hot hamburger buns, split and buttered. Cheese slices may be substituted for the onion filling.

Hamburger in Toast

  1½ pounds ground beef
  ½ cup finely chopped yellow cheese
  1 tablespoon minced onion
  ¼ teaspoon salt
  ¼ teaspoon mixed celery and garlic salt
    Dash of Tabasco

Mix well and shape into square cakes the size of a slice of sandwich bread. Brush with bacon drippings and broil.

Toast white sandwich bread, butter while hot, and stack on cookie sheet at back of grill. Lay finished hamburger upon a slice of prepared toast and pour about a teaspoon of hot barbecue sauce over it. Top with toast and serve immediately. Makes 6 servings.

Bacon-and-Cheeseburgers

Form hamburgers around a stick of Jack cheese in the shape of a frankfurter. Wrap each with a strip of bacon and skewer with toothpicks. For each serving figure on ¼ pound ground chuck, 1 ounce cheese, and 1 strip bacon. Barbecue 10 minutes over medium hot coals for medium done. Serve with split, buttered frankfurter buns and assorted relishes—mustard, catsup, and pickle relish.

Hamburger Supreme

  1 pound ground beef
 10 Brazil nuts, diced
  1 teaspoon salt
  ¼ teaspoon pepper
  1 tablespoon barbecue sauce or steak sauce
  1 tablespoon catsup
  1 slice white bread (minus crust), soaked in water and squeezed until just moist

Mix above ingredients and form individual patties. Broil in oven or cook on outdoor grill, 3 to 5 minutes on each side. Makes about 6 medium-sized patties.

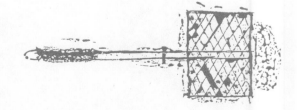

◆ Spicy Cheeseburgers

- 1 tablespoon each A-1 sauce, Worcestershire, and wine vinegar
  Dash of Tabasco
- 1½ teaspoons salt
- ½ teaspoon each pepper, sage, and celery salt
- ½ cup salad oil
- ½ cup catsup
- 1 small onion, grated
- 1 clove garlic, mashed or minced
- 2 pounds ground beef
- 1 cup fine dry bread crumbs
- 10 slices American cheese, cut ⅛ inch thick and 3 inches square

The day before you expect to use it, mix sauce: Combine the A-1 sauce, Worcestershire, wine vinegar, Tabasco, salt, pepper, sage, celery salt, salad oil, catsup, onion, and garlic in blender or beat well. Mix meat with sauce and bread crumbs. Divide meat into 20 parts; form each piece into a thin patty. Put 2 patties together with a slice of cheese between them; pinch edges together to seal. Grill on barbecue until browned on both sides. Makes 10 servings.

◆ Miniature Barbecue

Guests will have fun barbecuing miniature hamburgers and hot dogs on a brazier or outdoor fireplace. You'll need to set something on top of your grill so the small morsels of food will not fall into the fire. For this you can buy, at most hardware stores, stretched steel or welded (*not* galvanized) hardware cloth.

Buy cocktail frankfurters (about 2 dozen per pound), or cut regular frankfurters into pieces about 1½ inches long. Shape ground chuck into tiny hamburger patties. You can make about 20 small patties from a pound of meat.

Some bakeries will make miniature hamburger buns and frankfurter rolls if you order ahead, or it is easy to make them yourself with packaged roll mix. Prepare the mix as directed on the package. On a lightly floured board, roll out dough to ¼ inch thickness. Cut out the buns with a 2-inch biscuit cutter. We bent a

biscuit cutter (2-inch size) into the shape of a frankfurter to cut out these rolls.

Place rolls on a greased cooky sheet; cover and let rise until almost doubled in size. Bake in a hot oven (425°) about 15 minutes, or until browned. Plan on about 24 miniature buns or rolls from each package of roll mix. Have the baked buns split; cover to reheat them in the oven.

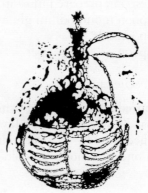

◆ Stretched Hamburger

- 1 pound ground beef
- 2 carrots, grated
- 2 stalks celery, finely chopped
- 1 sprig parsley, finely chopped
- 1 green pepper, finely chopped
- 1 onion, finely chopped
- 1 clove garlic, finely chopped
- 1 tablespoon steak sauce
- 1 egg
  Dash salt and pepper
- 2 tablespoons cooking oil or shortening
- 8 hamburger buns
- ½ cup melted butter or margarine
- 8 large tomato slices
  Sliced unpeeled cucumber

Mix all ingredients (except the last four listed) together well, using egg as binder. Roll into patties the size of hamburger buns and broil. Split hamburger buns into halves and toast cut sides, then brush with melted butter. Cover each hamburger with one slice of tomato and several slices of fresh, crisp, unpeeled cucumber. A little prepared mustard may be added, if desired. Makes 8 servings.

◆ Hukilau Hamburgers

    1   pound ground chuck or ground round
    1   cup prepared stuffing mix
    1½ tablespoons garlic butter
    1   tablespoon onion flakes, or 1 medium-
          sized onion chopped fine
    1   teaspoon parsley flakes, or 1 tablespoon
          chopped fresh parsley
    1   tablespoon prepared mustard
    ¼   teaspoon monosodium glutamate
    ¼   teaspoon salt
    ⅛   teaspoon ground pepper
    1   egg
        Barbecue sauce

Mix all ingredients lightly. Form into four patties. Coat lightly with your favorite sauce. Cook on sheet of foil set over your barbecue grill. Turn once; do not overcook. Makes 2 to 4 servings.

◆ Chef's Ground Beef

    1½ pounds ground lean beef
    1   teaspoon salt
    ¼   teaspoon pepper
    ½   teaspoon monosodium glutamate
    2   tablespoons butter or margarine
SAUCE
    1   tablespoon butter or margarine
    1   tablespoon chopped parsley
    1   tablespoon lemon juice
    ⅛   teaspoon salt
        Pepper and paprika

Blend the ground beef, salt, pepper and monosodium glutamate and form into a loaf about 3 inches wide and 1½ inches thick. Spread the butter over the loaf.

For the sauce, melt butter, and add parsley and lemon juice. Mix thoroughly, and add salt and a sprinkling of paprika and pepper.

Broil meat over coals, lowering grill so that the meat is close to the coals. (Extinguish serious conflagrations immediately.) Count on 5 or 6 minutes for each side, carefully turning the meat only once with a broad spatula. The result should be a loaf crusty brown on the outside, deliciously rare inside.

Place the loaf on a sizzling hot platter the instant it comes from the fire, and pour over it the lemon-butter sauce. Slice into individual servings and serve on warm plates without further delay. Makes 3 or 4 servings.

◆ Grilled Blue-Cheese Patties

The flavor of these thick grilled hamburger patties is enriched by blue cheese, deviled ham, and a preliminary marinating in wine.

    1   pound lean ground beef
    1   small can (2 or 3 oz.) deviled ham
        Pinch each salt and pepper
    4   pieces blue cheese, each cut about 1¼
          inches square, ½ inch thick
        Red table wine

Combine ground beef, deviled ham, salt, and pepper. Divide into 4 portions, and mold each around a piece of cheese. Place in bowl, cover with wine, and allow to marinate, covered, in refrigerator for about 3 hours. Remove from wine marinade and barbecue over charcoal until done. Makes 4 patties.

◆ Burgundy Burgers

    ¾   pound ground chuck
    2   tablespoons each chopped parsley
          and green onion
    ¾   teaspoon salt
        Freshly ground pepper to taste
    ⅓   cup dry red wine
        Roquefort or blue cheese

Mix together ground chuck, chopped parsley, and green onion; season with salt and pepper. Shape into 2 patties, making a depression in the center of each one. Place in a shallow pan, and pour wine over patties, pouring it into the depressions; chill 2 hours or longer. Broil over medium hot coals, 8 to 10 minutes for medium rare. Place a square of Roquefort or blue cheese on each meat patty just before serving so it will melt slightly. Makes 2 servings.

◆ Glorified Hamburgers

1 pound ground beef
1 cup cracker crumbs
1 cup tomato juice
1 egg
1 small onion, finely chopped
Salt and pepper to taste

Mix ingredients together. Shape into patties and broil. Makes 6 servings.

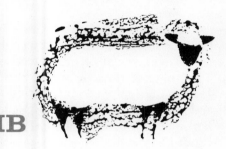

LAMB

◆ Ground Lamb with Pineapple Ring

Onion juice, lighter and gentler than chopped or grated onion, is used to flavor this lamb dish. The method of extracting onion juice is worth noting for use in other recipes.

1 large onion, minced
1½ teaspoons salt
1 pound ground lamb
2 stalks celery and leaves,
    chopped very fine
4 rings of pineapple
Paprika

Place onion in a small bowl, sprinkle with salt, and let stand for about ½ hour. Turn onion onto a square of cloth, roll it up, and twist ends to squeeze out onion juice over ground lamb. Add celery and leaves to meat; work with hand to mix well. Divide into 8 portions, then form each into a roll about 3 inches in length. Place meat on the grill and broil until nicely browned. Place pineapple rings on grill and sprinkle them generously with paprika; put on grill during last 10 minutes of cooking. Makes 4 servings.

◆ Lamb Choplets

For lamb choplets (stuffed lamb chops), have meat man remove breastbone from breast of lamb. Cut away first 2 or 3 ribs from point end of breast and remove boneless flank end. Cut meat and some fat from trimmings and, with an extra pound of shoulder meat, grind in food chopper. Season with salt, pepper, and ½ teaspoon mace. Then make a pocket in breast and stuff tightly with ground meat. Chill, cut between ribs, and grill over hot coals.

◆ Lamb Breast, Shanks

Either lamb breast or lamb shanks may be barbecued with rewarding success. Lamb breast may be placed directly on the grill, but lamb shanks should be precooked until tender before grilling. Braise shanks in small amount of water in a stout, covered pan.

Marinate 4 pounds lamb breast or 4 to 6 pounds precooked shanks in:

1 cup orange juice
½ cup lemon juice
2 tablespoons sugar

For last 2 hours, add ½ cup of chopped, crushed mint leaves to marinade.

Oil the meat well, place on grill over slow fire, and cook until thoroughly browned. While cooking, baste with a sauce made of ½ cup of the marinade mixed with ¼ cup of salad oil. Heat remainder of the marinade and serve as a sauce with the meat.

◆ Gypsy Lamb

Before barbecuing a roast of lamb or chops, rub with salt in which garlic has been mashed. Then place a layer of onion in the bottom of a pan or crock. Put in the meat and pile sliced lemon and sliced onion on top and around sides. Cover and let stand in cool place overnight, or longer if possible. Before cooking, shake plenty of paprika over the meat. The lamb is then ready to be roasted or grilled.

◆ Lamb Chops à la Castellane

3 tablespoons butter
3 tablespoons flour
1 cup rich beef stock or beef bouillon (undiluted)
¼ cup diced lean ham
1 tablespoon butter
3 tablespoons sherry
2 tablespoons minced green pepper
6 thick slices unpeeled eggplant
Butter or olive oil
6 loin lamb chops
Parsley or broiled mushroom caps for garnish

Make the sauce first: Melt the 3 tablespoons butter and add flour. Cook, stirring, until lightly browned. Gradually add beef stock and cook until smooth and thick.

In another pan, cook ham in the 1 tablespoon butter for a minute or two, then add sherry and green pepper. Add to sauce.

Brush eggplant on both sides with butter or olive oil, and broil over hot coals until nicely browned (a hinged broiler makes turning easy). Broil the lamb chops as usual, cooking so that they are pink and juicy inside, crisply brown outside. Reheat the sauce and pour on the eggplant slices. Put one chop on each slice of eggplant. Garnish with a plume of parsley or a broiled mushroom cap. Makes 6 servings.

◆ Barbecued Boned Leg of Lamb

At Basque barbecues we've attended, as many as 45 lambs were barbecued on open barbecue pits. In one instance, the fires were started at 3 A.M. in four pits, each 6 feet deep, 6 feet wide, and 20 feet long. Beginning at 9 A.M., the cut-up lamb sections were roasted slowly on racks high over the coals of oak wood.

We worked out this method for preparing legs of lamb on a home barbecue. You may need to devise a way of raising your grill to 1½ feet above the fire. The photographs on page 142 illustrate the steps described below.

Have your meat man bone the legs of lamb. For each leg (6 to 7 lb.) prepare a marinade of

¼ cup dry sherry, 2 tablespoons olive oil, and 2 teaspoons mixed herbs (you might use one of the prepared herb blends). Marinate the meat overnight. Drain, saving all the marinade.

Cut 3 or 4 deep incisions in the thickest parts of the meat and insert a seasoned bacon roll in each. (To make the bacon rolls, you'll need about 2 slices of bacon for each leg of lamb. Sprinkle each slice with finely chopped green onion or instant minced onion and mixed herbs, roll up like a jelly roll, then cut each roll crosswise to make 2 smaller rolls; insert deep into meat.)

Fold the boned lamb into a compact shape, tucking any ends inside. Skewer the meat together with metal or heavy wooden skewers. Then put the meat on a grill arranged about 1½ feet above the bed of glowing coals. Turn and baste often with the basting sauce (below). Barbecuing will take about 1½ hours. Each leg of lamb will serve 8 to 10 generously.

BASTING SAUCE

To the drained marinade (above) add for *each* leg of lamb: ½ cup catsup, ¼ cup wine vinegar, 1 can (6 oz.) tomato paste, 1 teaspoon liquid smoke, ½ teaspoon salt, 1 finely mashed clove garlic (or ⅛ teaspoon garlic powder), and 1 cup dry white table wine. Blend the mixture well and use to baste the lamb.

◆ Barbecued Split Leg of Lamb

Ask your meat man to bone a 5 to 6-pound leg of lamb without cutting through the meat. Insert 2 skewers through the meat at right angles (see photograph on page 141).

Place fat side down on the grill over medium hot coals. Turn once, using the skewers as holders. Meat will be medium rare in about 45 minutes. To carve, start at one end and cut meat across the grain into ¼-inch-thick slices. If you wish, marinate the meat ahead of time in your favorite red wine marinade, or brush with garlic butter during barbecuing. Makes 6 servings.

◆ Split Loin Roast

This method gives not ordinary barbecued lamb chops, but delicious small "lamb roasts" for each guest. The meat selected is a split loin of lamb—preferably hung for 8 to 10 days at the market before barbecuing. Have the meat man divide the split loin into about 6 chops, cutting through the bone but not completely separating the cuts. In this way the whole large piece can be cooked as one roast, yet easily divided into large loin chops for serving.

Rub the meat lightly with a cut clove of garlic, then roast on the grill over glowing coals. Turn as frequently as necessary for even cooking, and baste with a favorite barbecue sauce or not, as desired. Ordinarily 40 to 45 minutes should be long enough to allow for the roasting. Then, with a sharp knife, divide into chops and allow one for each serving. Makes 6 servings.

A half rack of lamb may be barbecued in the same way if you want to use the rib cut instead of the loin.

◆ Barbecued Lamb Steaks

If you look at the picture on page 141, you'll see a leg of lamb that has been cut crosswise into meaty lamb steaks. They are a good choice for a dinner party of about a dozen or so persons.

The steaks acquire flavor as they grill because you swish them with garlic butter. Cook them to your guests' order—crisply brown outside and rare or well done inside, as preferred.

Ask your meat man for a long-cut leg (it has the large loin in it) weighing between 7 and 8 pounds, cut crosswise into 12 steaks about ¾ inch thick.

Place on grill over medium hot coals and brush with warm garlic sauce, made by combining 4 cloves crushed garlic with 3 tablespoons *each* melted butter and salad oil. Grill 15 minutes altogether, or about 8 minutes on each side, for medium rare. Makes 12 servings.

◆ Chelo Kebab

Consider serving *Chelo Kebab,* a colorful meal-in-one dish, the next time you serve a patio dinner. Its striking appearance makes it a good choice for guests, yet it's easy and inexpensive enough to be suitable for a family meal.

Chelo Kebab is Persian for shish kebab; both pertain to any barbecued food, generally lamb. The dish includes lamb, tomatoes, and rice, so you need only a green salad and dessert to complete the menu.

      1½ pounds ground lamb
       1 large onion, finely chopped
       1 egg
       ½ teaspoon salt
       ¼ teaspoon pepper
       2 tablespoons flour
      1½ cups uncooked rice
       4 tablespoons butter
          Paprika (optional)
       3 tomatoes, halved
          Butter, salt, and pepper

Mix lamb, onion, egg, salt, pepper, and flour until smooth and creamy. Shape into oblong patties about 5 inches long, 1½ inches wide, and 1 inch thick; put aside.

Cook rice; sprinkle with cold water, shaking gently so kernels won't stick together. Drain 5 minutes. Melt butter in frying pan or shallow casserole (of a material which will stand direct heat) and pile the rice in it in a dome shape; sprinkle with paprika if desired. Place over low heat (on range or grill) for 10 minutes to dry rice. Meanwhile, cook lamb patties in a hinged wire broiler on barbecue. Broil for about 10 minutes on each side. Dot tomato halves with butter; salt and pepper and place on grill for about 8 minutes. Stack cooked lamb patties on rice dome; arrange tomatoes at bottom or on separate plate. Serve hot. Makes 4 to 6 servings.

◆ Peking Lamb

In China, where this dish originated, a special grill is used to provide the characteristic smoky wood fire. The cooking surface of the Chinese grill is oval and consists of broad strips of metal with very narrow spaces between, so that thinly sliced meat and vegetables will not fall through.

To grill the lamb and vegetables, we used a portable brazier in which we built a wood fire, using partly green wood to increase the smoke. You could use a hibachi or other small barbecue just as well. The wood fire is not a necessity, but if you use charcoal instead, you will probably want to add liquid smoke seasoning to the sauce (directions for this are given in the sauce recipe below).

You will need to place something over your grill so that the meat and vegetables won't fall through. A piece of expanded steel, available in metal shops and some hardware stores, or welded (*not* galvanized) hardware cloth is good (see photograph, page 143). Or use a hinged broiler or toaster rack.

For the meat a leg of lamb is the best choice. We found that one small leg (about 4½ pounds) made generous servings for 6 to 8 people. The meat should be sliced very thinly into long, narrow strips, about the way you cut beef for sukiyaki.

For the vegetables green onions and Chinese parsley are traditional. Chinese parsley somewhat resembles our parsley, but it has an interesting sharp, spicy flavor. It is usually available only in Oriental grocery stores. Cut the green onions and parsley into 1½ to 2-inch strips. Other vegetables can be substituted in this dish, such as fingers of eggplant, parboiled green beans, or thin slices of zucchini squash.

The dipping sauce is primarily soy. To ¾ cup soy add 1 tablespoon sugar and ¼ cup sherry (optional). You may also add 1 teaspoon liquid smoke seasoning.

Guests gather around the grill, take hold of meat and vegetables with chopsticks or forks, dunk them in the bowl of sauce, then set them on the hot grill. You might provide inexpensive wooden chopsticks, but remember that your guests must be quite proficient with them to handle the pieces of meat and vegetables over the fire. You'll want to have cooking forks or tongs handy, too. The broiling takes only about 2 minutes. The sauce drips into the fire and makes it spark and smoke. A slight char on the food seems to make it taste even better.

◆ Lela Ka Kabab

A spicy brown yogurt sauce serves as the marinade, basting sauce, and final meat sauce for the lamb steaks or chops. As you blend it, the quantity and varied fragrances of the eight spices may seem a little overwhelming; however, the meat turns out superbly seasoned.

    2 medium-sized onions, sliced
    2 tablespoons ground coriander or 6
        sprigs fresh coriander (Chinese
        parsley) plus 1 tablespoon ground
        coriander
    2 teaspoons each salt and ground cumin
  1½ teaspoons each black pepper, ground
        cloves, and ground cardamon
    1 teaspoon each ginger, cinnamon, and
        poppy seeds
    2 tablespoons *ghee* (see explanation at
        end of recipe) or 2½ tablespoons
        melted butter
    1 pint (2 cups) yogurt
    6 tablespoons lemon juice
   12 lamb steaks, round bone lamb chops,
        or rib chops

Put the onions, spices and seasonings, ghee, yogurt, and lemon juice in a blender, and blend until smooth. (Or grind the onions and fresh coriander with a mortar and pestle, adding spices gradually; add to ghee, yogurt, lemon juice.) Place chops in shallow pan, spoon over half of the marinade, and let marinate, refrigerated, overnight; or let stand at room temperature 2 hours. Barbecue over glowing coals for about 40 minutes, or to desired doneness. Baste occasionally with sauce. You can heat the left-over marinade and serve it as a sauce on the meat. Makes 12 servings.

Ghee, or purified fresh butter, is made by heating 1 pound butter in a 2 or 3-quart sauce-pan over very low heat for 1 hour, or until only butter fat remains. Strain through a cheese cloth. Its flavor is quite different from that of butter and it has a higher smoking point.

PORK

◆ Chef's Spareribs

> ¼ cup brown sugar
> 1 tablespoon salt
> 1 tablespoon celery seed
> 1 tablespoon chili powder
> 1 teaspoon paprika
> 2 to 3 pounds pork spareribs
> ¼ cup vinegar
> 1 cup canned tomato sauce or purée

Mix the dry ingredients and rub part of the mixture into the ribs. Combine remainder of mixture with the vinegar and tomato sauce for basting. Let ribs stand an hour or longer, if convenient, then spread on grill over slow fire, basting occasionally with sauce. To reduce cooking time, pre-cook ribs in kitchen oven until almost tender, then finish on barbecue grill. Makes 3 or 4 servings.

◆ Easy Rib Barbecue

Select meaty pork spareribs or lamb breast and cut in pieces. Place between wire toaster. Cook about 5 inches above bed of coals. Grill for 25 minutes, turning every 5 minutes, then brush with barbecue sauce and continue grilling for 10 to 15 minutes longer. Ribs may also be cooked in a revolving grill or on a spit.

◆ Spareribs with Onion

> Sweet onions, chopped fine
> Pork spareribs, cracked
> Salt and pepper
> Butter to sauté onions

Spread finely chopped onions on spareribs, roll up with onions inside and place in refrigerator or cooler overnight. Just before barbecuing, scrape off onions and season meat with salt and freshly ground pepper. Sauté onions in butter and serve with spareribs. No barbecue sauce required.

◆ Spareribs Encino

Cut 6 pounds lean pork spareribs into individual-sized servings. Broil over coals in barbecue, until golden brown. Brush with barbecue sauce (see below). Place in covered roasting pan and let steam on back of the barbecue grill for at least one hour. Do not allow ribs to dry out. Baste frequently with sauce and fat from bottom of roaster. Makes 6 servings.

SAUCE

> 2 large onions, minced
> 2 tablespoons olive oil
> 8 large, ripe tomatoes
> 1 green pepper, sliced
> ¼ cup chopped celery leaves
> 1 pinch each sage, oregano, thyme, rosemary, sweet basil
> Salt and pepper to taste
> 2 tablespoons white wine vinegar
> Sherry

In a large saucepan, sauté onions in olive oil until transparent. Quarter tomatoes and add to onions with green pepper, celery leaves, herbs, salt, and pepper. Cover and simmer slowly until tomatoes are soft. Put mixture through a coarse sieve to remove tomato seeds and other solids. Return mixture to stove, add vinegar, and let simmer to a thick paste, stirring frequently. When ready to use, dilute with ¾ cup sherry to ½ cup of barbecue paste. The paste may be made ahead in quantities and sealed in jars or bottles.

◆ Smoky Spareribs

3 pounds pork spareribs
Liquid smoke
1 clove garlic
1 onion
Few sprigs parsley
Salt
Pinch each of rosemary leaves, ginger,
  and coarsely ground black pepper
½ cup dry sherry
2 tablespoons tomato paste
2 tablespoons sugar

Cut ribs into serving pieces and swab generously with liquid smoke. Place in a shallow open baking pan. Chop garlic, onion, and parsley together until fine; toss over meat. Sprinkle with salt, rosemary leaves, ginger, and pepper. Cover pan with waxed paper and let stand overnight.

When ready to cook, remove from pan and grill over a slow fire. Mix sherry, tomato paste, and sugar, and use for basting sauce. Grill until ribs are browned and meat is tender, basting frequently with sauce. Makes 3 to 4 servings.

◆ Spicy Spareribs

2 pounds spareribs
1 can (8 oz.) tomato sauce
4 whole cloves
⅛ cinnamon stick
1 stalk celery, chopped fine (or ¼ teaspoon celery salt)
1 clove garlic (or ¼ teaspoon garlic salt)
2 dashes Tabasco
1 tablespoon steak sauce
2 tablespoons vinegar
1 tablespoon sugar
½ teaspoon chili powder
2 tablespoons chutney
⅛ teaspoon dry mustard
1 small onion, chopped fine

Leave ribs in one piece. Cook all other ingredients for 20 minutes or until blended to taste. Baste ribs frequently with this sauce during barbecuing. Makes 2 servings.

◆ Grilled Bacon

The best results are obtained by buying part of a side of bacon and having it sliced somewhat thicker than is customary. If there is a large crowd, the bacon should be first sliced and then replaced in its original block form and put into a bread pan. This is placed in the oven for 15 minutes at medium heat. In that way much of the surplus fat is removed, which reduces the possibility of flare-ups in cooking the bacon. Then place the bacon strips, separated, on the grill over a slow fire and cook, turning once or twice, until done.

◆ Perro Con Queso

Here's a novel way to cook the ever-faithful hot dog: Take any quantity of frankfurters (the short, chubby ones are best) and core them with a piece of thin-wall, ⅜-inch copper tubing, that has been sharpened at the cutting end. Cut strips of cheese ⅜-inch square, and stuff in the hole. Grill until the frank is cooked and the cheese melted inside. Serve in toasted hot dog rolls. The frankfurter cores have to be punched out of the tubing with a stick. Chop them up and add them to a fresh garden salad.

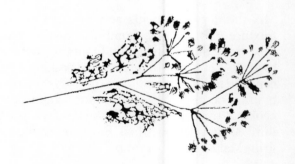

◆ Barbecued Canned Ham

Start the fire 3 hours before you eat. Open the canned ham; place the can in a large kettle (or dishpan) and pour in enough water so it comes to within 2 inches of top of can. Cover the kettle with a lid or aluminum foil. Simmer until ham is heated through, about 1½ hours for an 8 to 12-pound ham.

Remove meat from the can and place on a grill over low coals. Baste occasionally with the following mixture as the ham cooks: ⅔ cup catsup, ¼ cup white distilled vinegar, 2 tablespoons brown sugar, and salt and pepper to taste. Turning every 15 minutes, barbecue ham until it is lightly browned and crusty, from 1 to 1½ hours.

◆ Charcoal-Broiled Ham Steak

  1 slice tenderized ham, ½ to ¾ inch thick
  3 teaspoons dry mustard
  1 cup brown sugar
  ½ cup juice from a can of sliced pineapple
  2 to 3 slices canned pineapple

Put steak on grill and baste with a thin paste of the mustard, brown sugar, and pineapple juice. Use mustard sparingly at first, then add more to taste. Remove steak when brown. Put pineapple rings on grill and when they are a steaming brown, serve them on top of the steak.
  Serve with baked candied yams, hot rolls, and a green salad. Makes 2 or 3 servings.

◆ Spicy Ham Steak

  ¼ cup melted butter
  1 cup sherry
  1 cup pineapple juice
  2 teaspoons ground cloves
  ¼ cup dry mustard
  ⅓ cup firmly packed brown sugar
  ? teaspoons paprika
  ? cloves garlic, minced
  ? center-cut slice ham, 1 inch thick

Combine all ingredients except ham and mix well. Slash edges of ham and marinate in sherry and pineapple mixture for 3 hours; turn several times. Grill over low to medium coals for 20 minutes, basting frequently with marinade and turning occasionally. Carve ham into individual portions and serve hot. Makes 4 to 6 servings.

◆ Grilled Pork Chops

Take thick pork chops—soak for at least one hour (completely submerged) in juice from canned pears. Charcoal barbecue until well done.

FOWL

◆ Rosemary Barbecued Chicken

  ½ cup olive oil or other salad oil
  ½ cup melted butter
  ½ cup white wine
  1 teaspoon salt
  ¼ teaspoon freshly ground pepper
  1 teaspoon crushed rosemary
  1 clove garlic (minced or mashed)
  2 broiler-fryers (about 2 pounds each), cut into halves

Combine all ingredients except chicken and heat to bubbling hot. Brush chicken halves inside and out with sauce. Place cavity side down on grill about 4 inches above hot coals. Baste frequently and turn chicken about every 10 minutes. Total cooking time is 45 to 60 minutes. Makes 4 servings.

◆ Chicken Californian

Allow half a small broiler-fryer for each serving. Brush with olive oil, and broil over charcoal for 12 to 20 minutes on each side, or until done to your liking. For 6 servings make a sauce of ¼ pound (½ cup) butter or margarine, in which a split clove of garlic has been heated then discarded; ½ cup each sliced green and ripe pitted olives; and 4 ripe, firm tomatoes, peeled, seeded, and diced. Serve hot over the broiled chicken.

◆ Barbecued Chicken, Paprika

  2 broiler-fryers (about 1½ to 2
     pounds each)
  2 cups olive oil
  2 or 3 cloves garlic, well minced
  4 heaping tablespoons paprika
     Salt and pepper

Quarter chicken, wash quickly, and dry well; place in shallow pan. Mix together the oil, garlic, and paprika, then pour over chicken. Marinate for 3 or 4 hours, turning the chicken about every half hour. Season with salt and pepper and place quarters on grill. Broil over hot coals, baste frequently with the marinade. Makes 4 servings.

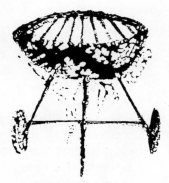

◆ Ranch-Style Chicken

Cut 3 broiler-fryers into pieces as for frying. Brush with melted butter, and place over coals for about 5 minutes to sear, and then turn. Brush with sauce and turn every 3 to 5 minutes, brushing with sauce at each turn. (If possible, make the sauce at least 24 hours before using.) Time required is about 35 minutes. Makes 6 servings.

BASTING SAUCE

  ½ cup white apple vinegar
  ⅓ cup salad oil
  1½ teaspoons Worcestershire
  ½ teaspoon minced onion
  1 clove garlic, minced
  3 teaspoons salt
  1 teaspoon paprika
  1½ teaspoons tomato paste
  6 to 8 drops Tabasco
  ¼ teaspoon dry mustard

◆ Barbecued Boned Chicken

  4 broiler-fryers (2½ to 3 pounds each)

MARINADE

  1 large or 2 small cloves garlic, put
     through press
  ½ cup wine vinegar
  ½ cup Chablis or sauterne wine
  1 cup salad oil
     Dash Tabasco
     Salt to taste

Using a very sharp boning knife, split the skin of each chicken down the back and dissect out the bony carcass—backbone, rib cage, and breastbone assembly—leaving only the legs and wings with their skeletal equipment. Save the carcasses for chicken broth later.

  Combine marinade ingredients. (If any is left over, it can be kept for several weeks in the refrigerator.) Marinate the boned chickens in a deep dish for about 2 hours. Longer marinating is unnecessary, since the juices enter the cut flesh easily.

  Arrange marinated chickens on a hinged, wire broiling frame, legs and wings akimbo, with the loose skin pulled and folded over the opening so that no flesh is in sight. Broil slowly over charcoal, 6 to 8 inches from the coals. If the day is windy, or you're in a hurry, invert a large roaster pan over the birds to help hold in the heat. They should be turned several times, and basted with marinade frequently. Cooking time: 30 to 45 minutes. Serve one half chicken per person.

◆ Barbecued Breast of Chicken

Select 6 large split breasts (almost ½ pound each). Rinse and dry thoroughly. Dip pieces, one at a time, into about ¾ cup melted butter, then shake in a paper bag with about 1½ cups flour, seasoned with salt and pepper, to coat thoroughly. Place pieces on greased grill 6 to 12 inches above hot coals (grill temperature should be about 375°). Cook 10 to 12 minutes on each side. Baste during cooking with melted butter (you will need about ¼ cup). Serve immediately. Makes 6 servings.

◆ Chicken Sukiyaki

Thin-sliced chicken takes the place of the usual beef in this sukiyaki. Cook it on a miniature barbecue as shown on page 139. The chicken can be cooked the day before the barbecue. Vegetables, too, can be prepared ahead and refrigerated in plastic bags to keep them crisp and fresh.

  1 chicken (about 3 pounds) or 1½
    pounds chicken breasts
  2 stalks celery
  1 medium-sized onion, sliced
  1 teaspoon salt
  4 tablespoons (¼ cup) butter or
    margarine
  1 bunch green onions, trimmed to about
    3 inches long and sliced lengthwise
  1 cup sliced fresh mushrooms
  ⅓ pound fresh spinach, cut into 2-inch
    lengths
  ½ cup thinly sliced celery
  ½ cup thinly sliced bamboo shoots
    (optional)
  ¼ cup soy
  ¼ cup chicken stock
  2 tablespoons sugar

Simmer chicken in water to cover, adding celery, sliced onion, and salt to the water. Cook just until tender enough to bone and slice. Cut from bone in slices; cover and refrigerate until used.

In a frying pan or sukiyaki pan, lightly brown chicken slices in butter or margarine. Push to one side or remove from pan. Add onions and mushrooms, and cook until lightly browned. Add spinach, celery, bamboo shoots, soy, chicken stock, and sugar. Cook until just tender, but still crisp. Put back chicken if it was removed from pan; heat.

Serve with hot cooked rice. Spoon liquid from pan over each serving or the sukiyaki. Makes 4 servings.

◆ Turkey Steaks

Here's a recipe that will leave your meatman shaking his head in disbelief and will stir your guests into pelting you with questions:

Buy a large, hard-frozen, eviscerated tom turkey—the bigger the better. Have your meatman cut it on his power saw into 1-inch transverse slices, starting at the front of the breastbone, and working back to about where the thighs join the body. If you're serving a large number of people, have him cut more slices—one slice will make two good servings. The two ends that are left can be kept frozen until you need them.

Now lay the frozen slices out in a large flat pan (you can stack them) and drizzle on enough cooking oil to coat each one. As the slices thaw, the oil and juices will make a fine marinade in the pan. This should be brushed back over the slices from time to time. When they are completely thawed, divide each slice into two steaks with a sharp, heavy knife. (You'll find that the cross-sections of breast and backbone will split quite easily.)

Have a good, hot bed of coals going in the barbecue. Arrange the steaks in toasting racks, brush with basting sauce (¼ pound butter, ½ cup dry white wine, salt, and pepper). Broil about 8 inches from the fire for around 10 minutes on each side. Turn them a couple of times during the cooking, and brush with more butter-wine mixture.

Serve them up, one to a person, with the remainder of the basting sauce heated and spooned over each serving, and have the guests guess what they're eating. You'll get quite a variety of answers—from pork, veal, to swordfish. The steaks don't taste like the customary roast turkey, but you'll agree that it is some of the best turkey you ever sank a tooth into. Once again, not too much cooking. Don't let them dry out.

◆ Barbecued Boned Half Turkey

This way to barbecue turkey on your grill doesn't require a spit. It is especially suitable for grilling the large tom turkey halves that are available in many markets and inexpensively priced.

You cut off drumstick and wing, then remove the meat in one piece from the carcass. When these pieces are slowly grilled, the result is moist tender meat with a distinct smoky flavor. The turkey is easy to slice and serve, although total cooking time has been only a little over one hour. (If you can't buy the ready-cut turkey halves in your area, have your meat man cut a whole turkey in half; wrap one half for your freezer.)

Follow the pictured steps on page 145 for cutting and boning the turkey, making sure the bird is completely thawed before you start to bone it; make slashes in pieces as pictured in step 6. Then prepare the following turkey marinade and allow the turkey to stand in it for 3 to 4 hours before grilling.

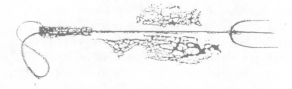

TURKEY MARINADE

  1 cup each salad oil and dry white wine
  6 tablespoons lemon juice
  ½ teaspoon each salt and Worcestershire
    Freshly ground pepper to taste
  3 green onions with tops, finely chopped

Start your barbecue fire, allowing enough time for all the fuel to ignite and burn down to a nice bed of coals (takes about 1 hour).

When ready to grill your half-turkey (times based on a 10-pound turkey half), place marinated drumstick, flat wing, drum wing, and body meat (skin side up) on a grill 6 to 8 inches above low, slow burning coals. Baste frequently with marinade. When turkey has browned on one side (takes about 15 minutes), turn and grill for 15 minutes on the other side.

Use kitchen tongs to get a good grip when turning turkey pieces.

Rotate pieces about once every 15 minutes for a total cooking time of about 1 hour and 15 minutes. Add the feather-shaped fillet piece during the last 45 minutes of grilling. When possible, keep dark meat in the center of the barbecue over the greatest heat, as it cooks slower than the white meat. To increase smoke flavor, place a sheet of foil loosely over meat during cooking. Slice to serve hot or cold.

◆ Grilled Young Turkey

  1 broiling turkey (6 to 9 pounds)
    Salt and pepper
  1 cup favorite barbecue sauce
    Dash liquid smoke
    Melted butter

Cut turkey in pieces as you would a frying chicken and lay in roasting pan. Sprinkle lightly with salt and pepper, and cover with barbecue sauce to which liquid smoke has been added. Marinate at least 5 hours, or overnight.

Split skin of turkey and rub sauce under it on meat, but do not remove skin. Grill turkey over charcoal coals, turning pieces frequently, and painting pieces with pastry brush dipped in melted butter. Cooking time, approximately 45 minutes. Makes 6 to 8 servings.

◆ Broiled Split Turkey

Split a 5 or 6-pound young turkey down the back and remove breastbone so it can flatten out like a thick steak. Have at hand a bowl of melted butter, mixed with a little chopped garlic and parsley. Broil the turkey like a steak over a deep bed of coals. Baste liberally with the melted butter.

Keep a bowl of water at hand. When flames spring up, sprinkle water (don't splash) on flames. By sprinkling lightly you create little steam clouds. After 45 minutes of this alternate steaming and broiling with frequent turnings you will have a broiled fowl that tastes the way pheasant is supposed to taste, and often doesn't.

◆ Charcoal-Broiled Duckling

Allow 1 young duck for 3 or 4 persons, depending upon its size. Have it split, and rub with soy. Broil over a medium hot fire, starting with cut side down; turn and continue broiling until the skin is crisp and brown and the meat fork tender. Because of the variance in tenderness, exact time cannot be given—45 to 60 minutes is usual. Toward the end of the cooking, brush with equal parts soy and honey.

◆ Boneless Breast of Mallard Duck

Breasts are removed in halves, filleted from the bone at the time of cleaning.

8 duck breasts
About 1 cup orange marmalade

MARINADE

1 cup soy
1 cup white wine vinegar
1 cup honey
4 cloves garlic, crushed or finely minced
1 tablespoon powdered ginger
¼ tablespoon dried tarragon

Remove duck breasts in halves. Combine ingredients for the marinade, and immerse duck breasts. Marinate for 24 hours in a cool place, but not in the refrigerator. Broil over charcoal for approximately 10 minutes on each side, or to desired doneness. Baste with marinade during the broiling.

Place on ovenproof platter and cover meat generously with orange marmalade. Place under oven broiler until marmalade bubbles and thickens. Garnish with parsley sprigs and serve. Serves 8 to 16, depending on heartiness of appetite for duck.

◆ Broiled Wild Mallard Duck

1 mallard duck (2 to 3½ pounds)
1 cup prepared French dressing
1 teaspoon dry mustard
2 teaspoons Worcestershire
2 teaspoons grated orange peel
1 teaspoon grated lemon peel

Split duck up backbone with poultry shears. Place breast side down on meat cutting board and break down breast bones by pressing with another board or by pounding gently with a meat tenderizing mallet.

Mix the sauce ingredients together and use mixture to baste the duck liberally. Insert the duck in a hinged wire grill and broil over hot coals until done to taste (7 to 10 minutes each side), basting it at least once more while cooking. Divide duck at breastbone into two portions and serve. Makes 2 servings.

◆ Wild Ducks – Grilled

Clean the ducks, wipe well, and split down the back. Season with salt and pepper, rub with fine olive oil and place on the grill. Let them cook from 7 to 10 minutes on each side, turning them over at least twice. A wild duck should never be cooked dry. Most chefs think it should just reach the point where the blood will not run if the flesh is pierced with fork in carving.

Place on a very hot dish and pour over them melted butter which has been mixed with lemon juice and minced parsley. Garnish with watercress or parsley sprigs.

Chinese Barbecued Duck

    2 or 3 young ducks, quartered
    1 cup sherry
    ⅓ cup honey or brown sugar
    1 tablespoon soy
    1 teaspoon grated fresh ginger (or
        powdered)
    1 teaspoon dry mustard
    Sesame seeds

Select lean, meaty young ducks. Trim off all excess fat possible. Pour marinade made of sherry, honey, soy, ginger, and mustard over quartered duck and let stand several hours, or overnight, in refrigerator. Place on grill over bed of coals and barbecue until done, about ¾ hour.

Baste duck with remaining marinade during cooking. Sprinkle with sesame seeds before serving. Makes 6 to 8 servings.

Squab

Split squab down the back. Brush with soy; barbecue 20 to 25 minutes, turning and basting occasionally with mixture of soy and melted butter.

Quail

Clean and wipe the birds well. Cut them through the back and spread. Rub them with melted butter and season with salt and freshly ground pepper to taste. Fasten a strip of bacon to breast of each bird with skewers. Place on the grill and cook for 15 or 20 minutes, according to size. Cook breast side up. Serve on buttered toast, allowing a slice for each bird.

Pheasant

Halve or quarter the bird, then marinate pieces in a mixture of half olive oil and half white wine. Sprinkle drained sections with paprika just before cooking. Broil on the grill, basting often with the oil-wine mixture. Add a little sprinkle of salt before serving. The oil-wine blend is used for basting because it does not dominate the natural flavor of the pheasant. Makes 4 servings.

GAME

Charcoal-Broiled Rabbit

If you've never barbecued rabbit, we think you'll find this an excellent method. The lemon-flavored marinade gives the rabbit pieces a crusty glaze so they aren't messy to pick up in your fingers.

    1 cup salad oil
    1 tablespoon celery seed
    1 teaspoon paprika
    2 teaspoons fresh thyme or ½ teaspoon
        dried thyme
    ½ teaspoon each salt and garlic salt
    2 tablespoons lemon juice
    1 young rabbit (2 to 2½ lbs.), cut in
        serving-size pieces

Mix together salad oil, celery seed, paprika, thyme, salt, garlic salt, and lemon juice. Pour over rabbit pieces and allow to marinate at least 1 hour. Slowly broil meat over charcoal about 30 minutes, or until tender. Turn frequently and baste often with remaining marinade. Makes 4 servings.

Charcoal-Broiled Venison Steak

This is venison at its best. Have steaks cut thick—never less than 1 inch, preferably 1½ inches. Rub with garlic, if you wish; brush with olive oil or butter, and broil over hot coals 8 to 14 minutes, depending on the thickness of the steak and rareness desired. Connoisseurs prefer venison rare; if well done meat is wanted, try another method of cookery, such as braising. If steaks have been cut thinner than 1 inch, pan-broil them, searing them quickly on both sides in a heavy, very hot frying pan or griddle.

◆ Barbecued Venison Chops

    1 tablespoon dry mustard
    1 tablespoon grated onion
    2 tablespoons minced parsley
    ½ cup (¼ pound) butter, soft but not
        melted
    6 venison chops, cut 1 inch thick
    ½ cup lemon juice
    ½ cup chili sauce
    1 teaspoon salt

Blend mustard, onion, parsley, and butter thoroughly. Shape into a small roll and chill until firm. Barbecue chops on a grill about 12 inches above glowing coals. Brush chops frequently with mixture of lemon juice, chili sauce, and salt; turn only once. Cook until done to your taste—8 to 14 minutes for rare. Remove to a heated platter and place a slice of spiced butter roll on each chop. Garnish with fresh herbs. Makes 6 servings.

◆ Saddle of Bear with Juniper

If the bear is young, this is a prize dish. Roast the saddle (the double loin) over charcoal, as you would lamb or mutton, basting with 2 cups red table wine to which you have added 1 sliced large onion and 2 teaspoons crushed juniper berries. Cook it to the extent you like, but if it is to be served rare, it must first have been frozen. Bear meat is delicious when cooked rare, but there is a danger of trichinosis if it is eaten that way. If the meat is frozen and held at —10° Fahrenheit for 30 days or longer, that danger is eliminated. Serve with braised celery and Roman sauce, or Napolitaine sauce.

ROMAN SAUCE
Combine 2 cups Espagnole sauce, 1 teaspoon sugar, ¼ cup currants, ¼ cup raisins, ½ cup pine nuts. Simmer for 10 minutes, correct seasoning, stir in 2 tablespoons red wine vinegar, and serve.

NAPOLITAINE SAUCE
Combine ¼ cup minced cooked ham, 1 teaspoon grated horse-radish, ½ cup sherry, ¼ teaspoon thyme. Simmer 10 minutes, then add ½ cup Espagnole sauce or brown gravy. Add ¼ cup seedless raisins, and salt and pepper to taste. Heat well before serving.

FISH AND SHELLFISH

◆ Sakana No Teriyaki

This is a Japanese way of broiling fish over charcoal. It's very easy, very quick. Select 2 pounds thick fish fillets, preferably sea bass or lingcod. Mix together 1 cup soy, ¼ cup sugar, and 1 teaspoon grated green or preserved ginger. Marinate fish 1 hour and broil over charcoal. Serve with rice and spinach that is cooked with a crushed garlic clove and a little salad oil. Makes 6 servings.

◆ Mackerel

Clean, cut off the head, and wipe with a damp cloth; do not wash. Split open and flatten out. Soak in a solution of salt and water (plenty of salt) for 24 hours. Then wash off all traces of salt and paint liberally with liquid smoke. Grill lightly for 5 minutes to a side over oak bark coals. Serve hot or cold.

◆ Trout

Trout, when wrapped in bacon, fastened with a skewer, and cooked on the barbecue grill is a dish fit for the gods. Cook over glowing coals in a hinged, double rack, and by the time the bacon is cooked crisp, the fish is done also.

◆ Grilled Fish With Herbs

Next time you broil fish outdoors, try this method so popular in Provence. Use any whole firm-fleshed fish. Clean, remove head if you wish, and make a few diagonal incisions in both sides. Brush with olive oil and sprinkle with salt and pepper. Lay a few branches of fennel across the fish on both sides, and fasten in a greased hinged broiler. (If you don't have fennel, use thyme, or bay leaves, or dill, preferably branches, though the crushed herbs may be sprinkled on.) Grill the fish on both sides, sprinkling a few times with a little more oil. When it's cooked, arrange it on a fireproof platter, and put a few heaps of dried herbs around it, douse with brandy, and light. When the flames die down, serve with lemon and sauce rémoulade (below).

SAUCE REMOULADE

To 1 cup mayonnaise made with olive oil and tarragon vinegar, add ½ cup each finely minced celery heart, white onion, and green pepper, 1 tablespoon prepared mustard, a pressed clove of garlic, and 2 teaspoons anchovy paste. A couple of chopped hard-cooked eggs may also be added.

◆ Grilled Lingcod

Buy unskinned lingcod fillets (2 lbs. for 4 servings). Baste with melted butter, season with salt and pepper, and place over a slow heat on your barbecue. Put skin side down; cook 10 minutes, turn, and cook 3 minutes more.

◆ Barbecued Sea Bass

For each serving:

    1 individual fillet of sea bass
        Salt and pepper to taste
    1 tablespoon melted butter
    ¼ teaspoon soy
        Juice of ¼ lemon
        Celery seeds
        Onion and green pepper rings
        White port wine

Arrange portions of fish in a large shallow container improvised from a double thickness of heavy aluminum foil, or in individual serving-size boats of foil. Season with salt and pepper, pour over butter, and sprinkle with soy, lemon juice, celery seeds, and onion and green pepper rings. Add white port until it's about ¼ inch up the side of the large container, or until each small container is about half full.

Place on barbecue, cover with hood (if your barbecue has one) or a sheet of aluminum foil, and cook just until the fish flakes.

Transfer to a hot platter and spoon juices over each portion as you serve at table, or if you are eating less formally, just serve the individual foil boats.

◆ Bass and Sausage

For a novelty, stuff bass with Mexican sausage, and grill over the coals. Type of sausage used is known as "chorizo."

◆ Rockfish Grilled in Skin

Ordinarily, you fillet a bony rockfish before cooking, but this isn't necessary—or even desirable—if you cook it on a hibachi or portable barbecue. Clean and scale starry rockfish, vermilion rockfish, Boccaccio (called red snapper), chilipepper, or other rockfish, and cook whole over low coals; no basting is required. The fish is turned just once, the cooked side is kept warm by a loose wrapping of foil. To serve, you peel off the skin and transfer the flaky fillets to waiting plates.

Select rockfish weighing 1½ to 2¾ pounds each. Allow about 1 pound fish for each serving. Clean, scale, and clip off side fins, remove head, if desired. Place fish on hibachi grill about 3 inches above ignited coals arranged one layer deep and spaced checkerboard fashion (take out extras and keep in a coffee can to add as needed). Cook fish 10 to 20 minutes on one side; carefully turn and cook an equal length of time, or until flesh flakes when tested along backbone just below head. (Cover loosely with foil to keep cooked side warm.) On serving tray, pull skin from one side of fish, lift fillet from bone; turn fish over and repeat.

Serve with savory lemon butter. (If fish chars, remove a few coals or raise grill.)

SAVORY LEMON BUTTER

Heat ½ cup (¼ pound) butter or margarine until lightly browned. Add grated peel and juice of 1 lemon, ½ teaspoon summer savory, ½ teaspoon salt. Makes about ¾ cup.

◆ Trout Barbecue

        ⅔ cup butter or margarine
        1 cup tomato juice
        1 cup dry white table wine
        ¼ cup (4 tablespoons) cider vinegar
        2 tablespoons brown sugar
    1½ teaspoons salt
        1 teaspoon each Worcestershire, paprika, and chili powder
        ¼ teaspoon pepper
        1 clove garlic, mashed or minced
        1 small onion, minced
        Small trout or larger trout cut in 3-inch pieces

Combine all the ingredients for the sauce and simmer for 10 minutes. When ready to cook trout, skewer cleaned fish on sturdy green sticks or long handled forks, dip in sauce, and roast over low coals for 10 to 15 minutes. Dip fish in sauce often to keep it moist.

◆ Bouillabaisse, Picnic Style

It's easy to cook bouillabaisse at a picnic when you take along a miniature barbecue or hibachi. Make the sauce ahead of time, and add the fish

and shellfish at the picnic spot. For larger groups, it's best to have a miniature barbecue and set of ingredients for each group of 4. Don't forget the bibs, and large soup plates for serving; also, be sure to include both soupspoons and forks.

        1 or 2 dozen small clams in the shell (optional)
        1 Dungeness crab, or ½ to ¾ pound frozen lobster tails
        ½ pound fresh or frozen shrimp
    1½ pounds assorted fresh or frozen fish (perch, cod, halibut, red snapper, bass—use 2 or 3 kinds)

SAUCE

        1 medium-sized onion, chopped
        1 or 2 cloves garlic, crushed
        2 tablespoons olive oil or salad oil
        ½ can (6 oz.) tomato paste
        1 teaspoon salt
        6 peppercorns
        1 bay leaf
        ¼ teaspoon turmeric
        ¼ teaspoon thyme
        1 or 2 lemon slices
        2 celery stalks with leaves
        1 sprig parsley
        1 cup wtaer
        ½ cup dry white wine

If clams are used, scrub thoroughly. Clean crab and cut or break into pieces; crack the legs. Slice the lobster tails crosswise into several pieces. Shell and devein shrimp. Remove bones from fresh fish; cut fish into pieces.

Prepare the sauce at home: Lightly brown onion and garlic in the olive oil or salad oil. Add tomtao paste, salt, peppercorns, bay leaf, turmeric, thyme, lemon slices, celery stalks, parsley, water, and wine. Carry this mixture in a jar or in a large kettle in which it will be cooked and served.

In the hibachi build a hot fire, using 2 quarts charcoal. Bring the sauce mixture to a boil in a large kettle. Add clams, fish, and lobster, if used; cover and boil for 2 minutes. Add shrimp and crab, if used; boil 4 to 6 minutes, or until fish flakes easily with a fork. Makes 4 generous servings.

◆ Broiled Salmon Steaks

An application of lemon juice adds greatly to the flavor of broiled salmon steaks. About an hour before cooking, brush both sides of each steak with lemon juice, cover loosely with waxed paper, and place in the refrigerator. When ready to cook, dust with flour, salt, and pepper. Then place on the grill.

◆ Tabangas Baked Fish

Select a good 5 to 7-pound salmon, striped bass, or steelhead. Clean, leaving head and tail intact. Stuff with this dressing:

2 cups chopped tomatoes
½ cup chopped onions
1 teaspoon ginger
1 teaspoon salt
Soy to taste
Lemon juice to taste
Dash of Tabasco
Minced garlic to taste

Fasten edges of fish together with skewers or toothpicks, and wrap whole fish in heavy foil or a large sweet leaf, such as banana. Bake over charcoal fire for about 2 hours. Makes 6 to 8 servings.

◆ Salmon Vinifera

The grape leaves protect the salmon from scorching and drying out; they keep the meat tender and very moist. The method should work equally well for steelhead.

Slice the salmon down each side, removing the bone. (Or purchase salmon fillets at the market.) If the salmon is large, cut off the salmon belly, which is thin, and discard it. Then cut in fairly small pieces as uniform in thickness as possible so one portion will not be overcooked while another is undercooked. Sprinkle with garlic salt.

Place each piece, skin down, on a slightly larger grape leaf. Put on rack or grill over barbecue fire, leaving a little space between leaves.

Cook for about 10 minutes. Then place another grape leaf over the top of each piece, turn over, and cook approximately 10 minutes more, until salmon is cooked through but not cooked dry. Remove from grill and serve.

◆ Salmon Barbecue for a Crowd

If you have a 20-pound whole fish, you can serve up to 20 people. You can have the fish filleted at the market where you buy it. Or if you are a sportsman and have caught your own salmon, sharpen a knife and fillet it yourself (see page 146).

Wait for the barbecue fire to form an even bed of coals and pass its peak of heat, for salmon is best cooked slowly.

To make the large fillets easier to handle on the grill and to serve, we laid each down on a piece of heavy duty foil and cut the foil just even with edge of fish.

Lift each fillet (including foil) and set it on your grill with the foil-covered skin resting on grill. You may want to consider putting one fillet on the grill 15 to 20 minutes after the first, so it will be hot for serving seconds.

If your barbecue has a hood, you can use several pieces of foil to cover the front completely and enclose the salmon on the grill. If it doesn't have a hood, you can make a foil hood for each fillet: Use a large sheet of heavy foil; shape the foil so that it will be 4 to 6 inches away from the fish all the way around. We rolled the edges of this foil hood around metal skewers, so it would not blow off in a breeze.

After the fish has cooked about 20 minutes, lift off the hood and brush the fish with lemon butter sauce: To make the sauce, melt 1 cup (2 cubes) butter, add ¼ cup lemon juice. Lift off hood and baste and check fish every 5 to 10 minutes until just tender enough to flake easily when tested with a fork—be careful not to overcook it. A 20-pound fish will probably cook in 25 to 35 minutes, depending on heat of the fire.

We found a large plank handiest for serving the fish. You might use a pastry board. By slipping two large spatulas under the foil lined skin, two people can easily lift the fillets from the grill to your plank. You can add a garnish of parsley, lemon wedges, and fresh tomato wedges to the plank before setting it on your outdoor buffet table. For a final touch of elegance have hot amandine sauce ready to spoon over each serving.

AMANDINE SAUCE

Melt 1 cup butter, add 1 cup chopped almonds, and 2 teaspoons minced onion; cook until lightly browned. Add 2 teaspoons lemon juice and salt and pepper to taste. If you wish, stir in also 1 tablespoon finely chopped chives.

Cut the salmon in serving sized pieces across fillets and just to the skin. Then it will be easy for each guest to lift his serving from the skin.

◆ Barbecued Steelhead

    A steelhead or small salmon (about
        5-pound size)
  2 teaspoons salt
  ¼ teaspoon pepper
  1 clove garlic, mashed
    About 10 slices bacon
  1 large onion, finely sliced
    About 3 sprigs parsley
    About 3 celery tops
  1 green pepper, finely sliced

Rub fish inside and out with salt and pepper. Rub inside with garlic. Fill inside with all remaining ingredients except for 2 slices of bacon. Reserve these for placing along each side of the fish as you wrap it in foil. Wind fine wire around all and place on barbecue grill over a medium hot fire. Turn three or four times during the cooking, which should take about 1 to 1½ hours. Makes 8 to 10 servings.

◆ Grilled Swordfish Steaks

  6 swordfish steaks
  ½ cup dry white wine
  ¼ cup salad oil
    Juice of 1 lemon
  ⅛ teaspoon crumbled dry tarragon
    Salt and pepper to taste
    Lemon wedges

Place swordfish steaks in marinade made by combining the wine, salad oil, lemon juice, tarragon, salt, and pepper; marinate about 2 hours. Place fish on a well-oiled grill. Grill over low fire until tender, about 7 minutes on each side, basting frequently with marinade. Serve with lemon wedges. Makes 6 servings.

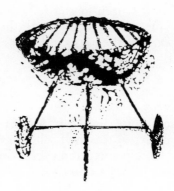

◆ Swordfish Barbecue

We suggest you use kitchen tongs to turn these fish steaks to prevent breakage.

  1½ to 2 pounds swordfish, cut 1 inch thick
  ½ cup soy
  ¼ cup catsup
  ¼ cup chopped parsley
  ½ cup orange juice
  2 cloves garlic, mashed
  2 tablespoons lemon juice
  1 teaspoon pepper

Marinate swordfish for 1 hour in a mixture of all other ingredients. Grill about 4 inches above hot coals for about 8 minutes. Turn fish and grill 7 minutes on other side. Brush on marinade frequently. Makes 4 servings.

◆ Lobster

Live or frozen whole lobsters, and frozen lobster tails, may be satisfactorily barbecued. If you buy live whole lobster, kill it by inserting knife in back between body and tail shells. Split lengthwise and clean under running water. Spread each half with Lemon-Butter (below). Grill cut side toward heat about 5 minutes. Turn, brush with Lemon-Butter, and grill about 5 minutes longer, or until meat is opaque.

Whole frozen lobsters have been cooked before freezing. Too much heat will toughen them. After thawing, spread each half of the split, cleaned lobster with Lemon-Butter; wrap each half in foil and place shell side down on a grill over medium heat until heated through, about 15 minutes.

To barbecue frozen lobster tails, thaw tails; cut away the under-shell. Bend shell back, cracking some of the joints. (If tails are large, split them lengthwise.) Grill same as live lobster.

LEMON-BUTTER

Cream ⅓ cup butter until soft. Add 2 teaspoons minced parsley, ½ teaspoon salt, dash of pepper, and 2 tablespoons lemon juice; beat until fluffy. Enough for 4 servings.

◆ Colby's Scampies

    6 large prawns, fresh or frozen
    ¼ pound (½ cup) butter or margarine
    2 tablespoons olive oil
    2 tablespoons steak sauce
    6 crushed garlic cloves
    1 teaspoon each crushed basil, tarragon,
        celery seeds
    2 tablespoons dry white wine
      Salt to taste

Shell and vein the shrimp and split each in butterfly fashion. Combine all other ingredi-

ents except salt in a sauce. Marinate shrimp in the sauce at least 1 hour. When coals in the barbecue have reached the glowing stage, spread tails out on the grill, turning them and basting often. When they show a little brown color, salt to taste, remove from fire, cut into 1-inch pieces, and serve immediately. Serves about 6 for hors d'oeuvres, 2 as an entrée.

◆ Barbecued Prawn Appetizers

    1 pound raw (green) prawns
    ½ cup dark molasses
    1 can (8 oz.) Spanish-style tomato sauce
    ½ teaspoon salt
    ½ teaspoon freshly ground pepper
    1 teaspoon dry mustard
    ¼ teaspoon Tabasco
      Pinch of thyme
    ¼ cup salad or olive oil

Wash, shuck, and clean raw prawns. Toss into boiling salted water, reduce heat, and simmer for 15 minutes. Drain and cool, but do not rinse as this tends to toughen them.

Mix all the rest of the ingredients together to make the sauce. If you do not like too hot a mixture, cut down on the pepper, mustard, and Tabasco. Add the cooked prawns and turn in the sauce until completely covered.

Scoop out the prawns and arrange on the barbecue grill or thread on skewers. Cook over hot coals. Turn prawns two or three times and baste frequently with the sauce left in the bowl. Serve hot, right from the grill. This is finger food, so have plenty of napkins nearby.

◆ Oysters in Bacon Wrap

Season oysters with salt and pepper, and wrap each oyster in a thin strip of bacon and secure the wrapping with wooden toothpicks. Arrange the "blanketed" oysters in a hinged, double, wire rack. Barbecue quickly over a hot bed of coals, turning often. As soon as the bacon has "sizzled" to your fancy, your barbecued oysters are done.

Serve with sliced lemon, a little drawn butter, A-1 sauce and Tabasco.

Celestial Shrimp

These shrimp are broiled in the shell, so serve them with plenty of enormous paper napkins or, in the Chinese manner, with hot, wet towels.

Select 2 pounds of jumbo green (uncooked) prawns; slit the backs with a pair of pointed scissors, then wash out the sand veins.

Marinate the prawns for 2 hours in the following mixture: ½ cup each of soy, salad oil, and sherry to which you have added a tablespoon of minced green or crystallized ginger.

Drain the prawns, put in a fine-meshed hinged broiler, and cook over coals for 3 minutes; turn and cook 2 or 3 more minutes, or until the shells are pinkly browned. Serve immediately. You'll have 30 to 40 prawns.

VARIETY MEATS

Broiled Brains

Beef, veal, or lamb brains may be broiled over charcoal. A beef brain serves three, a veal brain serves two, and a lamb brain serves one. Unless you are a master at fire control and charcoal cookery, we think it is best to parboil the brains first. Soak brains in cold water, then simmer for 15 minutes in water to cover. (Add 1 tablespoon lemon juice and 1 teaspoon salt to each quart of water.) Drain, and cover with ice water; remove discolored spots. Split brains and dip in melted butter, then roll in fine crumbs.

Broil over a slow charcoal fire, turning so that both sides will brown. Baste with a little more butter while cooking. The brains will broil in about 10 minutes. Serve them with lemon wedges, crisp bacon, and drawn butter or tartar sauce.

Charcoal-Broiled Liver

Liver is at its best when cooked over charcoal. Use beef, veal, or lamb liver, and have it sliced at least 1 inch thick. Brush well with melted butter, oil, or bacon drippings. Broil over a medium hot fire, allowing the meat to become crisply brown on the outside but not dry in the middle. Most persons prefer liver broiled medium rare (make a slit in the meat with a sharp knife to see degree of doneness). Serve with bacon and fried onions, or broiled tomatoes, or eggplant.

Charcoal-Broiled Liver'n Bacon

2 pounds calf's liver (approximately 4 pieces cut 1 inch thick)
1 teaspoon monosodium glutamate
8 strips lean bacon

MARINADE
½ cup oliv oil or salad oil
⅛ teaspoon pepper
⅛ teaspoon garlic salt or ¼ teaspoon onion salt

Have the meat man cut liver into 1-inch-thick slices and trim off veins and outer skin. Soak liver in a mild salt-water solution (1 teaspoon salt to 2 cups water) for 30 minutes. Remove and dry surfaces of liver. Sprinkle each side with monosodium glutamate. Take each piece, put a strip of bacon under it and another on top of it, and roll up together and secure with a skewer.

Mix marinade ingredients in a shallow dish or pan. Place liver in marinade, slosh it thoroughly over the meat, and place all in the refrigerator for 2 or 3 hours, turning twice during that time.

Place liver on grill over medium charcoal fire. Broil on each side, turning only once (approximately 15 minutes total cooking time). *Do not overcook*. The meat should be slightly pink on the inside with a mild brown crust on the outside. The bacon drippings that fall on the coals and make the fire flare up give the liver a wonderful barbecue smoke flavor. Makes 4 to 6 servings.

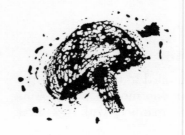

◆ Charcoal-Broiled Kidneys

Beef, veal, lamb, and pork kidneys may all be successfully cooked over charcoal. Split the kidneys and remove cores; brush with oil or melted butter, seasoned, if you wish, with garlic or with bacon drippings. Broil over a medium hot fire, but not too long or they will toughen. The kidneys will take from 5 to 15 minutes to cook, depending on size. They are done when brown on the outside but still juicily pink inside. Slice kidneys and serve with melted butter.

Kidneys may also be cut in pieces, wrapped in bacon, and charcoal-broiled. In this case it is not necessary to brush them with oil. Cook until bacon is very crisp.

◆ Broiled Beef Heart

If you like rare beef, you will like beef heart sliced ½ inch thick and broiled quickly over charcoal. The slices should first be marinated in equal parts wine and olive oil, or in melted butter. If cooked lightly, the heart will be tender. Do not attempt this method if you like your beef well done, for longer broiling will make the beef heart tough.

◆ Charcoal-Broiled Sweetbreads

You cook these exactly the same way you do brains (see recipe on page 51). Or they may be parboiled, cut in pieces, and threaded on skewers, alternated with mushroom caps. Dip filled skewers in melted butter and broil until nicely browned.

◆ Charcoal-Broiled Pigs' Feet

The pigs' feet must be boiled before they are grilled. Cook them, whole or split, in water to cover, with salt, an onion, and an herb bouquet. Simmer until tender—from 3 to 4 hours. Drain, brush well with softened butter, then roll in crumbs. Broil until nicely browned on all sides. Serve with charcoal-roasted potatoes and with sauerkraut heated at the back of the grill.

◆ Charcoal-Broiled Tripe

Tripe needs to be pre-cooked until fork-tender. Cook it in a pressure cooker or by boiling in salted water. Cut in strips, dip in melted butter, and broil on both sides until brown. Serve with individual dishes of melted butter and with wedges of lemon. Fried onions and green pepper, and charcoal-roasted potatoes go well with this.

FRUITS AND VEGETABLES

A hinged grill with narrow grids is the best way to handle the broiling of fruits and vegetables. They usually require brushing with butter or basting during the cooking.

◆ Fruits

APPLES. Cut unpeeled apples in thick slices and dip in butter. Broil on both sides, sprinkling with cinnamon and sugar toward the end of the cooking.

BANANAS. Peel bananas and cut in half. Wrap with bacon and broil on both sides. Or use unpeeled bananas and make a slit about 3 inches long in the skin. Force 1 tablespoon of honey into this opening and let stand for ½ hour. Place on grill and cook for about 8 minutes, turning frequently.

DATES. Remove pits, stuff with Cheddar cheese, wrap in bacon, and broil. These are for an appetizer.

FIGS. Wrap fresh figs in bacon and broil until bacon is crisp.

GRAPEFRUIT. Cut grapefruit in halves and remove seeds. Loosen segments from the skin and section membranes. Cover with brown or white sugar to start the juice running, and after half an hour, add more sugar, if desired. Dot tops with butter, pour about a tablespoon of sherry or rum over each half. Place on grill and broil until fruit is thoroughly heated.

ORANGES. Cut unpeeled oranges in thick slices, dip in melted butter, then dust lightly with flour. Broil on both sides.

PEACHES. Use fresh or canned peaches. If fresh, they should be peeled and halved. Brush with butter and broil, cut side down, until brown, then turn and fill cavities with butter and brown sugar, and continue broiling until brown on the bottom. If desired, put a little sherry or rum in the cavities and serve them as a dessert with cold sour cream or ice cream.

PEARS. Do these in the manner suggested for peaches.

PINEAPPLE. Cut a fresh pineapple of average size lengthwise into 8 sections. Place in baking pan and drip honey—about a tablespoon to a section—over the fruit. Let stand for ½ hour and then grill. Or, use sliced pineapple, either canned or fresh, and brush with melted butter before broiling on both sides.

◆ Vegetables

ARTICHOKES. Use cooked artichoke bottoms, and marinate them in French dressing before broiling.

CARROTS. Cook unpeeled carrots until just tender, peel, dip in butter, and broil.

CORN. There are many ways to cook corn on the cob over a charcoal fire, and these are just a few of the variations:

1. Use unhusked ears. Lay back husks and remove silk. Return husks to former position and wire into place (with any fine wire) at center and near tip of cob, covering the kernels as well as possible. Roast on the grill, turning 3 or 4 times so that all surfaces are exposed to the heat. Snip the wires with wire cutter, husk the ears (gloves are necessary) and serve.

2. Open husk at one end; let about 2 tablespoons of barbecue sauce run inside the ear. Smooth husk back in place; tie and cook as above.

3. Pull husks back, remove silk, brush corn generously with garlic butter. Replace husks and place ears on grill. Dip a clean burlap sack in warm water, wring it out slightly, and place it over the ears so that they will steam. Let the ears grill 5 minutes on one side. Remove burlap, turn ears, re-cover with burlap, sprinkle it with more water. Grill 5 minutes longer.

4. Strip ears down to last 3 or 4 husks and place in ice water 30 minutes or longer. Drain well and place on grill for only 15 or 20 minutes.

5. Husk corn, wrap in bacon, and broil until bacon is crisp and the exposed corn brown.

EGGPLANT. Cut unpeeled eggplant in slices or wedges. Marinate for an hour in garlic-seasoned olive oil, and broil until nicely browned, brushing with more oil during the cooking.

MUSHROOMS. Select large ones, remove stems, and dip caps in butter. Put in a hinged broiler and cook stem side down, then turn, fill cavities with butter (seasoned with tarragon, chives, or dill, if desired), and finish broiling. Serve as an appetizer, or serve with any meat, shellfish, or poultry.

ONIONS. Take big whole yellow onions just the way they come from the market, leave the dry outside skins on, wet them thoroughly, and place them on the grill. Roll them around while you're cooking steaks, spareribs, or whatever. By the time everything else is done, they'll be black on the outside and soft and creamy inside.

PEPPERS. Cut green peppers in quarters, remove seeds, and dip in olive oil before broiling.

TOMATOES. Cut firm tomatoes in halves, brush with butter, sprinkle with salt and pepper, and broil, cut side down. When brown, turn, brush with more butter, and continue cooking until barely tender. If desired, buttered toast crumbs may be sprinkled on the cut sides after turning.

◆ Foil-Wrapped Fruits

APPLES. Peel and slice; season with butter and sugar and with cinnamon, coriander, or mace. Wrap in foil and broil until fork tender.

BANANAS. Peel and slice or quarter; season with sugar and butter; wrap in foil and broil.

ORANGES. Peel oranges and divide into segments. Season with butter, sugar, and cinnamon or rosemary. Wrap and broil.

PEACHES. Peel and cut in slices. Season with butter and brown sugar. Wrap and then broil.

PEARS. Peel and slice; season with butter, sugar, and ginger, or add slivered candied ginger. Wrap and broil.

PINEAPPLE. Use pineapple chunks. Season with butter and sugar. Wrap and broil.

◆ Foil-Wrapped Vegetables

Shredded peeled beets, sliced carrots, corn cut from the cob, sliced peeled eggplant, sliced mushrooms, sliced onions, sliced green peppers, sliced or diced white or sweet potatoes, shelled peas, and sliced squash may all be foil-wrapped and cooked on the grill. Season them with plenty of butter and with salt and pepper before wrapping. If desired, vegetables may also be cooked in combinations. Onions and potatoes, corn and green peppers, and peas and mushrooms are good together.

SKEWER COOKING

◆ Skewer Cooking

When you decide to have a skewer dinner, toss rules and cookbooks aside. Just take an assortment of foods from refrigerator and cupboard, season them with imagination and curiosity, push them on a skewer, add a bit of showmanship, and grill over coals. Anything and everything which cooks in a reasonable length of time can go on a long or short metal skewer.

All kinds of meat, firm fish and shellfish, canned meats and sausages, almost any vegetable, and many fruits can be slipped over steel spikes for their turn over the grill. Pre-cooking gives you an even greater choice. Best of all, you have both meat and vegetables on one skewer, needing only some rice, a glistening green salad, and a well-browned loaf of French bread treated with garlic butter to complete the meal.

An assortment of food grilled on a skewer is colorful and gay. There's no monotony with such a meal because each bite is different— something like a box of assorted chocolates. And, if the foods have hugged close together while they cooked, they'll slide off the skewer and retain their shape on the plate.

Even the shape that the food takes on a skewer can be varied. Instead of using green

pepper squares, curve green pepper strips around another bite of food. In addition to looking attractive, the green pepper will keep fragile foods such as fruit from breaking off the skewer. Instead of cutting bacon or beef into squares, try weaving strips of either meat on the skewer. The trick to this is to use the skewer as you would a long needle and a short piece of thread and work close to the point.

Onions cut into quarters stay put if the skewer is run through the point and out on the other side. Tomato quarters will still be intact if they aren't too ripe and if the skin is left on to hold them together. Since mushrooms may split and fall into the coals if pressed too hard in the lineup, they are better when they are used as end pieces.

Bacon squares or strips and partially cooked sausage add fat and flavor to lean foods such as vegetables and fish or shellfish. Use oil, butter, or margarine in the basting sauce, too, to help with the browning as well as to add fat to some foods. Any barbecue sauce should·be heated so that it won't cool off the foods on the grill and will have a better chance to season well.

It's up to the cook to decide whether or not

to soak the filled skewers in a marinade before grilling—except in the case of shish kebab. Here the squares of meat cut from a leg of lamb must be marinated (preferably overnight) so that the herb and garlic-flavored wine and oil goes clear through them. Round steak strips or squares are better flavored and take on a crisper brown if soaked in a mixture of soy and a little mashed garlic. Worcestershire performs in much the same way.

For a new idea in patio entertaining, you can give your guests a chance to build their own dinners on skewers. Spread out an assortment of foods on a tray, furnish skewers and paper napkins, and see who will come up with the most amazing assortment—the "Dagwoods" of the grill. But it isn't wise to let each guest cook his own skewer meal after assembling it. That would be asking for burned meat and trouble. Here, however, is where the host can perform with mop and sauces.

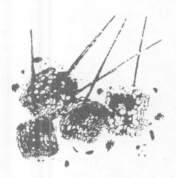

◆ Try a Skewer Buffet

Everybody has fun at a skewer buffet—the guest because he can select his own combination of food to slip on the steel spike; the host because he holds the center of the stage at the barbecue, basting and browning each personalized order; and the hostess because most of her work is done before the party starts.

A good assortment of skewer foods is colorful and gay looking. Best of all, foods can be simple. You can plan your buffet around several kinds of meat or fish. Add half a dozen vegetables, and fruits—and endless combinations are possible (see photograph on pages 152-153).

You can thread on a skewer any food that cooks in a reasonable length of time. Remember, however, that you can't mix short-cooking and long-cooking foods on the same steel spike.

To baste as large an assortment of foods as is shown on pages 152-153, you will need three different sauces:

SAUCE NO. 1: Soy, wine, and oil seasoned with mashed garlic.

SAUCE NO. 2: Tomato-base barbecue sauce.

SAUCE NO. 3: Lemon-butter seasoned with herbs.

You may wish to marinate some of the meats before arranging them in dishes. In this case, save the marinade, add extra oil or butter to insure better browning, and heat the mixture over the grill before using it as a basting sauce.

Here are the nine skewer combinations shown in the photograph:

1. Round steak with small green onion bulbs. Weave strips of meat around onion bulbs on skewer, working close to the point of skewer. Grill. (Sauce No. 1.)

2. Bacon-pineapple roll-ups; sweet pickle chunks. Grill slowly until bacon is done. Drippings provide natural basting sauce. Bacon keeps pineapple from falling off skewer.

3. Green pepper strips; whole small, white boiling onions (or canned onions); bacon; round steak strips. Roll up thin round steak strips loosely so meat cooks in center. Bacon supplies some fat. Grill slowly (Sauce No. 1 or No. 2).

4. Orange sections; ham and olive roll-ups. Ham supplies some fat so light basting of oil is sufficient.

5. Onion quarters; marinated lamb; green pepper; tomato. Add additional oil or butter to marinade for sauce.

6. Apple and ham. Butter or oil provides necessary fat; last-minute brushing with honey glazes meat, fruit.

7. Mushrooms; bacon; chicken livers. Weave bacon around chicken livers. Grill slowly. (Sauce No. 1 or No. 3.)

8. Ripe olives; prawns; pimiento. Food is cooked so needs only browning. (Sauce No. 3.)

9. Potato; chunks of frankfurter; canned artichoke hearts. Use cooked small potatoes or

canned potatoes. Skewer artichokes through the hearts. Needs only heating, browning. (Sauce No. 3 plus some prepared mustard.)

◆ Hors d'Oeuvres on Disposable Skewers

In Honolulu, kebabs made in miniature on disposable bamboo sticks—just 3 or 4 tempting bits to each tiny kebab—are popular party fare. The rules for making them are simple: (1) Cut foods so that each piece is bite size. (2) Use pre-cooked foods when necessary so the kebab will broil in 3 to 5 minutes. (3) Arrange foods on skewers with marinated meats between other foods to spread the juicy meat flavor; put firm bits on the ends to hold all the others in place.

Skewers should be about 4 inches long. Bamboo sticks in 6 to 10-inch lengths can be purchased in Japanese stores; cut these and sharpen one end. You may also use small applicator sticks available in most drug stores, or cut the skewers from an inexpensive match-stick bamboo place mat.

You may serve the kebabs Honolulu style—arranged ahead of time, with guests then broiling their own over a hibachi or other miniature barbecue. Or they can be broiled in the kitchen and served piping hot to your guests. Have ready as many different combinations as your

time and budget will allow. Here are some suggested combinations—some dipped or marinated before broiling, others broiled plain and served with one or more of the cold dunking sauces given below.

1. CHICKEN LIVER, BACON, MUSHROOM. Drop chicken livers into mixture of hot butter and sherry (use 4 tablespoons butter and 2 tablespoons sherry for 1 pound of livers). Cook about 1 minute on each side; cool, and cut into bite-sized pieces. Partially cook strips of bacon; cut into 2-inch pieces. Use canned small whole mushrooms. Alternate on skewers, starting with mushrooms; fold each bacon piece. Dip in Teriyaki Sauce before broiling.

2. BEEF, TOMATO, CELERY, GREEN PEPPER. Use top sirloin or other good quality lean beef; slice very thin. Cut in 1-inch pieces. Marinate for 1½ to 2 hours in Teriyaki Sauce. Fold meat pieces to put on skewers between raw vegetables. Use small pieces of green pepper, celery, and tomato (halves of cherry tomatoes or quarters of small Italian tomatoes are best if you can get them). Dip in sauce; broil.

3. CHICKEN, WATER CHESTNUTS, MUSHROOMS. Breasts of chicken (or turkey) are the best parts to use; cut into small squares. Marinate in a barbecue sauce about 1 hour, then sauté in a little butter or margarine to cook partially. Arrange on skewers with canned mushrooms and slices of canned water chestnuts, starting with mushrooms. Dip in sauce before broiling.

4. SHRIMP, MUSHROOM, GREEN PEPPER. Use small shrimp, shelled and deveined; drop into boiling water and simmer 5 minutes. Marinate shrimp about 1 hour in a barbecue sauce. Arrange on skewers with small pieces of green pepper and canned whole or sliced mushrooms. Dip in sauce before broiling.

5. PORK, APPLE, PINEAPPLE. Use fully cooked fresh pork roast (leftover roast is fine). Cut into small squares, and marinate about 1 hour in Teriyaki Sauce. Arrange on skewers with pineapple chunks and halved raw apple slices. Dip in sauce; broil. In place of pork, cubes of cooked duck or lamb roast are also delicious in combination with pineapple and apple.

6. FRANKFURTER, ONION, MUSHROOM, GREEN PEPPER. Cut frankfurters into small pieces; marinate in either Teriyaki Sauce or a barbecue sauce for about 1 hour. Put on skewers with canned or precooked tiny white onions, canned mushrooms, and pieces of green pepper. Dip in sauce; broil.

7. BEEF ON A STICK. Cut top quality beef sirloin (raw) into tiny cubes. They may be marinated for ½ to 1 hour in Sesame Soy Sauce, or just put on the skewers and dipped in the sauce, before broiling.

8. CHICKEN OR TURKEY ON A STICK. For this it would be best to buy chicken or turkey breasts and cut the raw meat into tiny cubes. These may be marinated or just dipped into the Sesame Soy Sauce; broil until brown and tender, about 5 minutes.

9. MINIATURE MEAT BALLS. Use lean ground chuck or round, mix with egg, and season well; or use recipe for meat balls. Roll into tiny balls. Put 3 or 4 on each skewer or alternate meat with chunks of banana or pineapple; broil. We liked them best dunked in Sour Cream-Onion or Cheese Rabbit Sauce.

10. BACON, PINEAPPLE, BANANA. Partially cook bacon strips. Weave on skewers around chunks of canned pineapple and slices of banana; broil. Cheese Rabbit Sauce makes a good dip.

11. BEEF, PINEAPPLE, BANANA, PAPAYA. Use top sirloin or other good quality lean beef; slice very thin. Cut in 1-inch pieces. Fold pieces of beef and arrange on skewers between small chunks of banana, pineapple, and papaya (or mango); broil. Use Guacamole or no sauce at all with these delicate, tropical flavors.

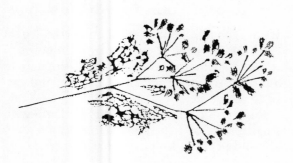

12. CHICKEN, BACON, AVOCADO. Use chicken or turkey breasts or leftover roast turkey. Cut into small cubes. Brown uncooked poultry in a little butter until tender. Partially cook bacon; cut firm avocado into chunks. Weave bacon skewer around chunks of chicken and avocado; broil. You might serve it with Guacamole Sauce.

TERIYAKI SAUCE

Soy is the principal ingredient in this sauce which is typical of those used for Japanese teriyaki. It can be varied to suit your taste by adding ginger, garlic, or sherry.

  1 cup soy
  ½ cup sugar
  1 teaspoon monosodium glutamate
  ¼ cup olive or salad oil
  2 teaspoons grated fresh ginger or 1 clove garlic, chopped (optional)
  ½ cup sherry (optional)

Combine all ingredients and stir until blended.

SESAME SOY SAUCE

If you have an electric blender, you'll find it takes the work out of grinding sesame seeds for this sauce. The flavor is unusual and very good. The recipe makes a large amount, but it keeps indefinitely.

  1 cup sesame seeds
  1 cup soy
  1 cup water
  1 clove garlic, crushed
  1 tablespoon sugar
  ½ cup vinegar
  ½ cup sherry
  1 large apple, finely grated

Put the sesame seeds into a deep frying pan; stir continually over medium heat until they are brown. Remove from heat. Using a mortar and pestle, grind about ¼ cup of the seeds at a time until they reach the consistency of peanut butter. (Or combine sesame seeds and soy, and whirl in a blender.) Add all the remaining ingredients. Let stand at least 24 hours to blend flavors. Makes about 1 quart.

CHEESE RABBIT DIP

Prepare cheese rabbit from your own recipe; cool. Or buy prepared cheese rabbit in a can or jar.

SOUR CREAM-ONION DIP

Blend a package of onion soup with 1 pint sour cream; let stand several hours so flavors blend.

GUACAMOLE DIP

Mash 2 large avocados with 1 large tomato (peeled, chopped, and drained). Add 1 small onion, chopped fine, 1 tablespoon wine vinegar, salt, pepper, and chopped green chili peppers to taste; mix well.

LAMB

◆ Shish Kebab

Buy 1 pound of leg of lamb per person, plus 2 or 3 extra pounds. Lamb shoulder may be used, too. Plan on 1⅓ "shish" (skewer load) per person.

> 1 medium-sized onion per person
> Salt
> Cayenne
> Italian red pepper
> Black pepper
> Dried oregano
> ½ cup wine, wine vinegar, or cider vinegar
> 2 tablespoons olive oil
> 1 medium-sized green pepper per "shish"
> 1½ medium-sized tomatoes per "shish"

A day ahead of time prepare the meat as follows: Cut the boned leg of lamb into steaks, crosswise down the length of the leg, about 1¼ inches to 1½ inches thick; then into cubes. Cut out any gristle. A small strip of fat may be left on the cubes if desired.

Place meat in a bowl and salt to taste. Pepper with the three different kinds of pepper, but not too much for it will kill the flavor of the meat. Add about 1 rounded tablespoon of oregano for each leg of lamb. Cut onions into thin strips and place in the bowl with the meat. Pour over all the wine or vinegar and olive oil. Mix well and allow this to marinate in your refrigerator overnight.

Save the lamb bones and leftovers to make the broth used in preparing pilaff, an accompanying rice dish, the recipe for which is given in the chapter on accompaniments.

Cut the tomatoes into chunks about the same size as the meat. Do not skin. Small Italian pear-shaped tomatoes are good used whole. Cut the peppers into pieces big enough to bend and be skewered. Beginning with a piece of meat, then tomato, and pepper, skewer three of each alternately on each "shish." Broil for 15 to 20 minutes over a good bed of coals, basting frequently.

Heat the marinade, add chopped tomatoes to suit taste, and use for sauce.

◆ Lamb and Ham Shish Kebab

Using about 7 pounds of shoulder or leg of lamb for 7-8 people, cut the lamb in cubes.

Soak 6-8 hours in claret wine—enough to almost cover meat; add slices of onion and garlic to your taste.

Place on skewers, alternating the lamb with small pieces of tenderized ham. Season with salt and pepper. Broil over charcoal fire.

◆ Chinese Shish Kebab

Dip cubes of lamb or pork in a mixture of soy, cornstarch, and peanut oil. If available, add fresh ginger root, mashed. Skewer between slices of green pepper and cook over coals. Serve with sauce made from 1 part prepared mustard to 3 parts catsup.

◆ Lamb or Beef Kebabs

1½ pounds meat (use either beef round or lamb shoulder) cut in 1-inch cubes
½ cup tomato catsup
1 teaspoon salt
2 tablespoons sugar
2 tablespoons beefsteak sauce
2 tablespoons cider vinegar
2 tablespoons Worcestershire
¼ cup water
2 tablespoons salad oil or shortening

Place cubed meat in bowl; combine remaining ingredients in saucepan and heat to boiling. Pour over meat; let stand several hours or overnight in marinade. String on skewers and broil over hot coals. Reheat marinating liquid for sauce. Serves 4.

◆ Lamb in Onion Juice

2 pounds lean lamb
2 medium-sized onions
½ cup salad oil
1 bay leaf
1 teaspoon salt
½ teaspoon thyme
Pinch of sage
3 peppercorns, crushed
1 cup sherry (or red wine)

Cut the lamb into cubes about an inch square and put them in an earthen bowl. Run the two onions through the food grinder, using the finest blade. Place the onion pulp in a small muslin sack or a cloth and squeeze the juice onto the meat. Add the oil, bay leaf, and seasonings, working them into the meat. Add the

wine and let everything stand—at least overnight. Then spike the meat on skewers and broil to your taste. You can alternate pieces of bacon, onion, green peppers, or even very small tomatoes with the lamb.

◆ Lamb en Brochette

4 tablespoons olive oil
6 tablespoons soy
¼ teaspoon freshly ground pepper
1 large onion, grated fine
3 tablespoons lemon juice
3 to 4 pounds lean lamb meat

Mix ingredients together to make a marinade. Cut lamb into cubes and leave in the marinade for an hour or longer, turning and rubbing the seasonings into the meat. Thread on skewers and broil. Makes 6 servings.

◆ Skewered Minted Lamb

For each serving:

3 pieces lean lamb, cut in squares
2 whole small green tomatoes
2 slices onion, cut ½ inch thick
6 squares sliced bacon

Marinate meat for 30 minutes in sauce given below. Alternate the above items on skewers. Broil, basting frequently with sauce until done.

MARINADE AND BASTING SAUCE
½ ounce dry mint leaves
1 teaspoon dry tarragon leaves
½ cup vinegar
¾ cup brown sugar
1 teaspoon dry mustard
½ teaspoon salt
½ cup butter
Juice of ½ lemon and grated peel
½ cup sauterne

Put all ingredients except sauterne into a saucepan and bring to a boil. Remove from heat, cover pan, and let steep for about 30 minutes. Strain, and add sauterne. Cool.

BEEF

◆ Rolled Steak

Slice sirloin tip across the grain with a very sharp knife, making thin slices about the size of the palm of the hand. Cut fat bacon lengthwise into narrow strips about ⅛-inch wide. Put a strip inside the slice of beef and roll up; pin with toothpicks. Slide roll on skewer and broil.

◆ Beef Skirts-Kebab

On a beef, there is a strip running along the bottom of each flank called a skirt steak. Two of these adequately serve four persons. Get your butcher to cut these skirts in two, lengthwise, and you will wind up with four long pieces of meat about 2 inches wide and 18 inches long.

> 2 skirt steaks, cut into 4 lengthwise strips
> ¼ cup salad or olive oil
> 1 cup dry red wine
> 1 clove garlic, crushed
> 1 medium-sized onion, minced or grated
> ½ teaspoon pepper
> 2 tablespoons soy
> 2 tablespoons prepared mustard
> Fresh mushroom caps, quartered; onions, green peppers, and tomatoes as desired

Soak the meat in the marinade (all the remaining ingredients except the mushrooms, onions, peppers, tomatoes) for at least 5 hours—the longer the better.

When the charcoal fire is ready, thread the meat on metal skewers in a ribbon style, alternating with mushrooms and other whole ingredients.

The fire should be 6 to 8 inches from the skewers. Cooking time is between 45 minutes and 1 hour. When you serve, give each of your guests a Skirt-Kebab, sliding it deftly off the skewer. Makes 4 servings.

◆ Foil Kebabs

To cook kebabs in foil: Thread meat, onion, green pepper, and tomato cubes on a skewer or a thin stick. Wrap in a double thickness of foil, place on coals, and cook for about 14 minutes.

◆ Skewered Round Steak

Buy whole slices of top round, cut ⅜ inch thick. Allow 1 slice for 3 people (or for 2 if they have "outdoor" appetites). Weave meat on 2 skewers so the length of the meat runs parallel to the skewers. Weave skewers about 1 to 1½ inches in from the side edges of the meat. Rub both sides of meat with a cut clove of garlic and salad oil.

Hold meat over low coals 3 minutes for each side, or until half done. Sprinkle with salt, pepper, and any other seasonings you wish; then, using 2 forks, bunch the meat together on the skewers so it "ripples." Continue cooking until each side is crusty brown.

Pull meat off skewers and cut crosswise in 2 or 3 servings. The sections of meat folded inside the ripples will be rare and juicy and the outside sections will be crusty. For an even better browning, brush the meat with a barbecue sauce after you have bunched it together in ripples.

◆ Steak with Orange Sauce

> 2 pounds skirt steak, sirloin, or top round
> 1 teaspoon salt
> Freshly ground pepper
> ¼ cup sugar
> 2 tablespoons vinegar
> 1⅓ cups fresh orange juice
> 2 teaspoons lemon juice
> ½ teaspoon dry mustard
> 2 beef bouillon cubes
> ½ cup heavy cream

Cut steak into bite-sized chunks and thread these on small bamboo or metal skewers. Rub meat with salt and pepper. Caramelize the sugar in a heavy skillet over low heat, stirring constantly. Add vinegar and orange juice; cook and stir until sugar dissolves again. Cool. Add lemon juice and mustard, and pour over steak pieces. Cover meat and marinate overnight in refrigerator.

Remove meat from marinade. Pour marinade into a small pan, add bouillon cubes, and simmer until about half as much remains. Add cream, stirring rapidly so it doesn't curdle; remove sauce from heat.

Broil skewered steak pieces over hot coals. Reheat orange sauce. Serve meat on toasted hamburger buns; spoon orange sauce over the meat. Serves 4.

◆ Steak Kebabs

Secure bay tree sticks from the hills. (Any green sticks may be used but the bay sticks add aroma and flavor.) Wash and whittle them to a point at the smaller end.

Pieces of steak cut about 3 or 4 inches square are spiked on the stick, leaving about an inch or so between each 2 pieces. This, of course, is to allow the meat to cook on all sides. Salt and pepper the meat and then hold or prop your stick over the fire until the meat is done to your own liking. It usually takes 20 to 30 minutes. Top round steak from good beef may be used for this.

◆ Skewered Beef Chunks

Fillet of beef or top round, cut 3 inches thick.

SAUCE
- ½ cup olive oil
- 3 tablespoons wine vinegar
- ½ tablespoon garlic salt
- 1 tablespoon paprika
- 1 teaspoon monosodium glutamate

Trim fat, then cut meat in 3-inch squares. Thread 3 cubes on each skewer, so the grain of the meat is a right angles to the skewer. Leave 1 inch between each chunk of meat. (If you use lightweight skewers that are not grooved or notched, stick 2 skewers into each set of chunks so the meat won't slide around.)

Brush meat with sauce and let stand for 30 minutes. Brush sauce over meat again, then barbecue until meat is cooked, about 20 to 30 minutes.

To slice meat, place point of skewer on cutting board; slide chunks down, very close together. Cut down through chunks, across the grain, and make thin slices. Serve slices on hot split and buttered French rolls. Have mustard and catsup ready in case they are desired.

◆ Skewered Steak and Mushrooms

Well marinated squares of tender beef, and fresh mushrooms, threaded on skewers and broiled, make good outdoor eating.

- ½ cup Burgundy or claret wine
- 1 teaspoon Worcestershire
- 1 clove garlic
- ½ cup salad oil
- 2 tablespoons catsup
- 1 teaspoon sugar
- ½ teaspoon salt
- ½ teaspoon monosodium glutamate
- 1 tablespoon vinegar
- ½ teaspoon marjoram
- ½ teaspoon rosemary
- 1 pound sirloin steak
- 12 large fresh mushrooms

Mix wine with Worcestershire, peeled garlic clove, salad oil, catsup, and seasonings. Cut meat into 2-inch squares. Wash mushrooms thoroughly. Marinate steak squares and mushrooms in wine mixture for 2 hours.

Alternate meat squares and mushrooms on skewers. Broil, turning on all sides, basting frequently with remaining marinade. Makes 4 servings.

◆ Ground Beef

> 1 pound ground meat
> 2 eggs
> ½ cup dry bread crumbs
> 1 tablespoon prepared mustard
> ½ teaspoon salt

Combine ground meat with eggs (beaten), bread crumbs, mustard, and salt. Divide into 6 or 8 parts and squeeze each portion of meat around the skewer. Broil. Makes 6 to 8 servings.

VARIATION

Use the above combination of ground beef and form into 6 or 8 thick patties; encircle each with a strip of bacon and let stand for several hours. Skewer patties crosswise.

◆ Skewered Hamburgers

> Garlic, finely chopped
> Salt and pepper
> ½ cup olive oil
> 1 pound ground beef
> ½ cup finely chopped onion

Put finely chopped garlic, salt, and pepper into olive oil and stir thoroughly. Place hamburger in large bowl and cover with onion. Add olive oil mixture, and combine. Knead with hands to mix onions thoroughly through meat and to permit complete absorption of oil.

Take barbecue skewers and form meat around skewers to about 1½-inch diameter. Length of meat along skewer may be varied to suit size of buns into which it will be placed. Barbecue over charcoal, turning continuously to keep juices in and upon meat.

Push meat off skewers into buns and serve. Have mustard and catsup ready in case it's needed. Makes 6 servings.

◆ Hamburgers en Brochette

Form seasoned meat loaf mixture into balls the size of a small egg. String 2 or 3 meat balls on skewers, alternating with onion and quarters of unpeeled tomato. Sprinkle with salt or brush with barbecue sauce. Grill until done.

VARIATION

Mold seasoned meat around skewer, and wrap with a slice of bacon. Dip in sauce when done.

◆ Veal Sati

> 2 pounds veal steak, cut in 1-inch squares
> ¼ cup soy
> Juice of 1 lemon
> 2 tablespoons oil

Run each skewer through the center of 4 to 6 meat squares. Mix the rest of the ingredients and pour over the skewered meat. Let stand 3 or 4 hours. Broil over glowing coals 15 to 20 minutes, or till a golden brown. Turn as necessary to cook evenly and baste with the sauce once during the broiling. Makes 4 to 6 servings.

◆ Skewered Veal Barbecue

> ⅓ cup soy
> 1 large onion, chopped
> 2 tablespoons salad or olive oil
> 1 tablespoon dried oregano
> 2 or 3 veal steaks, ½ to ¾ inch thick
> Burgundy or claret wine
> 1 can (1 lb. 13 oz.) sliced pineapple

Mix together the soy, onion, oil, and oregano. Cut the veal steaks into 1 to 1½-inch squares, depending on the thickness of your skewers. Put the veal squares in a bowl, pour in the marinade, then add enough Burgundy to cover the meat when packed down in the bowl. Let the meat marinate all day and turn it in the marinade from time to time. Cut the pineapple slices into quarters.

About 2 hours before time to barbecue, string the meat on the skewers with a piece of pineapple between every two pieces of meat. You'll have to work carefully on the pineapple as it is apt to split if skewers are large. Arrange the skewers on a shallow pan, pour over the sauce and marinate, turning occasionally, until time to barbecue over coals. Barbecuing takes about 20 minutes in all, turning 4 times. Baste with the marinade when you turn skewers. This fills 6 good-sized skewers. If you have any pineapple left over, drain well, then sauté the pieces in small amount of butter until lightly browned.

VARIETY MEATS

◆ Parboiled Sausage

Parboil sausage briefly and string with slices or cubes of unpeeled apple.

◆ Liver

Skewer calves-liver cubes with bacon and whole mushrooms. For chicken livers, alternate with small bacon squares. Broil.

◆ Lamb Liver

  1 whole lamb liver (1-1½ pounds)
  5 medium-sized onions
  4 cloves garlic, mashed
    Salt and allspice to taste
  1 large bunch celery

Buy the freshest lamb liver you can get. Cut it into 1-inch cubes and place in bowl. Add onions, cut in 4 parts lengthwise (do not cut the bottom stem, just peel outside skin, otherwise the onion sections will fall apart). Add the mashed garlic and seasonings. Chop the bunch of celery, including the leaves, and place in

bowl. Mix all ingredients together and set in refrigerator for 2 hours.

Place on skewers, alternating an onion quarter with 3 or 4 cubes of liver, and broil. Use remaining vegetables for salad. Makes 2 to 4 servings.

◆ Skewered Chicken Livers

  18 chicken livers
   6 slices bacon
     Salt and pepper
     Mushrooms
     Olive oil
     Bread crumbs
     Butter, melted
     Lemon juice
     Parsley

Wash chicken livers, and dry well with clean cloth. Season with pinch of salt and pepper. Cut livers in half. Broil bacon slices, one minute to each side, and cut each slice into 6 pieces.

Take 6 skewers, run one through center of liver slice, then a mushroom, then a piece of bacon, and repeat until all skewers are filled. Roll in olive oil, dip in fresh bread crumbs, and broil over coals.

Arrange on a hot dish, and over them pour melted butter to which lemon juice and chopped parsley have been added. Makes 6 servings.

◆ Chicken Livers with Water Chestnuts

Use fresh (wash thoroughly) or canned water chestnuts; slice into 3 parts. Slice chicken livers and dip in soy; place slice of water chestnut between two slices of chicken liver, wrap in thin strip of bacon, place on skewer, and broil.

◆ Broiled Chicken Hearts

Many "chicken parts" markets sell hearts at a very low price. They are delicious when broiled, either as a main course with a casserole of rice or noodles, or as an appetizer. Marinate washed hearts in equal parts soy, sherry, and cooking oil, seasoning with garlic or ginger, if you wish. String on skewers and broil for about 8 or 9 minutes, turning to cook on both sides.

GAME

◆ Ripple-Skewered Venison Steak

    1¾ to 2-pound good quality venison steak
           (about 1½ inches thick)
     1 cup Rosé or white table wine
           (or 1 cup bouillon)
     2 tablespoons lemon juice
     1 tablespoon honey
     1 teaspoon seasoned salt
        Few drops Tabasco
    ½ cup catsup
     6 French rolls or frankfurter buns
        Chopped green onion

Cut steak across the grain into diagonal strips about ½ inch wide. Combine the wine, lemon juice, honey, seasoned salt, and Tabasco. Pour over meat, and marinate several hours or overnight. Drain meat well, saving marinade. Thread steak strips onto skewers, ripple fashion; grill, close to the barbecue coals until rare or medium-rare. In the meantime, add the catsup to drained marinade; heat to boiling. Heat or toast 6 split and buttered French rolls or buns. Slip venison strips from skewers into rolls. Spoon hot sauce over meat and sprinkle generously with chopped green onion. Makes 6 servings.

FOWL

◆ Soy-Broiled Chicken Squares with Green Onion

Cut the meat from a 1¾ to 2-pound broiler chicken (or from a 1-pound package frozen chicken breasts) into 1-inch squares. Cut about 10 green onions into 1½-inch lengths. Thread chicken and green onions on thin wooden or metal skewers — about 3 pieces of each per skewer. Place in sauce made by combining ¾ cup each soy and unsweetened pineapple juice and 3 tablespoons sugar. Quickly broil over hot coals, about 5 minutes on each side. Baste twice during broiling. Serve hot, sprinkled with cayenne pepper if desired. Makes 3 servings.

FISH AND SHELLFISH

◆ Fish-Kebabs

     1 bottle (5 oz.) soy
     1 medium-sized white onion, chopped
     2 tablespoons grated fresh ginger or
           washed candied ginger
     2 cloves garlic, finely chopped
     2 teaspoons dry mustard
     1 teaspoon prepared horse-radish
    ½ teaspoon curry powder
     2 pounds large shrimp
     1 pint medium-sized oysters
    ½ pound very lean bacon
     4 to 6 tomatoes
    12 to 16 pearl onions
     2 green peppers

Prepare marinade by combining soy, white onion, ginger, garlic, dry mustard, horseradish, and curry powder. (The marinade can be mixed the night before, allowed to stand overnight in the refrigerator, then brought out about 6 hours before broiling to allow it to come to room temperature.)

Shell and vein shrimp, then marinate at least 2 hours.

Puff oysters slightly in hot water and cook bacon to the limp stage. Then wrap oysters in half slices of bacon, using toothpicks to hold. Cut tomatoes into quarters, leave onions whole, and cut peppers into bite-size chunks. Interlace all ingredients on skewers and broil over a medium hot charcoal fire for 3 to 5 minutes, or until done to taste, basting frequently with heated marinade during the broiling.

Serve as an entrée with fried rice, or serve as hors d'oeuvres with any remaining marinade kept hot in a chafing dish for dunking purposes. Makes 6 to 8 servings as an entrée, at least twice that many for hors d'oeuvres.

◆ Campfire Oysters

Use skewers, or cut long green sticks, peel and sharpen ends. Cut thin strips of bacon into fourths. Alternate on the stick with drained oysters, ending and beginning with a piece of bacon. Three large oysters and four pieces of bacon are sufficient for one sandwich. Cook until bacon is well broiled and edges of oysters curl. Push off onto bread or bun. Season with salt and pepper and squeeze a little lemon juice over oysters.

◆ Barbecued Halibut

    4-pound piece of halibut
½ cup soy
 1 cup dry white wine
 2 tablespoons lemon juice
 2 cloves garlic (minced or mashed)
 1 teaspoon powdered ginger
½ cup salad oil
 2 tablespoons fresh rosemary
 6 tablespoons fresh chopped parsley
 1 pound fresh mushrooms, sliced
⅓ cup butter

Cut halibut into pieces about 1 inch wide, 2 inches long, and 1 inch thick. Combine soy, wine, lemon juice, garlic, ginger, and salad oil. Pour over fish pieces, and marinate 4 hours.

Pour off marinade and save. Sprinkle fish pieces generously with the rosemary and parsley. Skewer carefully or slip inside wire toaster and place over the barbecue grill over low coals. Cook until fish flakes when tested with a fork, about 10 to 15 minutes, basting occasionally with remaining marinade. In the meantime, sauté mushrooms in butter; add remaining marinade, heat through, and pour over broiled fish. Makes 8 servings.

◆ Swordfish on a Skewer

The swordfish is an excellent choice for outdoor cooking. Its firm, white, boneless meat holds together well and is easy to manage on the barbecue. When properly prepared, swordfish is moist and has a meaty flavor different from that of any other seafood. It becomes dry when overcooked.

 2 pounds swordfish
 1 tablespoon salad oil or olive oil
 1 tablespoon salt
 1 tablespoon chopped parsley
¼ teaspoon pepper
  Juice of 1 lemon
  Bay leaves

Cut swordfish into 1½-inch pieces. Combine in a small bowl salad oil, salt, parsley, pepper, and lemon juice. Dip fish in this sauce. Thread fish on skewer, placing a bay leaf lengthwise between every two pieces of fish. Grill about 4 inches above hot coals for about 5 minutes. Turn and grill 5 minutes on other side. Brush with sauce during grilling. Serve with oil and lemon sauce (below). Makes 4 servings.

OIL AND LEMON SAUCE
 3 tablespoons olive oil
 3 tablespoons lemon juice
 1 tablespoon chopped parsley
 1 teaspoon dry mustard (optional)
 1 clove garlic, mashed (optional)
  Salt and pepper to taste

Combine all ingredients and mix or shake in a small bowl or jar with a lid.

Shrimp

Skewer whole large shrimps or prawns with dividers of pineapple wedges and bacon. Broil.

VARIATION
Peel large shrimps. Dip in soy, drain, skewer, and broil over coals.

FRUITS AND VEGETABLES

This method of cookery requires a slow fire and careful watching. Most fruits cook quickly, but the vegetables, in many cases, should be parboiled first. The pieces are strung on skewers and are usually basted during the broiling.

Fruits

UNPEELED APPLE QUARTERS. Roll in melted butter and sprinkle with sugar.

PEELED APPLE. Cut in cubes, wrap in bacon, and broil until the bacon is crisp.

CANNED APRICOT HALVES. Dip in butter after skewering, and broil until brown.

PEELED BANANAS. (1) Cut in 4 pieces, dip in melted butter, and brown. Then roll in chopped salted almonds. (2) Cut in 1-inch slices, wrap in bacon, and broil until bacon is crisp.

ORANGE OR TANGERINE SECTIONS. Dip in butter and broil lightly.

PINEAPPLE CHUNKS. (1) Alternate with green pepper squares and brush with butter. Cook until lightly browned, but with the pepper still crisp. (2) Alternate with bacon squares; cook until bacon is crisp. (3) Brush with butter; alternate with thin slices of preserved ginger.

Vegetables

UNPEELED EGGPLANT CUBES. Marinate in garlic-flavored olive oil, and alternate with cherry tomatoes on the skewers. Cook until the eggplant is brown and tender.

PEELED EGGPLANT CUBES. (1) Wrap in bacon; broil until bacon is crisp. (2) Marinate in French dressing; alternate with green pepper and 1-inch-long pieces of green onion. Broil tender.

MUSHROOM CAPS. (1) Dip in dill-seasoned French dressing; broil until lightly browned. (2) Dip in butter; alternate with quartered tomatoes or small cherry tomatoes; cook lightly.

SMALL CANNED OR PARBOILED POTATOES. Dip in butter and broil until brown. After cooking they may be sprinkled with minced parsley or dill.

SMALL PARBOILED ONIONS. Alternate with squares of green pepper and squares of bacon. Cook until brown.

CUBES OF PARBOILED YAMS OR SWEET POTATOES. Alternate with chunks of pineapple, and brush with butter before broiling.

QUARTERED GREEN TOMATOES. Wrap in bacon and cook until the bacon is crisp.

SMALL ZUCCHINI. Cut in 1-inch slices, or use small green summer squash. Marinate in French dressing, and broil until tender. You may alternate the squash with onions, green pepper, or cherry tomatoes.

ROASTING ON THE SPIT

◆ Roasting on the Spit

Spit roasting is the oldest form of cooking, and many experts still consider it the best. Actually, it is the only *true* roasting, for foods cooked in the oven are really baked.

The superior flavor and extra juiciness of spit-cooked meats are unquestioned, for the meats are self-basted with their own juices while turning, and the only loss is that of excess fat. Spit cooking has another big advantage in that it needs little supervision once the meat is properly spitted over a well-built fire.

◆ Trussing and Balancing

Unless the meat—or fish, or fowl—is correctly trussed and balanced, there will be trouble. The small electric motors with which spits are equipped are not powerful enough to offset the jerking and stopping caused by meat that is spitted off center. The motor may break down; and even if it doesn't, the food will be unevenly cooked.

In all cases, the food should be as compact as possible. This means that it should be tied or trussed so that wings and legs of poultry will lie close to the body, and no small, oddly shaped pieces will protrude from the main mass of other meats.

Care must also be taken to assure that the meat will not slip around on the spit but will turn with it. This means that holding forks must be properly adjusted and tightened. In many cases, especially when several pieces of food are on one spit, one or two extra skewers —long ones—must be inserted so that all will turn together.

The important thing in balancing is to have the spit pass through the center of gravity. This takes some experience; only way to judge the success of your effort is by eye and by the way the spitted meat comes to rest when you hold the ends of the spit in either hand or put it on props of equal height. Even when the meat is properly balanced at the beginning of the roasting period, it may not remain that way. Sometimes more fat renders out from one part of the roast than from another. Several charcoal grills on the market today are equipped with a weight compensator. This makes balancing very easy. At least one such compensator can be adjusted while the cooking is actually in progress.

◆ Fire and Direction of Turn

The fire for roasting should, generally speaking, be a little lower than for broiling.

It is best to have the spit turn away from the cook when at the top of the turn (clockwise when you are facing the right end of the spit). The fat drops off on the upswing, not at the very bottom of the turn. If the spit turns away from you, you can catch dripping fat in a pan placed in front of the fire (the fire itself should be toward the back of the firebox). This arrangement prevents flaring, so that you may leave the roast unattended except for an occasional check of the fire.

If it is not feasible to have the spit turn in that direction, push the coals into a circle and put a pan in the center to catch drippings. This is less satisfactory because, as stated above, the drippings do not fall at the exact bottom of the turn.

◆ Basting

A roast properly spitted and turning in the right direction will automatically baste itself with its own juices. If the spit turns evenly, as it will if well balanced, the meat will brown evenly too. We do not attempt here to suggest bastes for all the meats mentioned in this chapter, because most cooks have their own favorite ones. However, some are given here and there are more in the chapter on sauces and marinades.

We do want to point out, however, that unless the meat is very lean, basting is not really necessary.

◆ Timing

Cooking time is bound to vary greatly for a number of reasons—size and temperature of the uncooked meat, temperature of the fire, temperature of the air, whether there is a wind, and, if so, whether the spit is shielded from it.

For all these reasons, it is most satisfactory to use a meat thermometer to determine when the meat has reached the degree of doneness desired.

The times suggested in this chapter are based on meats started at room temperature; remember that a large roast taken from the refrigerator will take 6 or 8 hours to reach that temperature.

One more point should be emphasized in regard to timing and temperature: All roasted meats, but particularly the larger ones, continue cooking after they are removed from the fire or the fire is doused. For this reason, the temperatures given here as a signal to end the cooking may increase from 5° to 10° by the time the meat is served. If the roast is allowed to turn on the spit after the fire is out, the juices will increase and carving will be easier.

BEEF

◆ Standing Rib Roast

A rib roast of any size, from 2 ribs to 8, may be roasted to perfection on the spit. Have the ribs cut short and the back cord and chine bone removed. If the roast is larded with fat, it should be securely tied in place. A standing rib roast should be spitted on the diagonal—this makes balancing much easier.

Insert one end of the spit into the cut side just below the ends of the bones. Force it diagonally through the length of the roast, so that it emerges toward the top of the other cut end. Adjust holding forks and tighten screws securely. Balance the roast and respit if necessary. Insert the meat thermometer in the center of the meat, making sure that it will not touch a bone or the spit. Roast over a medium slow fire until the thermometer reaches the point you desire. A 5-rib roast will take from 2 to 2½ hours to reach from 125° to 140°.

◆ Spencer Roast

This is a rib roast with the bone and most of the end fat removed. It may be spitted through the center of the meat, or on a diagonal. It should be securely tied. A whole one, weighing about 14 to 16 pounds, makes a fine roast to serve a large party of 20 or more. It will cook rare in about 2 hours, well done in 3½. Again, we recommend a meat thermometer.

SPIT ROASTING TIME

Variety of Meat	Cut of Meat	Size or Weight	Warm-up Time for Frozen Meat		Recommended Heat of Fire*
			In Refrigerator to 40°	In Room 40° to 70°	
Beef	Standing Rib	3 to 5 Ribs	36 to 40 Hrs.	8 Hrs.	Hot-Medium
	Rolled Rib	6 to 7 Pounds	36 to 40 Hrs.	8 Hrs.	Hot-Medium
	Spencer	8 to 10 Pounds	36 to 40 Hrs.	8 Hrs.	Hot-Medium
	Rump	3 to 5 Pounds	24 to 30 Hrs.	6 Hrs.	Medium
	Tenderloin (Whole)	4 to 6 Pounds	12 to 18 Hrs.	10 Hrs.	Hot
	Sirloin	5 to 7 Pounds	18 to 24 Hrs.	8 Hrs.	Hot-Medium
Fish	Large, Whole	10 to 20 Pounds	30 to 40 Hrs.	12 Hrs.	Slow
Ham	Smoked	We do not recommend roasting cured ham over charcoal. If you wish to do			
Lamb	Leg	4 to 8 Pounds	15 to 40 Hrs.	5 to 7 Hrs.	Medium
	Rolled Shoulder	3 to 6 Pounds	15 to 30 Hrs.	4 to 6 Hrs.	Medium
	Saddle	6 to 16 Pounds	15 to 36 Hrs.	6 to 10 Hrs.	Medium
	Rack (Ribs)	4 to 7 Pounds	12 to 24 Hrs.	5 to 6 Hrs.	Medium
	Baby Lamb, Kid	12 to 25 Pounds	30 to 54 Hrs.	12 to 15 Hrs.	Medium
Pork	Loin	5 to 14 Pounds	28 to 36 Hrs.	6 to 10 Hrs.	Medium
	Shoulder	3 to 6 Pounds	24 to 30 Hrs.	6 to 8 Hrs.	Medium
	Fresh Ham	10 to 16 Pounds	30 to 48 Hrs.	10 to 15 Hrs.	Medium
	Spareribs	1½ to 3½ Pounds	4 to 7 Hrs.	2 to 3 Hrs.	Medium to Hot
	Suckling Pig	12 to 20 Pounds	30 to 54 Hrs.	12 to 15 Hrs.	Medium
Poultry	Chicken	3 to 5 Pounds	10 to 12 Hrs.	4 to 5 Hrs.	Medium
	Cornish Hen	12 oz. to 1 Pound	8 to 11 Hrs.	2 to 3 Hrs.	Medium
	Squab	10 to 14 Ounces	8 to 11 Hrs.	2 to 3 Hrs.	Medium
	Turkey	10 to 25 Pounds	15 to 36 Hrs.	8 to 10 Hrs.	Medium
	Junior Goose	4 to 7 Pounds	13 to 20 Hrs.	5 to 7 Hrs.	Medium
	Goose	8 to 15 Pounds	20 to 30 Hrs.	6 to 9 Hrs.	Medium
	Duckling	4 to 6 Pounds	13 to 18 Hrs.	5 to 7 Hrs.	Medium
Veal	Leg	8 to 14 Pounds	24 to 36 Hrs.	7 to 10 Hrs.	Medium
	Loin	10 to 13 Pounds	20 to 30 Hrs.	6 to 9 Hrs.	Medium
	Shoulder (Rolled)	3 to 5 Pounds	15 to 24 Hrs.	4 to 6 Hrs.	Medium
Venison	Leg	9 to 12 Pounds	20 to 40 Hrs.	7 to 10 Hrs.	Hot-Medium
	Shoulder	5 to 7 Pounds	15 to 24 Hrs.	4 to 6 Hrs.	Hot-Medium
	Saddle	12 to 18 Pounds	18 to 40 Hrs.	8 to 12 Hrs.	Medium

* Hot fire, 325° or over; medium, 250 to 300°; slow, 150 to 225°. Check with thermometer.

AND TEMPERATURE CHART

Approximate Time for Cooking						Comments
Very Rare 120°-130°	Rare 130°-135°	Med.-rare 135°-145°	Medium 145°-155°	Well-done 155°-180°		
1½ to 2¼ Hrs.	1¾ to 2¼ Hrs.	2 to 2¾ Hrs.	2½ to 3 Hrs.	3 to 4½ Hrs.	1	1. Start with very hot fire; let it burn down to medium.
1¾ to 2½ Hrs.	2 to 2¾ Hrs.	2¼ to 3 Hrs.	2¾ to 3¼ Hrs.	3¼ to 5 Hrs.	1	2. If meat is larded (wrapped in fat), it will take somewhat longer to cook.
1½ to 2½ Hrs.	2½ to 3 Hrs.	2¾ to 3½ Hrs.	3 to 4 Hrs.	3½ to 5½ Hrs.	1	
1¼ to 1¾ Hrs.	1½ to 2 Hrs.	1¾ to 2½ Hrs.	2½ to 3 Hrs.	3 to 4½ Hrs.		3. Handle fire as for rib roast, above.
25 to 40 Min.	35 to 45 Min.	45 to 60 Min.	50 Min. to 1¼ Hrs.	1 to 2 Hrs.	2	
1 to 1½ Hrs.	1¼ to 1¾ Hrs.	1¾ to 2¼ Hrs.	2¼ to 3 Hrs.	3 to 4 Hrs.	3	4. Thawing time varies, depending upon shape of fish.
Cook to 135° or 140° internal temperature.					4	
so, follow timing for fresh ham (below).						
50 to 65 Min.	1 to 1¼ Hrs.	1¼ to 1½ Hrs.	1½ to 2 Hrs.	2 Hrs. or More	5	5. Some believe lamb is tenderer and more flavorsome when cooked rare.
50 to 65 Min.	1 to 1¼ Hrs.	1¼ to 1½ Hrs.	1½ to 2 Hrs.	2 Hrs. or More	5	
— — —	¾ to 1¼ Hrs.	1 to 1½ Hrs.	1¼ to 1¾ Hrs.	2 Hrs. or More	5	
— — —	¾ to 1 Hr.	1 to 1¼ Hrs.	1¼ to 1½ Hrs.	1¾ Hrs. or More	5	
— — —	— — —	— — —	2 to 2½ Hrs.	2½ to 3½ Hrs.		
— — —	— — —	— — —	— — —	2 to 4 Hrs.	6	6. Pork should be cooked to 185° internal temperature.
— — —	— — —	— — —	— — —	2 to 3½ Hrs.	6	
— — —	— — —	— — —	— — —	4 to 6 Hrs.	6	
— — —	— — —	— — —	— — —	1 to 1½ Hrs.	6	
— — —	— — —	— — —	— — —	3 to 4 Hrs.	6	
— — —	— — —	— — —	— — —	1 to 1½ Hrs.	7	7. Eviscerated weight. Use leg joint test for doneness.
— — —	— — —	— — —	— — —	¾ to 1 Hr.	7	
— — —	— — —	— — —	— — —	¾ to 1 Hr.	7	
— — —	— — —	— — —	— — —	2 to 4 Hrs.	7	
— — —	— — —	— — —	— — —	1¾ to 2½ Hrs.		
— — —	— — —	— — —	— — —	2 to 3 Hrs.		
— — —	— — —	— — —	— — —	1 to 1½ Hrs.	8	8. Whole wild duck cooks in 20 to 30 minutes to very rare stage.
— — —	— — —	— — —	— — —	2 to 3 Hrs.		
— — —	— — —	— — —	— — —	1½ to 2½ Hrs.		
— — —	— — —	— — —	— — —	¾ to 1½ Hrs.		
1 to 1¼ Hrs.	1¼ to 1½ Hrs.	1½ to 1¾ Hrs.	1¾ to 2¼ Hrs.	2 Hrs. or More		
50 to 65 Min.	1 to 1¼ Hrs.	1¼ to 1½ Hrs.	1½ to 2 Hrs.	2 Hrs. or More		
— — —	1¼ to 1½ Hrs.	1½ to 1¾ Hrs.	1¾ to 2¼ Hrs.	2 Hrs. or More		

◆ Rolled Rib Roast

This is usually cut from the large end, the bones removed, and the remaining meat and fat tied in a roll. It is most easily spitted if done on the diagonal. It will take a little longer than a Spencer roast.

It is excellent for serving a crowd; it is easy to slice in convenient serving-size pieces. Have your meat man roll a rib of beef. Make several small incisions in the surface of roast and insert small pieces of peeled onion and fresh thyme. Rub surface of roast lightly with smoked salt. Place on spit and roast, basting frequently with barbecue sauce. Cooking time is 1½ to 2 hours. Slice in rounds to serve. Makes 14 servings.

◆ Tenderloin Roast

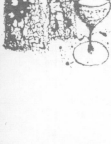

Here is a boneless cut that is actually better in a lower grade of beef than prime or choice. Good, standard, or commercial tenderloin makes a fine, tender, and economical roast, as the fat content is less than in the higher grade. It should be basted with butter or oil, or wrapped in fat. Such a roast will cook rare in half an hour. It may be spitted through the center of the meat, but it must be tied securely.

◆ Rump Roast

This is a fine cut for roasting, if prime or choice beef is used. It should be trimmed and tied compactly. A thermometer is essential with this cut, as the shape varies considerably. For this reason not even approximate timing can be given.

◆ Buttered Beef with Rosemary

This is an easy meal to fix for family or friends, yet it has distinction.

Use a 6-pound boneless rump of beef, one of choice or prime grade. Roast on the spit until the meat thermometer reaches 120°. (This will be very rare.) In a large skillet, heat 1 cup (½ pound) butter or margarine—more if you are feeling lavish—with 1 tablespoon finely minced rosemary, along with any juices that gathered

while the meat roasted. Slice the meat thinly, and dip in the herb-seasoned butter. Add a little salt and pepper before serving on slices of French bread with some of the herb butter and juices. For those who prefer their meat less rare, it is a simple matter to cook the meat in the skillet until done to their liking. Makes 10 to 12 servings.

◆ Veal

Veal roasts may be successfully cooked on the spit, but, because of their tendency to be dry, they should be well basted or well larded. Spit in the same manner as like cuts of lamb, and cook until the thermometer reaches 160° to 165°, or until well done.

◆ Sirloin Roast

Here is a very choice roast, better known in England than it is here. It is the same cut as a strip or top sirloin or club steak, but it should be cut at least 5 inches thick. Spit on the diagonal, and cook with a thermometer. It will take less than an hour for rare.

LAMB

A leg of lamb or mutton should be spitted more or less parallel to the bone. A rolled boneless shoulder may either be spitted on the diagonal or straight through the meat. Both roasts take about the same length of time to cook: medium rare (145° to 150°) in an hour or a little over, well done up to 2½ hours.

◆ Leg of Lamb

Make several cuts in a short-cut leg of lamb (5 to 6 pounds), and insert 4 split cloves of garlic and a mixture of ½ teaspoon crumbled dried oregano and 1 teaspoon salt. With any remaining oregano and salt, rub the outside of the meat. Insert the spit almost parallel to the bone and place over medium coals. Mix 4 tablespoons melted butter and the juice of 1 lemon, and brush the meat. Basting once or twice, barbecue 1¼ to 1½ hours (140° on a meat thermometer) for medium rare. Makes 6 to 8 servings.

◆ Breast of Lamb

Have breast left whole, and allow 1 pound for each person. Marinate overnight in a mixture of 2 cups red wine or tomato juice, ¼ cup vinegar, 1 teaspoon sweet basil or rosemary, 2 crushed cloves of garlic, 2 teaspoons salt, a little pepper, and a sliced onion. When ready to cook, weave the meat on the spit and roast over charcoal, basting with the marinade. It will take an hour or so for the lamb to become crisply brown and tender.

◆ Saddle and Rack

The saddle and rack of lamb are other good cuts for spit roasting. Have the flank of the saddle rolled inside, and tie compactly. The rack may have the flank folded over the ends of the chops. It, too, should be tied.

◆ Lamb Shoulder

       4 cloves garlic, minced
       2 large onions, minced
       1 green pepper, minced
       2 tablespoons salt
       1 tablespoon freshly ground pepper
       2 cans (6 oz.) tomato paste
       1 pint water
         Rosemary and thyme to taste
         Dried celery leaves to taste
         Dash of Tabasco
       1 pint red wine
       4 lamb shoulders

Simmer sauce ingredients except wine for about 1 hour, stirring often. Remove from stove, cool, and stir in the red wine. Place about 1 pint of the sauce in a jar (saving the rest for later) and take it to your meat man. Have him bone the lamb shoulders, cover the insides well with the contents of your jar, and then roll them as any rolled roast.

Bring the rolled roast home, spit it over a good bed of coals, and baste frequently with the remainder of the sauce. Cooking time 1½ to 2 hours. Makes 24 servings (6 to each lamb shoulder).

PORK

A fresh shoulder or ham may be nicely roasted over charcoal. It should be done slowly and cooked to 175°. It will then be safely cooked but not dried out. A 12-pound fresh ham takes 4 hours or more. Spit like lamb.

Pork loins make a fine roast. Two loins may be tied together so that the fat is on the outside giving the appearance of a rolled piece of meat. Spit through the center. A single loin takes from 2 to 2½ hours to cook.

Suckling pigs are spectacular and delicious. Select one weighing 18 pounds or less. Tie the legs together and truss them close to the body. The pig may be stuffed, if desired. Cook, brushing with heavy cream or butter occasionally, for 3 to 4 hours, or until the thermometer reaches a temperature of 185°.

Spit roasting is an ideal way to cook spareribs, as they will cook slowly without flaring. They should be left in one piece and woven on the spit. Basting is usually preferred. The ribs will cook to a shiny tender brown in from 1 to 1½ hours. Do not overcook or the meat will be dry.

◆ Garlic Spareribs

       6 pounds (or more) spareribs
       4 large cloves garlic
       1 tablespoon salt
       1 cup chicken stock or consommé
       1 cup orange marmalade
       ¼ cup vinegar
       ¼ cup catsup

Figure on at least 1 pound of spareribs per person. Leave the sides whole so you can thread them on a spit later. Crush the garlic with the salt. Add the chicken stock, marmalade, vinegar, and catsup. Marinate the spareribs for at least 12 hours in the garlic marinade, turning several times. Weave the whole strips on a spit. and cook over low coals for 1 to 1½ hours, or until shiny brown and fork tender. Baste with the marinade during the cooking. Makes 6 servings.

◆ Roast Leg of Pork, Hawaiian-Style

When we tested this recipe, we ordered a whole leg of fresh pork, had the meat man bone and roll it. (Net weight was 12 pounds.) Prepare the pork marinade (recipe follows) and marinate the pork for at least 1 hour. Place on your spit, and roast over medium coals until well done, 6 to 7 hours for the 12-pound roast (internal temperature on meat thermometer should read 185°). Baste frequently with the marinade as it roasts. When done, remove from spit, slice and serve on a large platter. Makes 12 servings.

MARINADE

    1 can (1 lb.) apple sauce
    ¾ cup dry white wine
    ½ cup soy
    2 tablespoons salad oil
    1 cup chopped onion
    1 clove garlic, minced or mashed
    1 teaspoon ground ginger

Combine ½ of the apple sauce (1 cup) with all other ingredients and mix well. When roast is ready to serve, add the remaining 1 cup of apple sauce to the marinade that's left; heat, and serve as sauce to go with the meat.

◆ Roast Suckling Pig

Ask your meat man to provide you with a cleaned, tender suckling pig about 15 to 20 pounds in weight. A young pig any smaller will be nothing but skin and bones when cooked.

Stuff with a sage or fruit dressing. Don't stuff it in too tightly, as the dressing will expand. Sew it in with heavy string and lace it closely and tightly.

Leave the skin on. Head and feet can be cut off either before or after cooking; it is easier done before—but it won't look much like a pig. Insert a piece of wood in the mouth to simplify adding an apple later. Truss the legs with cord in a kneeling position, and place pig on spit over a deep bed of hot coals. Coals should be arranged in such a way to allow for a pan to be placed in the center to catch the drippings from the roasting meat; drippings should be used for basting. The pig can be basted with oil, but it will lose some of its flavor. Cooking time: 6 to 10 hours, depending on the fire.

When done, remove from the spit, place a red apple in the mouth, cranberries or cherries in the eye sockets, and place it on a bed of watercress. Various garnishes of vegetable flowers, radish roses, stuffed stewed apricots and prunes, or holly berries, may be added.

Bring the roast pig to the table with the head separated from the body, the cut ringed with a wreath of watercress and flowers. In carving, first separate the shoulder from the carcass, and remove the legs. This will leave the ribs open to the knife. Cut down the backbone, remove the loins and serve the tender chops from sliced loins.

◆ Barbecued Ham

Make your fire of prune or fruit wood, approximately two or three inches in diameter, and enough charcoal to keep the bed of coals at an even heat. If ham still has some of the rind, cut it off. Leave fat on and score.

Spit or skewer the ham (one weighing about 7 pounds), and cook it about the same length of time you would bake it (follow directions on label for the type ham you have). Baste ham as it cooks. The outside fat will char black, but dont let that worry you. Just don't let it burn. Keep the fire constant.

When ham is done, break off charred fat with a knife. Put back on spit for another 10 or 15 minutes and use up remainder of basting

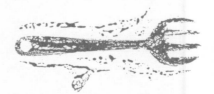

sauce. Remove ham, cut off excess fat, slice, and serve. Makes 6 to 8 servings.

BASTING SAUCE

    1 tablespoon cinnamon
    1 tablespoon dry mustard
    1 tablespoon ginger
    ½ tablespoon whole cloves
    1½ to 2 ounces whisky or gin
    2 tablespoons brown sugar
    ½ tablespoon molasses
    ⅔ cup wine vinegar
      Pineapple juice

Place the cinnamon, mustard, ginger, and cloves in a mortar, or small jar, and cover with the whisky or gin. (The alcohol will dissolve the essential oils, and that's what gives the flavor.) Let set for an hour or so. Put the brown sugar, molasses, and vinegar in a pint jar. Grind the spices with a pestle, or stir well, and add to the vinegar-sugar solution. Pour in enough pineapple juice to make a pint. Stir well.

Now you are ready to paint your ham. Mix the sauce each time you baste, so that the spices are evenly distributed. Don't leave any dregs in the jar, put them all on the ham to get the full, spicy flavor.

◆ Barbecued Wild Boar

Wild boar was the entrée one evening when *Sunset* entertained the Wine and Food Society of San Francisco at dinner in Menlo Park. Several cooks and consultants collaborated in the production.

Since a wild boar may weigh from 25 to well over 200 pounds, every man who cooks one must to some extent improvise his own cooking method to match his equipment. For this particular dinner, the object was to cook a 150-pound boar whole, where the process could be watched by a gallery of spectators.

MEAT PREPARATION: Clean and dress the boar just as soon as possible. If the skin is to be left on, scrape off bristles at this time, dipping carcass in hot water as necessary to make this job easier. Otherwise, skin the animal when you dress it out. In either case be sure to leave the head intact.

Hang the carcass in a freeze locker. Remove it in ample time to thaw before cooking. Cut off legs well above the hoofs. Rinse the cavity with a mild salt water solution.

FIREBOX AND SPIT: Only real essential is some apparatus strong enough to hold the boar absolutely steady as it turns above the fire. *Sunset's* boar was cooked over a temporary firepit of concrete block, measuring about 10 feet long, 3½ feet wide, and 1½ feet deep.

SECURING ON THE SPIT: First, a long spit—square in cross section—impaled the boar lengthwise. Then 10 special "hooks" that lock into the spit went through the meat from side to side to keep it stretched as flat as possible; the meat was fastened to the hooks with washers and nuts. (A final wrap-around with strong twine is frequently advisable to secure any floppy sections.)

BARBECUING AND BASTING: The glowing coals, in a bed about 6 inches deep, were pulled back to the edges before the already-spitted boar was mounted on the A-frame supports at either end (see photo, page 148). A couple of chain hoists attached to an overhead bar were extremely helpful in this process.

The boar cooked for about 6 hours and was basted frequently with a simple sauce mixed in these proportions:

    2 gallons hard cider
    4 cloves garlic, crushed
    3 ounces juniper berries, crushed

After the boar was removed from the spit, it was mounted on a long plank and garnished with orange, grapefruit, sliced pineapple, and maraschino cherries (two for the eyes). Three men carried it to the dining area to display before the seated guests, then made quick work of the carving to serve on individual dinner plates.

FOWL

◆ Chicken

This makes a fine spit-roasted meal. Truss it compactly and spit from just in front of the tail (through the bone), diagonally to a point near the apex of the wishbone (again through the bone, which is very soft at this point). A chicken is best basted occasionally. It may or may not be stuffed. It will cook in 1 to 1½ hours, depending on its size and tenderness. The best test for doneness is to wiggle the leg—when it moves easily at the joint, the chicken is done.

◆ Roast Chicken Parts

Figure on about 1 drumstick and 1 thigh per serving. Soak chicken parts for 2 hours in the following marinade:

 1½ cups soy
 ½ cup water
 ¼ cup salad oil
 ¼ cup gin
 1 finger fresh ginger root, shredded
 2 cloves garlic, minced
 ⅓ cup sugar

Put marinated chicken in wire basket and fasten it to spit to revolve over large but low fire (no hood). Baste with remaining marinade until chicken is done. (This will take an hour or more.) Makes enough marinade for 10 to 12 servings.

◆ Turkey

It may be stuffed or not. Spit in the same way as chicken; you may need a hammer to drive the spit through the breastbone. As a rough guide, figure on spit barbecuing a turkey slightly more than half the time you would oven roast it in a moderately slow oven (325°). As in oven roasting, a stuffed bird takes 20 to 30 minutes longer than an unstuffed one. Test it by moving the leg, or insert a thermometer in the fleshy part of the thigh and cook to 170°

to 175°. (Remember that all large roasts continue cooking after they are removed from the heat of the fire.)

◆ Roast Turkey

Remove bird from refrigerator 2 or 3 hours before cooking. Loosen neck skin and cut off neck close to the body, leaving the flap of skin. Put neck, heart, and gizzard to cook in about 1½ quarts of water with several sprigs of parsley and celery tops, and a sliced onion; simmer until very tender, then drop in the liver and cook 15 minutes longer. Set aside to use in making stuffing and/or gravy. Rub inside of bird with salt and pepper, then stuff with dressing.

Stitch or skewer the flap of neck skin to back of bird, and sew up or skewer and lace the body opening. Truss bird into compact shape, and slide on spit. Test it for balance, then lock in place with locking tines. Rub it all over with melted turkey fat or oil, and place bird in position over coals. As it cooks, baste with Chicken or Turkey Sauce, page 111.

Clear an oval in the coals and place a pan in center of the ring of coals to catch drippings from the roasting bird. Scoop out drippings with a long-handled spoon and add to basting sauce.

BREAD STUFFING

Allow about 1 cup bread crumbs for each pound dressed weight.

 3 quarts soft white bread crumbs
 1 to 2 teaspoons rubbed sage, thyme, or marjoram (or all three)
 2 to 3 teaspoons salt
 ½ teaspoon black pepper
 2 medium-sized onions, chopped
 1 cup celery tops, finely chopped
 ¾ to 1 cup melted butter or margarine
 1 cup broth from cooked giblets

◆ Roast Boneless Turkey

Boning a turkey is a tedious task, but a novice can handle it in about half an hour. It demands more patience than skill. The photographs on page 150 show you how to bone, stitch, stuff, skewer, and barbecue a 10-pound hen turkey. A large tom turkey, likely to weigh 18 pounds or more, is more cumbersome and therefore rather difficult to bone and spit barbecue.

This method of roasting a turkey offers several advantages. The turkey cooks in approximately half the time needed for oven roasting. It carves into beautiful, neat, crosswise slices because it lacks bones in its body cavity. It acquires a delightful, smoky flavor, even more pronounced when the meat is served cold.

A 10 to 12-pound hen turkey is an ideal weight to bone and spit barbecue. Meaty and compact, it regains its shape as it turns on the spit and its juices plump it up to a full-bodied, golden brown bird. This size serves a large family group of 14 to 16 persons, allowing ¾ pound per serving.

One caution: It is *essential* to use a fairly dry stuffing. When boned, the turkey has a "rag doll" limpness; the stuffing firms it up again and restores it to a recognizable shape. If the stuffing is too moist, however, the bird will be difficult to balance on the spit, and, as it revolves, it will lose its shape. You can use your favorite stuffing recipe, cutting back liquid if necessary. Or for a 10-pound turkey, try this quick, sausage-seasoned stuffing.

1 pound bulk sausage
1 large onion, chopped
½ cup (¼ pound) butter or margarine
2 packages (8 oz. each) seasoned
   stuffing mix
1 cup hot turkey or chicken broth

Sauté sausage with onion; melt in butter or margarine; toss with stuffing mix. Pour over turkey or chicken broth. Stuff the front cavity and body cavity, carefully plumping and shaping bird as you stuff and truss it. Sew openings closed and bind with twine.

It's a tricky job to insert the spit in the turkey so it will be balanced as it revolves over the coals. Because the bird lacks body bones, you must skewer it on the diagonal, instead of down the center. After you insert the spit in the turkey, give it a trial on the barbecue to see that it

turns easily. If it does not, remove the spit and try again.

The time over the coals is the same as for an unboned bird. After the turkey is removed from the barbecue, let it sit for 15 to 20 minutes before carving.

◆ Duck, Goose

Duck, goose, and other birds are trussed and spitted in the same manner as chickens. A duck will take 1¼ to 1¾ hours; a junior goose, from 1¾ to 2½ hours; a regular goose, 2 to 3 hours. A squab takes about ¾ of an hour or more; a Cornish game hen will cook in less than an hour; and wild ducks and wild geese will cook in 15 minutes to 45 minutes (for duck), and 45 minutes to 1½ hours (for geese), depending upon how rare you like them.

◆ Spit Barbecued Duckling

A 4 to 5-pound duckling will make 4 servings. Truss it compactly and spit it from just in front of the tail (through the bone), diagonally to a point near the apex of the wishbone (again through the bone). Spit-roast the duckling 1½ to 2 hours over a medium to low barbecue fire. Baste frequently with this sauce:

Combine ½ cup orange juice, ¼ cup soy, 1 teaspoon honey, ½ teaspoon monosodium glutamate, and ⅛ teaspoon pepper. Heat on the side of the grill and brush it warm on the bird. Using poultry shears, cut duckling into quarters to serve.

◆ Roast Goose

Buy a small (6 to 9-pound) goose. If the goose has been frozen, be sure it is completely thawed, and dried thoroughly. Rub the inside with salt and a cut half of lemon.

Spit the goose, securing it firmly. Roast over medium coals for 1¾ to 2½ hours, or until it is fork tender and the skin is crisp. (We have found that 2¼ hours is long enough for a 6 to 7-pound goose.)

FISH AND SHELLFISH

Because fish tends to fall apart when cooked, it is usually more satisfactory to broil split fish or fish steaks, or even a whole fish. However, if the whole fish is wrapped well in chicken wire and fastened securely, it may be spit roasted. Insert the spit the length of the fish, in the center, and use holding forks.

The best fish for roasting whole are salmon, sturgeon, bass, tuna, or any large firm-fleshed fish. Roasting will take from 30 to 60 minutes, depending on size. A fish is done when the thermometer reaches 155° or 160°, or when the flesh flakes easily with a fork. Be careful not to overcook any fish.

Smaller fish may be spit roasted, but it is questionable whether this isn't more trouble than it's worth. The fish broils so quickly that the extra time spent in spitting is probably wasted. However, if it is done, put several fish on one spit, spitting them through the middle, sideways, have one head faced one way, the next in the opposite direction, alternating the length of the spit.

◆ Lobster

Whole lobsters may be spitted right through their shells, from head to tail. They will cook to a juicy tenderness in 12 to 15 minutes.

VARIETY MEATS

◆ Lamb Kidneys

Lamb kidneys are delicious when cooked on the spit. Have them left in their fat, and tie more pounded fat over them where they are exposed. Impale 6 or 8 of them on the spit and fasten holding forks at both ends. Run an extra long skewer through all of them diagonally. Roast for 25 to 45 minutes, depending on the degree of doneness you prefer.

◆ Charcoal-Roasted Liver

Select a whole calf or lamb liver, and tie it into a compact piece. Lard it or tie strips of salt pork on the outside. Fasten on the spit and rotate over a medium hot fire for about an hour, or until a meat thermometer reads 150° for juicily pink, 160° for well done.

◆ Charcoal-Broiled Tongue

Tongue needs pre-cooking, but it's very good broiled until crusty outside. Cook tongue in a pressure cooker or in boiling water until tender. Drain, skin, and trim. Put tongue on spit and cook over charcoal for about 45 minutes, basting with ½ cup melted butter, ½ cup dry white table wine, and 1 teaspoon each chopped chives, parsley, and tarragon.

FRUIT AND VEGETABLES

If your barbecue equipment has multiple spits, you may like to spit-roast some fruits and vegetables. They will take longer to cook by this method than by ash-roasting, but they will be more uniformly cooked. Whole green peppers, acorn squash, potatoes, onions, yams, apples, and eggplant can all be cooked in this manner.

FIREPIT COOKING

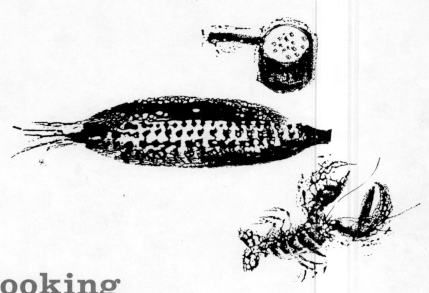

◆ Firepit Cooking

In this chapter, we have included recipes for cooking on and under the coals from a wood fire. The first few pages describe the science of cooking underground—a method of cooking that was practiced many years ago by the Indians and by the white scouts and hunters and trappers who roamed the country. The rest of the recipes in the chapter use the exposed embers for such techniques as open-pit barbecuing, roasting in the coals, and plank cooking.

◆ Cooking Underground

This method for cooking beef is still favored by many barbecuers, especially at such all-out community occasions as round-ups, rodeos, fairs, and farmers' picnics. It works well with meats other than beef, and it's famous with beans. And, most important to the way we live today, you can do pit cookery in a small way just as successfully as you can with a whole side of beef.

Essentially, cooking underground is a primitive version of roasting meat in an oven, with two important exceptions: 1) You can't peek into your "oven" to see whether the meat is done, or you may destroy the effectiveness of your coals. 2) Because the meat is tightly wrapped, it is really steam-cooked under pressure rather than roasted.

Steam-cooking keeps the meat moist while it is in the pit but is no guarantee against overcooking. It doesn't prevent overcooked meat from drying out and losing its flavor as soon as it is exposed to the air. In pit barbecuing, meat doesn't get the kind of searing that seals in juices when you roast it in the oven or cook it over an open fire.

How do you control the process? You can't read dials on the oven or on a meat thermometer. You have to control the cooking by the way you handle the fire and by your timing. The important elements are these: 1) size of the pit, 2) kind of wood, 3) length of time the fire burns before you put on the meat, 4) preparation of the meat for cooking underground, 5) covering of the meat and the fire, 6) cooking time.

Two examples of firepit cookery are shown in step-by-step photographs on pages 154 and 155.

◆ Size of the Pit

The experts on pit barbecuing don't agree among themselves as to the proper size of the pit. Actually, you can figure out the best size for your own operation if you understand the method.

LENGTH AND WIDTH. Obviously, these dimensions should be large enough so you can spread the meat out on the coals, in one large package or several small ones. In addition, there should be a little extra space all around the meat, so that heat from the outer coals will cook the outside edges of the meat. On a small-scale job, you might cheat a little on the outside edge and make the pit about 1½ feet wide. For easy handling of the meat and general convenience, a 3-foot width is about maximum. Length can be anything required by the quantity of the meat.

DEPTH. Here you just add up the thickness of each layer you intend to put in the pit.

Many experts like to line the bottom (and sometimes part way up the sides) with bricks or with large round stones, which should be hard and dry, without crevices or porous sections holding water that might later make the rock explode under steam pressure.

When the pit is ready for cooking, the first thing you must add is the bed of coals; recommended depths range from 1 to 2 feet (depends on cooking time you favor). Next comes the meat; some put it right on the coals, and others bank the fire and protect the meat from possible burning with about an inch of pre-heated dry sand. Finally comes the layer of dirt (right on the meat package or on a cover of metal or canvas); recommended depth is about 1 foot.

Add up these figures and you get a depth of about 2½ to 5 feet. It varies according to the depth of the bed of coals, the size of the meat packages, and, if you use a cover, whether you put it right on the meat or a few inches above it. (If you use galvanized iron, burn off the coating beforehand so it won't add an undesirable flavor to the meat.)

If you cook a pot of beans underground, you can use a smaller, shallower pit. The bed of coals may be as little as 6 inches deep, although a little extra depth won't matter.

◆ Kind of Wood

The aim is to prepare a bed of coals of the approximate size and consistency of charcoal. All the pieces of wood should be burning or be thoroughly charred. Any uncharred pieces should be removed before the meat is placed on top.

Wood has to be fairly hard if it is to burn slowly enough to pile up a bed of coals. Anything as soft and fast-burning as pine is likely to leave ashes and very little else.

Favorite woods for this purpose include oak, alder, hickory, mesquite, ironwood, and the wood from most orchard trees—walnut, pecan, apple, orange, lemon. Needless to say, the wood should be thoroughly dry. It burns best if pieces aren't more than about 4 inches thick.

◆ How Long Should the Fire Burn

When you stoke your preliminary fire, you are really heating up an oven—the bottom and sides of your pit—so that the stored heat will continue to cook for the next several hours. The principle is very much like that of the igloo-shaped Mexican oven, in which you build your fire, then scrape it all out and do your cooking with the heat stored in the walls.

In the pit barbecue, you should keep replenishing the fire until the bed of coals reaches the desired depth. Each expert has his own timing on this step, but the majority would agree that 3 to 6 hours should be enough to develop a 1 to 2-foot depth of coals. Less than 3 hours may not pre-heat your "oven" enough; more than 6 hours may get it too hot, and you'll probably be consuming more wood than necessary.

◆ Preparing the Meat

Standard practice is to wrap the chunks of meat in one or more layers of closely woven white cloth, parchment, or foil, and tie with twine; then wrap in one or more thicknesses of burlap and secure with wire. Each package is sprinkled or doused quickly in water before it goes on the coals.

Before wrapping, you can use any of the seasonings you might use with a roast. You can sprinkle the meat with liquid and dry seasonings. You can inject marinades with a syringe. Some like to put a little fat in each package of meat. Others always add a bouquet of herbs.

The traditional large-scale barbecue calls for whole quarters or whole sides of beef. But without a whole corps of meat cutters on duty, it is difficult to carve such huge pieces fast enough to serve the meat while it is still hot. For this reason many now prefer to bone the meat beforehand and tie it in reasonably small rolls that can be carved fast and easily. You can keep each piece wrapped until the cutter is ready to go to work on it. This method is definitely best for any family-size pit barbecue.

◆ Covering the Pit

The most primitive method is to pile the layer of dirt right on the meat packages—and do it fast before they have a chance to burn. A good idea here is to wrap a length of thick but soft wire around each package and let it stick up above the layer of dirt; you'll have no trouble pulling out each piece of meat and won't have to grapple for it with either a shovel or pitchfork.

For a more sanitary job, and especially if you'd like to use your burlap again for the same purpose, put a cover over the meat before throwing on the dirt. Canvas is used occasionally, but by far the most popular covering is thick sheet iron or corrugated galvanized iron (with the coating well burned off).

Some improvise a frame inside the pit in order to get the cover close to the meat. Others put pipes or rods across the top of the pit to support the cover; then they mound up the dirt on top.

In either case, work fast. Shovel dirt until you see no smoke or steam escaping. Some prefer to stamp on the dirt as it is being piled up. Others use a little water and seal the top with mud.

About every half hour, make an inspection to see that no steam is escaping. If it is, cover with dirt and stamp it down.

◆ Cooking Time

Here is the supreme test of artistry. You have to know your fire and what it will do. You also have to gauge time by the size of your pieces of meat, much as you gauge oven cooking times by the size of your roast. Generally, meat in 6 to 10-pound pieces will require about 5 hours cooking time; in 20-pound pieces, 8 to 10 hours; hindquarters of beef (100 to 150 pounds, dressed), 15 to 18 hours; pots of beans, 4 to 6 hours.

The theory is that if your preliminary firing is right, the heat will subside after the first few hours of cooking is done. You do have some latitude, but don't trust this theory too far.

Before your first trial, study the step-by-step directions in the various recipes in this chapter. You'll have to do some experimenting and adjusting to fit these directions to your cooking job.

It's worth noting that the most reliable experts in this field are not improvisers at all. After trial and error, they've learned exactly what to do (pit, fire, and timing) with a certain quantity of meat. They have developed a set routine and they know it well, and they don't mind repeating it over and over again.

◆ Imu Cookery

Prepare the firepit by digging a hole about 2 feet deep, lining the bottom and sides with medium-sized stones. Do not use sandstone or wet rocks from a creek bed. Build a good fire of wood in the pit, and put a few more rocks in it. When it burns down to coals, remove the extra rocks and the coals and save them for future use. Line the pit with fresh grass or leaves. If you use leaves, be sure that they are not bitter because this would impart an unpleasant flavor to your food. Taste them to be sure they are sweet.

Season your meat and wrap it securely in aluminum foil or plain wrapping paper. Do the same with your potatoes (either peeled or in their jackets, as you prefer), and other vegetables, wrapping them individually and securely. Carrots, turnips, onions, squash—all these and many others are delicious when cooked by this method.

Place your wrapped meat and vegetables on the bottom of the pit, cover with a thick layer of grass or leaves, and cover with the hot stones. Now replace the still-hot coals on top of the stones. And, last but not least, cover with the earth from the original excavation, making sure that it is airtight so that there is no steam or smoke escaping.

After 3 or 4 hours, depending upon the size and type of your meat, you are ready for a piping hot dinner.

◆ Barbecue for a Crowd

> 20 pounds beef shoulder roast (needn't be an expensive grade)
> Salt
> Garlic salt
> 3 large onions
> 2 tablespoons Worcestershire
> 2 or 3 bay leaves
> Pinch of oregano

Dig a pit 2 feet wide, 3 feet long, and about 2½ feet deep. Have enough wood on hand to fill the pit at least 3 times. Start the fire about 15 hours before serving time. Keep adding wood as needed until the fire has been burning about 3 hours.

Meanwhile, salt the meat generously, then add a few dashes of garlic salt. Cut up the onions and scatter them over the meat. Dash the meat with the Worcestershire. Add bay leaves and oregano. Wait until the fire has burned down to a bed of hot coals about a foot thick.

For the last stage, you need: aluminum foil; a 10-foot length of butcher paper; heavy twine; 2 burlap sacks; wire; 1 or more sheets galvanized iron (enough to cover the pit); 2 pipes about 3 feet long.

Put all pieces of meat together and wrap in aluminum foil as a single package, folding edges to retain juices. Then wrap in 3 or 4 thicknesses of heavy butcher paper and tie with heavy twine. Place package in a burlap sack; then wrap another sack around it and tie with wire.

Dip package in a tub of water, or wet thoroughly with a hose. Drop directly on the coals (when ready), place pipes across the pit, and cover with galvanized iron. Waste no time in covering the top with at least a foot of dirt, until you see no signs of smoke or heat. Sprinkle with a hose. Check again in 30 minutes; if dry spots have appeared, shovel on more dirt.

Meat will be ready to serve in 10 to 12 hours. Makes 20 to 30 servings.

◆ King Salmon

A 40-pound king salmon will serve about 20. To pit-barbecue a king salmon, first dig a 3-foot pit in the usual manner. A 40-pound king salmon will probably measure about 40 inches in length, so you'll need a pit 4 or 5 feet long, depending on the size of the fish. Build a fire

of hardwood, and let it burn down until it forms a bed of coals 8 to 12 inches deep.

Meanwhile, place the fish on a large sheet of parchment, fill the stomach cavity with chopped onions, celery, and parsley. Squeeze lemon juice over the outside, and sprinkle all over with pickling spices. Then wrap it snugly in parchment, 3 or 4 layers of newspaper, and three gunny sacks. Fold the burlap neatly and wire in place with light wire.

Turn the hose on the package until the burlap and newspapers are soaked through. Place the bundle in a chicken wire sling and lower it into the pit on top of the coals. Cover with a piece of sheet metal, and shovel a foot of dirt on top of the covering. Build a small fire on the dirt, and keep it burning until 1 hour before removing the fish. Cook 6 hours.

◆ Hawaiian Luau

Many simplified versions of the Hawaiian's special feast, the *luau,* have been brought back to the mainland by visitors to the islands. Not too often, however, does the feast assume the proportions of cooking a whole pig. Here, and in the photographs on page 154, we retrace step by step a luau at which two 130-pound pigs were pit-cooked for 275 people.

You can easily make adjustments in the procedure described here. It's best to figure on buying one pound of dressed pig per person. Naturally, the size of the pig or pigs—determines the size of the pit.

The whole pig—cleaned, well shaven, and scrubbed thoroughly with a weak soda-and-water solution—is prepared for pit cooking this way:

Make about 24 two-inch-long slashes into the back of the pig, cutting deep enough to penetrate the fat. Lift the pig onto a large rectangle of chicken wire on which a single layer of ti leaves (or corn husks) has been arranged. Place pig on its back. Slash deeply into the meat where the legs join the body. These cuts should be wide and deep enough so a small hot rock can be forced into each of them.

Rub the inside of the pig with crushed fresh ginger root (or powdered ginger), soy sauce,

and rock salt. Figure on approximately 1 pound of salt for a pig weighing from 75 to 85 pounds dressed, more for a larger pig. Season inside the pockets cut in front of each leg, also.

Loop pieces of stout cord around each leg at this time, so that later all four legs can be tied together quickly after the body cavity has been filled with hot rocks. These rocks, almost red hot from about 2½ hours of close contact with the hardwod fire in the pit, are rammed into place in the body cavity. Use volcanic rocks that won't break up under heat—or firebrick as a substitute.

Hawaiians use *kiawe* for fuel, but equally good is any hard wood such as oak which gives out an intense heat.

After the pockets and cavity of the pig are filled with the hot rocks, tie the legs together, wrap the chicken wire up around the pig, and fasten with baling wire. Lower the pig into the pit, and cook under a covering of ti and breadfruit leaves and wet earth. The two 130-pound pigs cooked in 6½ hours (60-pound pigs pit-cook in 4½ hours).

◆ Pit-Cooked Pig

    1 leg (10 to 15 pounds) fresh pork

MARINADE

    ½ gallon dry sherry
    ⅓ cup soy
    1 can (6 oz.) frozen lime juice or frozen limeade
    1 cup frozen or canned papaya, or about half of a fresh papaya, mashed
    1 or 2 small fingers of ginger root, grated or crushed
    1 large clove garlic, peeled and crushed
    3 tablespoons seasoning salt

Have the meat man bone and trim off all excess fat, then roll the meat. Mix together all marinade ingredients. Marinate meat overnight.

Start your fire in a rock-lined pit about 8 A.M., and by noon the pit should be full of

glowing embers. Remove pork leg from marinade, wrap in ti leaves (available from florists), then in clean sheeting, then in burlap. Tie with wire, which serves as a handle. Saturate the burlap and sheeting with the remaining marinade, then bury the meat in coals. Cover the coals with sand and dirt until you no longer see any smoke.

Take the afternoon for swimming and resting for a big evening. About 8 P.M., remove meat and serve. Makes 16 to 24 servings, depending on appetites.

◆ Tuna Luau

  1 long fin tuna, about 25 pounds
 12 large banana leaves (if not available, 4 clean wet gunny sacks)

SAUCE

  2 big bulbs of garlic, ground in food chopper
 ½ bottle Tabasco
  1 cup sugar
  1 bottle Worcestershire
 ½ cup prepared mustard
  2 bottles catsup
 ½ pint vinegar
  1 quart olive oil
 ½ gallon sauterne
   Salt and pepper

Build fire in 2½-foot-deep, stone-lined pit and keep burning for at least 10 hours.

Do not clean the fish. Wrap tuna in dampened banana leaves or wet gunny sacks. Place in pit on top of hot stones, cover with ashes a foot deep, then place a layer of earth 6 inches deep over the ashes. After about 6 hours, build a fire of charcoal on top of the pit and let it burn down for about 3 hours. Combine the sauce ingredients and simmer for about 10 minutes, stirring constantly.

Now you are ready to dig out the tuna. With a shovel, place the steaming tuna on a big wooden plank, peel off the wrappings, the skin, dispose of the innards. The pieces of tuna are eaten Polynesian style with the fingers, dipping the tuna into the bubbling sauce. Serve with dry white wine. Makes 15 servings.

◆ Bean-Hole Beans

  3 pounds dried beans (any kind you prefer)
 ¾ pound bacon or salt pork
 ½ cup brown sugar
  2 cans (8 oz.) tomato sauce
  1 tablespoon salt

Dig a hole twice as wide as your kettle and deep enough so top will be at least 6 inches below surface. Arrange rocks on bottom and sides. Build a fire and keep it burning for at least 2 hours.

Wash beans—or drain if previously soaked overnight. Place in large kettle and fill about ¾ full of water. Bring to a boil and boil 15 minutes. Cut up bacon or salt pork, add to beans; boil for another 15 minutes. Stir in brown sugar, tomato sauce, salt.

Remove all burning embers from hole. Put lid on kettle, wrap it thickly in newspapers, then wrap whole package in two thicknesses of wet burlap. Spread hot coals evenly, then cover with ½ inch dirt or sand. Set wrapped kettle in hole; cover with at least 6 inches dirt or sand. Dig out pot after 6 hours, serve. Makes 12 servings.

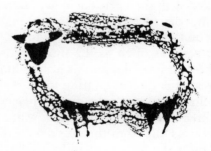

◆ Open-Pit Barbecue

Ordinarily the meat chosen for a barbecue of this type is a small pig, lamb, or calf. Here are directions for cooking it:

Select first-class meat weighing from 35 to 50 pounds. Remove the head near the shoulders. Cut off the feet at the first joint. Saw the backbone through the middle lengthwise so that it will open out flat, but do not cut the carcass in halves. For lamb and veal cut off the thin flanks with a circular cut.

Run sharpened iron rods or oak sticks lengthwise through the hams and shoulders just under the skin and under the ribs. This will permit the thick parts to come nearer to the fire for better cooking and, if the rods are run through in such a way as to support them, the ribs will not fall out when the meat is tender. These rods should be long enough to rest on the banks of the pit, and also to furnish hand holds for lifting and turning. Three or four smaller rods must be stuck through the sides at intervals and held to the main rod by baling wire. This prevents the cooked meat from falling off.

The pit should be 16 inches deep and as wide and long as needed to accommodate the meat. The hardwood fire should have been started several hours in advance of the cooking, to be burned down to a good bed of coals. At one end of the pit, away from the meat, or in another pit, should be an auxiliary fire from which coals can be taken to add to the cooking fire as needed.

Place the meat over the fire, meat side down, until warm. Then turn meat side up and baste, using a large swab, with a strong solution of warm salt water containing a little cayenne pepper, and turn back again. The meat is cooked with the open side down, skin side up, during the first part of the cooking.

A quart of salt will be needed for a 50-pound pig. Baste as often as the meat becomes dry, and repeat until the meat is nearly done. Then increase the heat by putting more coals under the thick sections of the meat. Then baste two or three times with plain warm water to wash the excess salt from the outside. At this point the meat should be carefully watched to prevent burning. When nearly done, baste with the barbecue sauce (recipe given below).

When done and very tender, remove some of the coals from the pit and turn skin side down to brown and crisp. While meat is browning, meat side should be basted frequently with salt water and barbecue sauce. (Keep both salt water and sauce warm throughout cooking.)

When carving to serve, put the skin pieces in one pan and the meat in another. Baste the meat with the barbecue sauce, but leave the skin pieces as they are, for basting makes them gummy instead of crisp and brittle as they should be.

BARBECUE SAUCE

 2 pounds butter
 2½ quarts water
 1½ tablespoons dry mustard
 ¼ cup sugar
 3 tablespoons salt
 3 tablespoons chili powder
 ½ teaspoon cayenne
 2 tablespoons Worcestershire
 1 cup vinegar
 2 teaspoons Tabasco
 3 tablespoons black pepper
 4 tablespoons paprika
 1 onion, chopped fine
 1 clove garlic, minced

Mix these ingredients and boil together gently for 30 minutes before using.

◆ Salmon Barbecue

To begin with, get strictly fresh fish, and allow one pound "on the hoof" for each person to be served. Silver, Spring, and Sockeye are the best varieties for the purpose. If the weather is warm, pack fish in ice until ready for use.

Start the fire 4 hours before serving time, on level ground. Choose a cleared spot away from any inflammable material. The fire should be long and narrow—1 foot wide and 3 feet long for the first one or two fish, then an additional 3 feet in length for every two more fish thereafter. Start it with anything handy, but feed it with half-dry alder poles. If no alder is available, use any hardwood, such as vine maple or maple. In cooking, a slow steady fire should be maintained.

Frames against which the fish are supported during the process of barbecuing are built by placing a rail the length of the fire (on both sides if more than a single salmon is to be barbecued) supported by stakes at each end. This rail should be about 2 feet from the fire and 18 inches above the ground.

Using a sharp knife, with plenty of water at hand, scale and clean the salmon in the usual manner. Then cut out the backbone by making an incision down each side of it on the inside (flesh side), being careful not to cut through the skin. After the backbone has been removed, the fish can be flattened out, flesh side up. It is in this position that two long wooden skewers, ½ inch in diameter, are thrust entirely through the body of the fish from side to side, about 12 inches apart. These should be long enough to project about 10 inches on either side. Then salt should be rubbed generously into the fleshy side of the fish.

Next, the salted and skewered fish are stood against the rails, supported by the ends of the skewers, in a slightly slanting position. The flesh side must be toward the bed of coals. The cooking now takes about 2½ to 3 hours, and all the cook can do is watch and keep the slow, even bed of coals going.

When the fish are thoroughly done, turn each one around so that the skin side is toward the fire and allow it to cook that way for a half hour longer. This adds much to the flavor by driving the oils, which have collected in the skin, back into the meat.

◆ Plank-Cooked Salmon

To hold an 8-pound salmon, choose a board about 18 inches wide, 36 inches long, and ¾ inch thick. Other equipment you need includes: about 2 dozen small nails, 6 yards of lightweight wire, tin scissors, and a stake about 5 feet long.

Clean and scale fish; remove head, tail, fins. Working from inside of fish, split down middle so it lies flat but is still in one piece. Cut bones away from meat. Alternate method for uncleaned fish (round): Cut off head; cut along back and slide knife down backbone and along

rib bones, folding meat to one side, keeping belly side intact. Repeat on other side. Slip fish into plastic bag containing the following marinade, and let stand in cool place for at least 1 hour before cooking.

MARINADE
1 cup lemon juice
1½ teaspoons salt
¼ teaspoon pepper
3 tablespoons brown sugar
2 teaspoons dry mustard
¼ cup (4 tablespoons) grated onion
½ cup salad oil

Combine lemon juice with salt, pepper, brown sugar, mustard, and grated onion. Stir in salad oil and beat until blended. Use both as marinade and basting sauce. Makes 1⅔ cups.

Build fire in front of rock or hill, which will reflect the heat. Mount salmon as follows: Cover one side of plank with heavy aluminum foil. Drive nail part way into each end of plank. Slide marinated fish out of bag; center on plank, skin side down. Lay 2 strips of bacon—overlapped slightly in center—across fish in 5 places. With nails, tack bacon at center and edges of fish. Cut 5 lengths of wire, wrap each piece around board at place where bacon covers fish; twist ends together. Fasten stake to nail at end of plank.

With stake for a prop, stand plank at about 75° angle in front of hot fire. Slip sheet of aluminum foil under bottom of plank and crimp edges upward to catch juices and keep sand off plank. Cook fish 30 minutes, basting occasionally. Unfasten plank from stake, turn plank upside down, put back in place to cook 30 minutes longer, or until meat flakes with fork. Makes 12 to 14 servings.

◆ Planked Steak

Let a 2-inch thick porterhouse steak reach "room temperature." Place steak in a hinged broiler and sear over fire until a good brown color on one side. Lace steak, uncooked side up, to a well-oiled hardwood plank (see below). Prop upright about 18 inches from fire. Arrange fire along length of board, extending on either side; add enough fuel to maintain a low flame. Allow about 20 minutes for rare steak, 25 to 30 minutes for medium, about 35 to 40 minutes for well done. (Insert meat thermometer in side of steak.) If the board chars, brush with water. Unlace the steak, carve, and serve.

Plank for steak: Use a hardwood plank (such as oak) large enough to allow a 3 to 5-inch margin around steak. Nail an evenly spaced row of upholstery tacks 1 inch from each edge along wide sides of plank; nail about 5 on each side. Center steak on plank. Drive 2 six-penny nails against top and bottom sides of steak to prevent slipping. Lace meat to board by looping stainless steel wire (available in sporting goods stores) around tacks. (See photo page 157.)

◆ Chuck Roast

   3 pounds chuck roast, cut 3 inches thick
   1 clove garlic
   ¼ cup olive oil
   ½ jar prepared mustard (approximately)
     Salt

Put the meat in a flat pan or on a platter. Rub it thoroughly with garlic, then smear it with olive oil. Spread plenty of mustard on it, and pat in all the salt that will cling to it. Repeat on the other side. Let stand an hour or more.

Let your fire burn down until you have a deep bed of glowing coals. Gently place the meat right on the coals—no grill. Turn only once during cooking, and allow 20 minutes to a side for rare. To serve, slice the meat in strips. Makes 4 generous servings.

(Note: The oil and mustard absorb a considerable amount of salt, thus forming a coating which adheres to the meat. This salty crust prevents the meat from becoming charred and, in addition, keeps the juices inside.)

◆ Steak on Foil

Steak is broiled on foil, not in it. Arrange the steak on a sheet of foil, but do not wrap. Place directly on top of the hot coals and broil, turning once. The length of time required for broiling depends on whether you like rare or well-done steak.

◆ Salt Steak

Wet and pack 5 or 6 pounds of rock salt around a 2 or 3-inch steak and place in paper sack. Salt coating must be at least 1 inch thick.

Bury in deep bed of glowing coals and leave 25 to 40 minutes. Break away salt crust and slice meat.

◆ Hamburgers in Foil

Hamburger patties, sliced potatoes, and carrot sticks can be cooked together in a foil slipcover. Don't forget the salt, pepper, monosodium glutamate, and a layer of prepared mustard on the meat. This combination will require about 15 minutes of hot coal cooking.

◆ Veal Chops in Foil

Marinate 4 thin veal round steaks in about ½ cup salad oil for 6 to 8 hours. Place in refrigerator and turn chops occasionally. Lightly butter (on one side) 4 pieces of heavy duty foil (or double thicknesses of regular foil), cut large enough to wrap the chops completely. Drain veal chops and lay one chop on each piece of foil. Sprinkle with salt and pepper. Mix together ⅓ cup chopped fresh mushrooms, ¼ cup chopped onion, and 2 teaspoons each chopped parsley and green olives. Drop 2 tablespoons of this mixture on each chop and dot with butter. Roll veal over filling and fold foil tightly around each chop (using a drugstore fold) so no steam or moisture will escape. Roast in low coals about 30 minutes or until tender. Makes 4 servings.

◆ Lamb on a Tepee

Three poles and fuel enough to keep a fire going for 4 hours are all you need to barbecue a hind of lamb for 25 hungry people.

Sprinkle a hind of lamb (about 22 pounds) with salt. If necessary, cut through flesh joining legs to flatten lamb as much as possible. Insert a meat thermometer in fleshy portion of leg or loin.

To make the tepee: Bind together with heavy twine or wire 3 poles (each approximately 2 inches in diameter and 6 feet long) about 14 inches from the ends. Stand upright tepee fashion. (See photo, page 156.)

Loop wire or heavy cord tightly around each leg of the lamb and tie each against a pole 30 inches up from the base. Cavity side should be up. Cut two small gashes through meat near front of the loin on each side of back bone and loop wire through; secure against third pole 30 inches up from base. Spread tepee open to pull lamb taut, and set over a bed of well ignited coals (wood and charcoal). Arrange coals in a triangle under the lamb, keeping the center area clear. Border with slow burning logs; add fuel as needed. Baste occasionally, if desired, with Burgundy wine. Turn lamb every hour (release each leg and attach to opposite pole). Total cooking time will be about 4 hours or when meat thermometer registers 170° to 180°. Remove to a large tray and carve. Makes about 25 servings.

◆ Mollusks-Roasted

Clean and scrub shells thoroughly and place on coals. Serve with butter, salt, and pepper.

◆ Baked Trout

> 1 12-inch trout
> ¼ teaspoon salt
> ¼ small onion, diced fine
> 1 thin strip bacon
>   Maple or other sweet leaves

Prepare 1 trout for each person to be served.

Clean trout and cut off the head and tail. Sprinkle the salt and onion evenly inside the trout, then place the strip of bacon over the diced onion so that it will not fall out. The trout so dressed is then ready to be wrapped firmly with wet leaves, so that the entire surface is covered. The leaves will prevent the fish from sticking to the mud, and will prevent any loss of moisture from the meat.

Make a mold of wet earth or clay 2 inches thick over the side and ends of the fish, patting the mud down solidly so that the fire can reach no portion of the meat. This mud must be wet enough to mold but not so wet that it will lose shape.

After the fish is prepared in this manner, bury it in the red hot coals of the campfire. The fire should be raked back over the fish and kept burning slowly for one hour.

Then take the fish from the fire and break open the mud shell. The skin of the trout will stick to the leaves. The fish should then be split open and the backbone removed, and the trout is ready to be served.

FOIL-WRAPPED FRUITS AND VEGETABLES

To cook fruits or vegetables in ashes, first wrap them securely in a double layer of foil, then place in or around the ashes. Turn once or twice during the cooking. Using a long-pronged fork, test for doneness by piercing through the foil.

◆ Fruits

ROASTED APPLES. Core apples and fill holes with sugar and a piece of butter, also cinnamon or nutmeg, if desired. Wrap in foil and cook for 30 minutes, or until fork tender.

ROASTED BANANAS. Wrap unpeeled bananas in foil and roast like apples. Or peel, dip in melted butter, and sprinkle with sugar before wrapping.

◆ Vegetables

ROASTED BEETS. Wrap whole unpeeled beets in foil and roast until tender. Serve with butter and lemon wedges, and let guests peel and season their own beets. Or peel beets before roasting and wrap in foil.

ROASTED CORN. Husk corn, brush with butter, and wrap in foil before roasting. Turn occasionally during the cooking. Corn will take 10 to 15 minutes. Another method of roasting corn is in the husks: Peel back husks, remove silk with a brush, replace husks, and wire or tie ends. Soak in cold water for half an hour before roasting in or around the ashes.

ROASTED EGGPLANT. Wrap a whole eggplant in foil and roast it over the coals, placing it on the spit if desired. When fork tender, the skin will peel off easily. Eggplant may also be roasted on a spit without the foil wrapping.

ROASTED ONIONS. Wrap whole peeled or unpeeled onions in foil, and roast until fork tender. Serve with butter.

ROASTED POTATOES. Wrap unpeeled potatoes in foil and roast as you would onions. Or, if you like a hard, blackened skin—and many do—roast potatoes without wrapping. Cook potatoes until fork tender, and turn during the cooking. They will take from 30 to 60 minutes. Serve with plenty of butter, or with sour cream and chives.

ROASTED SWEET POTATOES OR YAMS. Cook exactly as directed for white potatoes.

SMOKE COOKING

◆Smoke Cooking

The tantalizing flavor and rich mahogany color of smoke-cooked foods are tempting many an outdoor cook to try out the technique of smoke cooking. Whether you buy a commercial "smoker," or build a traditional Chinese oven or one of its homemade cousins, you will enter a new realm of taste experience. There's no limit to the variety of meats and fish that you can smoke-roast. Not only will the food have a wonderful smoky flavor, but also, as a consequence of the slow cooking process, meat and fish will retain their natural juices and flavors.

In hot smoke cooking, a wide variety of foods may be cooked in a 250° to 400° oven filled with aromatic smoke. Although cold smoke curing can be done in a smoke oven, hot smoke cooking is the simplest way to impart a mild smoke flavor to meat, fish, and poultry.

Timing varies with each food. In a Chinese oven with no direct heat, times are comparable to those for ordinary oven cookery—perhaps a little shorter. With a heat source directly below, you have to avoid charring the underside of the food.

You can best judge timing by experience, and in the beginning, by using a good ther-mometer. For roasts and heavier cuts of meat, your best bet is a standard meat thermometer. Air temperature thermometers are recommended by some experts, scorned by others. For smaller pieces of meat, you'll have to develop a practiced eye—and slice off an occasional sample.

If your oven is designed to burn wood, you can get a consistent, natural smoke by using green, freshly cut wood or by soaking dry wood in a bucket of water before placing it on a hot bed of coals. If you are limited to charcoal as a fuel, or want to increase the quantity of smoke, add chips of specially prepared aromatic wood, fresh prunings, or hardwood sawdust or shavings soaked in water.

Every smoke enthusiast has his favorite wood —only hard-and-fast rule is never to use pine or any soft wood that gives off a resinous, sooty smoke.

SMOKE BARBECUING IN A CHINESE OVEN

Smoke cooking borrows much from the centuries-old method of the Chinese oven, and this type of masonry oven is still preferred by many barbecuers because of several general reasons:

- You can do any kind of open fire cooking from low temperature cold smoking to high temperature "flash broiling."
- You can hang great quantities of food from the top of the chimney-like oven for large-party entertaining.
- You can maintain an even temperature for indefinite periods without disturbing food that is cooking.
- You can use any kind of fuel and you can add it conveniently whenever additional heat is required.
- Your fire is indirect—grease drippings can't fall on the coals to cause unwanted flames or a greasy smoke.
- You can control smoke flavor by adding smoke-producing fuel as often as you wish. Some true Chinese oven experts use dry wood and prefer no smoke at all; others stand by with a bucket of wet sawdust and make the air blue with a moist, aromatic smoke.

◆ Fish

Both salmon steaks and fresh trout are delicious cooked in a smoke oven. Either needs only a good rubbing with salt and pepper and an occasional basting with equal parts of melted butter and hot water. Use a good white wine with the butter if you prefer, but the smoke flavor is more pronounced with only the butter-water sauce. Time: 30 minutes for small trout, 45 minutes for inch-thick salmon steaks. Do not try to turn the fish, as it will crumble.

Save several of the smoked trout (if you can) and chill them in the refrigerator. Boned and cut in small pieces, they make mouth-watering hors d'oeuvres.

◆ Smoked Salmon Hors d'Oeuvres

Cut a salmon fillet carefully into finger-size pieces, including 3 or 4 "leaves" of meat in each piece. Marinate for 30 minutes or more in a lemon or wine base marinade that includes a small amount of salad oil. Place pieces of salmon on a sheet of aluminum foil and cook in a very slow, very smoky Chinese oven until done to your taste. These hors d'oeuvres are neat enough to serve hot or cold right from the aluminum "platter." The small size of each piece allows it to take on an especially smoky flavor.

◆ Salmon Lovers' Salmon

> Whole salmon, 6 to 8 pounds
> 1 cup lemon juice
> 1 cup dry white table wine
> 2 teaspoons salt
> ½ teaspoon pepper
> 1 medium-sized onion, chopped fine

Have the salmon cleaned and filleted with the skin left intact. Marinate both fillets in the lemon juice, wine, salt, and pepper mixture for at least 30 minutes. Lay the salmon, skin side down, on a piece of hardware cloth and spread the onion over the top. Bake in a very slow Chinese oven (200° to 250°) about 45 minutes.

◆ Chicken

Rub well with salt, pepper, brown sugar, and tarragon vinegar. Turn and baste the chicken occasionally with a mixture of butter and warm water for moist, even cooking. Smoking will impart a golden-orange color to the chicken unlike any you've seen before. Time: 2½ to 3 hours.

◆ Smoke-Glazed Chicken

1 broiler-fryer (2 to 3 pounds)
2 strips hickory-smoked bacon

After washing and removing the giblets, place in smoke oven. Set a pan of hot coals, either charcoal or briquets (from hardwood only), about 8 inches below the fryer. Lay the 2 strips of high grade hickory-smoked bacon on top of the fryer. To make smoke, occasionally lay on the coals some small pieces of green spicy wood (our preference is green apple wood, but green oak or grape is also good).

As the bacon melts, it absorbs smoke from the green wood and forms a glaze on the fryer. As soon as the chicken is rich brown on one side, turn it over and change the bacon again to the top side. About 1¼ hours in a light smoke, with the oven all but closed, produces a flavor quite distinct from anything else we've met. Makes 2 to 4 servings.

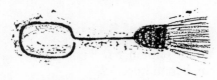

◆ Surprised Squab

4 squabs (or Rock Cornish game hens)
3 tablespoons soy
¼ teaspoon monosodium glutamate
1 tablespoon brown sugar
3 tablespoons Scotch whisky
   Salt and pepper to taste
1 medium sized onion, chopped
4 squab gizzards, sliced
3 tablespoons butter
2 cups diced white bread
3 medium sized cooked shrimp or 6
   dried Chinese shrimp, broken
   in small pieces
6 water chestnuts, sliced
1 cup milk
1 teaspoon salt
¼ teaspoon pepper
   Salad oil

Marinate the squabs in a mixture of the soy, monosodium glutamate, brown sugar, whisky, salt and pepper for about 1 hour. Brush the in-

side and outside of each bird with this mixture several times during the hour.

Fry the onion and gizzards in 1 tablespoon of the butter until brown. Add the remaining 2 tablespoons of melted butter and mix with the diced bread, shrimps, water chestnuts, milk, salt, and pepper.

Fit this stuffing inside each bird, and sew up the openings. Skewer together each pair of legs or tie with light wire. Brush skins with oil and hang in a moderate (300° to 400°) Chinese oven for about 1 hour and 15 minutes. Brush the skins with salad oil once again during the cooking process. Serve one juicy squab per person.

◆ Marinade for Chinese-Oven Chicken

2 tablespoons soy
1 cup boysenberry or loganberry jelly
2 tablespoons lemon juice
1½ teaspoons powdered ginger
½ teaspoon freshly ground pepper

Mix together soy, jelly, lemon juice, ginger, and pepper. Heat gently in a saucepan until jelly is melted. Marinate chicken—the inside as well as the outside—in this mixture for about 1 hour, then hang in a Chinese oven. About 10 minutes before you expect to remove the chicken from the oven, lift it out, brush it liberally with marinade, and return it for the final cooking.

This quantity of marinade should be ample for two chickens.

◆ Chinese-Oven Pig (Sui Gee)

Take a 15 to 20-pound pig, remove most of the shoulder bones, and split the backbone from the inside, taking care not to cut the outer skin. Replace the shoulder blade and pelvic bone with bamboo sticks so the pig won't lose its shape. Rub salt and pepper and a barbecue sauce with a catsup base in the cavities, wire the pig, and hang in the oven which has been preheated so the masonry walls are very hot. Put the cover in place and cook for ½ hour.

Remove the pig and puncture holes through the skin with an ice pick over the entire surface of the animal to allow some of the fat and juices to escape. Wash with hot water to which a little honey has been added, return to the oven and cook until done, usually 1 to 2 hours. Seal lid of oven with wet sacks to retain heat.

◆ Smoked Sirloin

  3 to 4 pounds sirloin tip, cut to
    1¼ inches thick

MARINADE
  4 tablespoons salad oil
  2 tablespoons paprika
  1½ teaspoons salt
  ¼ teaspoon coarsely ground pepper
  ¼ teaspoon monosodium glutamate
  1½ teaspoons onion salt
  ¼ teaspoon garlic salt
  1 tablespoon soy
  ½ teaspoon dried oregano, crumbled
  ½ teaspoon Tabasco (or less, according
    to taste)
  2 tablespoons white port wine
  ½ teaspoon dry mustard

Immerse steak in marinade for about 2 hours. Hang from top of smoke oven. Cook about 11 minutes at 450°—or longer as necessary, depending on the efficiency of your oven. Steaks will be a little on the rare side. Makes 6 to 8 servings.

◆ Smoked Beef Tongue

Buy a fresh beef tongue and smoke it 6 to 8 hours—long enough to give it a pronounced smoky flavor, but not long enough for it to acquire an undesirable dark smoky coating.

Put it in a pot with a carrot, celery stalk, onion, and a bay leaf or two. Cover with water. Cover the pan and simmer 4 to 6 hours, until the meat is tender but not limp. (Save the broth the tongue cooks in; it is the basis for a wonderful lentil or bean soup.) Makes 4 to 6 servings.

◆ Turkey in a Smoke Oven

MARINADE
  ½ cup soy
  ¼ cup each honey and sherry
  1 tablespoon freshly grated ginger root
  3 cloves garlic

FRUIT STUFFING
  4 tart apples, quartered (unpeeled)
  ½ cup water
  ¼ cup brown sugar
  1 cup cooked, pitted dried prunes
  1½ cups cooked mixed dried fruits
    (apricots, pears, peaches)
  ¼ teaspoon each cinnamon, nutmeg,
    and mace
  ½ cup dry sherry

Marinate a 12-pound hen turkey overnight in a mixture of the soy, honey, sherry, ginger, and garlic.

To make the stuffing, simmer apples in water and brown sugar until barely tender. Add prunes, mixed fruits, cinnamon, nutmeg, and mace. Pour over sherry. Stuff turkey lightly, and skewer openings closed. Truss with string, and make a double loop at the drumstick end so that you can hang the bird from a hook.

Build a small fire in smoke oven, using charcoal and fruitwood, and place bird on hook in chimney. Smoke-cook at a temperature between 300° and 350° until the meat thermometer registers 180°, or approximately 5 to 5½ hours for a 12-pound bird. (Figure about 25 per cent longer than for oven roasting at 325°.)

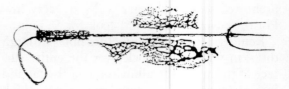

◆ Smoked Spareribs

3 sides spareribs
3 small onions
2 bay leaves
12 peppercorns
1½ cups soy
2 cans (1 lb. each) chunk style pineapple,
　　　with the juice
½ cup soy
½ cup honey

Parboil ribs slowly with onions, bay leaves, and peppercorns for 45 minutes to 1 hour. Remove ribs and put in smoke oven for approximately 1 hour, turning three or four times and basting frequently with a mixture of the 1½ cups soy and 1½ cups of the juice from the pineapple. Remove ribs from oven, cut into serving size pieces, brush each piece lightly with a mixture of the ½ cup soy and ½ cup honey, and pack in a fairly deep baking dish with the pineapple chunks mixed in. If you wish, you can keep the ribs for two or three days in the refrigerator. Before serving, heat in a 350° oven. Makes 12 generous servings.

◆ Chinese Ribs

2 sides pork spareribs
¼ cup soy
1 teaspoon pepper
4 tablespoons honey
¼ cup sherry
2 teaspoons monosodium glutamate

Marinate whole sides of the spareribs in a mixture of the soy, pepper, honey, sherry, and monosodium glutamate for at least 30 minutes. Remove the ribs from the marinade and allow to dry thoroughly.

Hang the ribs from the top of a moderate (300° to 400°) Chinese oven for 1¼ to 1½ hours. The closer you place the ribs to the actual fire, the more carefully you have to watch for charring.

SMOKE-BARBECUING ON A COVERED GRILL

One of the latest trends among barbecue cooks is to give foods a mild smoking as they cook on the barbecue, and you can now buy special barbecue equipment designed for just this purpose. The new devices for smoke-barbecuing on a covered grill offer several advantages over an ordinary brazier. Because the hood completely covers the firebox, foods cook partially by reflected heat as in any oven. Large portions of meat such as a whole turkey or a roast will cook evenly from all sides, so a rotisserie attachment is not necessary (although some models include it). You can use such a unit to cook almost an entire meal; for example, while the meat barbecues, you might heat a covered casserole dish, bake a potato, or roast corn.

With most units, you control heat by (1) raising or lowering grill level, and (2) opening and closing drafts. For highest heat, open drafts or dampers wide; the more air, the hotter the fire. Nearly close dampers for low heat, but never close them completely; fresh air movement is necessary for browning and to keep fuel burning. Use a grill thermometer to measure barbecuing temperature most accurately. Use a meat thermometer inserted into the meat to judge when done.

If your barbecue has the type of hood that half encloses the grill, you can fashion a foil hood to complete your smoke oven. Use 4 strips of wide heavy-duty foil, each about 2½ feet long. Lay the strips side by side and fasten them together securely using the drug store fold along the foil edges. With the center seam of your foil blanket in the center of the opening of your barbecue, shape the foil over the opening—a pair of asbestos gloves helps prevent burned fingers. Use a length of wire around the barbecue from top to bottom to hold the foil tightly in place. Let the foil hang loosely at the lower edge, to admit enough air to keep your fire going. You control the heat of your oven by the amount of ventilation you allow, so you may want to part the foil at the lower edge of the center seam a few inches to speed the cooking.

SMALL CUTS, STEAKS, CHOPS, CHICKEN HALVES, HAMBURGERS: Use direct heat. Place foods directly on grill above charcoal. Put cover on the barbecue unit. Remove cover and turn meat once during cooking.

Recommended grill temperatures are 350°-375° for steaks, hamburgers, lamb chops, kebabs, fish; 300°-325° for pork and poultry. The time it takes to cook in a covered smoke cooker will tend to be slightly shorter than you used when open-barbecuing.

LARGE CUTS, WHOLE MEATS, ROASTS (either on the grill or on rotisserie spit): Use indirect heat. By this we mean that you build the charcoal fire as usual, but before cooking, use long handled tongs to arrange glowing charcoal at sides or back of grill; place drip catching pan directly beneath meat centered on grill. (These drip pans may be purchased, or you can fashion one yourself from heavy foil. Fold a sheet of foil double so it is about 3 inches longer than meat to be prepared. Fold in all edges 1½ inches. Lift folded edges and turn triangle-shaped corners outward. Pinch corners together and fold to side to close square pan corners.)

Recommended cooking temperature for all meats, whether on the grill or at spit-level, is 300°. Smoke-cooking will require about the same amount of time as open-spit-roasting similar cuts. For an *approximate* index, calculate 15 minutes per pound for fish, poultry, and rare beef; 25 minutes per pound for lamb; 30 minutes per pound for pork.

If you want a pronounced smoke flavor, put wood on coals just before you put the meat on to cook, and continue to add wood as needed to provide continual smoke throughout the cooking period. If you want a more subtle smokiness, put the wood on coals just a few minutes before removing meat from the grill.

Try various wood smokes with various foods to determine your favorites. Experiment with light and heavy smoking. Try keeping the fire temperature extremely low and smoke a large piece of meat for several hours to achieve a result much like smoke curing. When you barbecue fresh salmon over low heat this way you achieve a flavor mildly like kippered salmon. Beef tongue deliciously absorbs a subtle hickory smoke. (See recipes below.)

◆ Hickory-Smoked Beef Tongue

Cook a medium-sized beef tongue in simmering water until tender; skin and trim. Cover grill and smoke-cook with hickory smoke over very low indirect heat for 2 hours. After an hour's smoking, baste occasionally with mixture of 2 tablespoons each tomato purée and melted butter, ¼ teaspoon crumbled dried basil, and ⅛ teaspoon crumbled dried tarragon. Slice thinly and serve either hot or cold for sandwiches. Serve cold for hors d'oeuvres.

◆ Chicken and Fruit with Brandy Baste

Salt and pepper 2 broilers, split. Set on grill over direct heat, cover grill, and cook about 40 minutes, basting occasionally with mixture of ½ cup melted butter and ¼ cup *each* lemon juice, brandy, and brown sugar. In a shallow pan fashioned of foil, place 1 cup fresh (or drained canned) dark sweet cherries; in another pan put 12 ripe fresh apricot halves, cut side up. Brush fruits with chicken baste. Cook and smoke over direct heat during last 10 minutes that chicken cooks. Serve fruit alongside chicken. Makes 4 servings.

◆ Smoked Fresh Salmon Fillet

Place a 1-pound piece of fresh salmon fillet on a sheet of heavy foil; place on grill over charcoal arranged for indirect heat. Keep temperature low (not over 275°), cover the grill, and smoke (adding wood as needed) for 2 hours. Salt to taste. Use for hors d'oeuvres, sandwiches, or entrée. Makes 20 generous canapés of salmon on buttered bread, or 4 entrées.

◆ Slow-Smoked Garlic Swordfish on Lemon Slices

Very thinly slice 1½ lemons over bottom of shallow pan fashioned of heavy foil. Lay a large swordfish steak (1 inch thick, about 1½ pounds) on lemon. Pour garlic butter (made by heating 1 large clove garlic, minced or mashed, in ⅓ cup butter) over steak. Sprinkle with salt and pepper to taste. Place on grill over indirect very low heat (not over 275°). Cover grill and smoke for 2 hours. Baste with juices in pan. Makes 4 servings.

◆ Smoked Oyster and Lemon-Topped Beef Fillet

Broil 1½-inch-thick beef fillets (1 for each serving) directly over charcoal fire (allow 5 minutes each side for rare steaks; leave uncovered to sear for 1 minute on each side, then cover to finish smoke-cooking). For each serving, place on a sheet of heavy foil 1 *each* of the following: thin crosswise slice of onion, thin crosswise slice of lemon, drained large oyster. Brush with melted butter. Place on grill to heat and smoke as steaks cook. Stack on each steak an onion slice, a lemon slice, and a smoked oyster; grind black pepper over top.

◆ Roast Pork on Smoked Melon Ring

Place a 4-pound rolled pork loin roast over indirect charcoal heat (meat-level temperature about 300°). Cover grill and roast with smoke for 2 hours or until meat thermometer registers 185°. Brush ½-inch-thick peeled slices of cantaloupe (1 for each serving) with butter, place on foil sheet; place on grill to heat and smoke for 10 minutes (while you slice pork roast). Beat 2 small packages (3 oz. each) cream cheese with chives with 8 tablespoons heavy cream until fluffy. To serve, place a thick roast slice atop a melon ring. Top with a spoonful of whipped cheese. Makes about 12 servings.

◆ Smoked Steak

Start with a good lean cut of tender steak, at least 2 inches thick and without bones. Using any hard wood, get a flaming wood fire going in your barbecue grill. Roll steak in olive oil or salad oil until it's drenched. Then place over the fire and sear it on all sides. Remove and cut diagonally in ¼-inch-thick slices. Lay slices in tiers along one side of a roasting pan with a cover, salting the meat as you go. On the opposite side of the pan, lay a burning ember of wood, put the cover on the pan, and leave it on for 60 seconds. Remove cover and taste meat. If you'd like it smokier, repeat the process.

You can serve the meat now or, for varied tastes, place the roast pan back on your grill. In very short order, the bottom tier will be well done, the middle medium, and the top still rare.

◆ Garlic Leg of Lamb with Coffee Baste

Insert about 5 peeled cloves garlic in a 5 to 6-pound leg of lamb; rub with salt and pepper. Place over indirect charcoal heat (meat-level temperature about 300°). Cover and roast with smoke about 2 hours or until meat thermometer registers 170° (higher, if you prefer it well done). Baste during last half of roasting time with ⅓ cup *each* strong hot coffee and melted butter mixed with 1 teaspoon grated lemon peel. Slice and serve while hot. Makes 8 to 10 servings.

◆ Cumin Steak Strips and Cheese

Barbecue 1 flank steak (about 1½ lbs., not scored) over very hot direct heat with the cover on grill for smoking—5 minutes each side. Place on board and slice very thinly, on the diagonal, as for London Broil. Arrange hot steak strips on top of hot bread slices as an open sandwich, alternating and overlapping steak with ½ pound Meunster cheese, sliced thin. Sprinkle with powdered cumin. Makes 4 servings.

SAUCES AND MARINADES

◆ Sauces and Marinades

There is no mystery about the composition of barbecue sauces and marinades. They are simply a blend of three main ingredients: oil, seasonings, and a food acid such as lemon juice, vinegar, wine, or tomato juice. They are used to sharpen the flavor of meats, fowl, or fish, and to supply fat to meats that are lacking in natural oils. Some cooks believe that the food acids help to tenderize the meat.

Meats are soaked in marinades to flavor, and sometimes to tenderize them before they are put on the grill or spit. Some durable cuts profit from prolonged marinating—two or three days; most need only to be left for a few hours in the flavorful bath. Usually the marinade may also be used as a basting sauce.

Sauces are used primarily to supply flavor and oil to meats as they broil over charcoal. The liquid may be sloshed on with a basting brush or spooned over the meat. Some can be mixed with drippings to make gravy; some are served as is.

◆ Smoky Sauce

Add 1 tablespoon or more of liquid smoke, according to strength desired, to about 1 pint of your favorite barbecue sauce. Let meat or shish kebab stand in sauce for several hours or overnight to absorb flavors; use as basting sauce while the meat is barbecuing.

◆ Special Barbecue Sauce

    ½ cup chopped shallots or green onions
    ¼ cup olive oil
    2 cups sauterne
    1 cup soy
    2 cups catsup
    ½ cup prepared English mustard
    ¼ cup sugar
       Salt and pepper to taste
    ¼ cup chopped parsley

Cook chopped shallots in olive oil for 5 minutes. Add sauterne and let reduce about half. Add all remaining ingredients except parsley. *Do not boil at any time.* Remove from fire, correct seasoning to taste, and add parsley. Makes about 1 quart sauce which can be kept in refrigerator until needed.

To use for barbecued meat: Rub meat with sauce and wait 10 minutes before broiling. Then broil meat slowly until tender.

◆ Circle J Sauce

1 clove garlic, minced
1 small onion, minced
¾ teaspoon dry mustard
1 tablespoon grated fresh horseradish
1 tablespoon mixed minced herbs
    (thyme, marjoram, parsley)
2 tablespoons vinegar
3 cups water
¾ teaspoon salt
1 tablespoon A-1 sauce or Worcestershire
⅔ cup butter
½ cup catsup
½ teaspoon juice from a bottle of
    Tabasco peppers
2 teaspoons sugar
¾ teaspoon chili powder
¼ teaspoon black pepper, freshly ground

Combine all ingredients and cook slowly for 45 minutes. Use to baste meat or fish while cooking, or dip slices or chunks of hot cooked meat into the heated sauce before serving. Makes 3 cups.

◆ Garlic Sauce

1 clove garlic, minced
½ cup salad oil, olive oil or melted butter

Put the garlic to soak in oil the night before the barbecue. Or, if butter is used, melt and keep warm, with the clove of garlic floating in it about 2 hours before the meat is to be grilled. Use for basting grilled steaks or chops.

◆ Sauce Jerez

¼ pound process Cheddar cheese
½ cup sherry
1 teaspoon dry mustard
½ teaspoon seasoning salt
¼ teaspoon paprika
Salt to taste

Melt cheese in double boiler and add wine, a little at a time, stirring constantly. When well blended, add seasonings, stirring thoroughly. Serve hot over steaks, lamb chops or other meat dishes.

◆ Thick Sauce

2 tablespoons lard or shortening
2 tablespoons flour
4 small cans (8 oz.) tomato sauce
1 tablespoon Worcestershire
5 tablespoons chili powder
Few drops Tabasco
2 cloves (or powdered equivalent)

Heat fat until very hot. Add flour and stir until slightly browned. Add the rest of the ingredients and cook until thick. If too thick, add a little water, but it should not be a thin sauce.

◆ Steak Sauce

1 bunch green onions
3 cloves garlic, minced
Butter for sautéing
1 cup catsup
½ cup wine vinegar
1 teaspoon Worcestershire
½ teaspoon each of celery salt, garlic salt,
    onion salt, chili powder, dry
    mustard, and dried mixed herbs

Cut up green onions and garlic in small pieces and sauté in butter until brown. Mix remaining ingredients in a bowl, then add the sautéed onions and garlic. Marinate steaks in this mixture for 3 hours before grilling.

◆ Barney's Barbecue Sauce

¼ cup vinegar
¼ cup catsup
½ cup Worcestershire
¾ cup water
1½ teaspoons dry mustard
¾ teaspoon salt
2 tablespoons butter, melted
¼ cup chopped onion
½ teaspoon sugar
¼ teaspoon chili powder
Small clove garlic
Dash of red pepper

This sauce is good with spareribs, venison, or may be served over steamed wild rice. May be used as either marinade or basting sauce.

◆ Quentin Barbecue Sauce

  1 good-sized onion, finely chopped
  3 or 4 cloves garlic, minced
  1 sprig parsley, minced
  2 cups catsup
  ½ cup wine vinegar
  1 cup olive oil
  2 tablespoons Worcestershire
     Freshly ground pepper to taste

Put ingredients in order given into a quart jar, cover and shake so ingredients will be well blended. Let stand 24 hours, shaking occasionally during the day. Use as a basting sauce.

◆ Easy-to-Make Sauce

  1 can (8 oz.) tomato sauce
  4 teaspoons Worcestershire
  ¼ teaspoon each celery, onion, and
      garlic salt
  4 tablespoons sherry
  1 tablespoon wine vinegar
  2 tablespoons olive oil
  1 clove garlic, minced

Combine all ingredients. Place in a covered jar and let stand in refrigerator overnight, or at least for several hours.

◆ Alki Point Sauce

  2 tablespoon finely minced onion
  3 tablespoons finely minced green pepper
  1 tablespoon butter
  ½ cup water
  1 medium-sized tomato, diced
  ½ teaspoon salt
  ⅛ teaspoon pepper
  ¼ teaspoon Kitchen Bouquet
     Dash of celery salt

Sauté onion and green pepper in the butter until they are golden brown. Add water, tomato, and seasonings. Bring to a boil. Simmer for 10 minutes, stirring frequently. Makes enough sauce for 4 meat servings.

◆ Marinade

  1 cup Zinfandel
  1 cup olive oil
  2 or 3 cloves garlic
  1 bay leaf
  2 or 3 sprigs rosemary
  2 or 3 sprigs thyme
  2 or 3 sprigs marjoram

Mix all ingredients and set away in refrigerator. This preparation will keep indefinitely and will do for several barbecue occasions. The herbs may be strained out after the mixture is well flavored.

Cover steaks with the sauce and let stand from 6 to 36 hours before barbecuing. The sauce may also be used for basting when the meat is on the grill. Apply with a long stalk of celery, using the leaves on the end as a swab. The celery also adds flavor.

◆ Western Sauce

  1 can (1 lb.) tomatoes
  2 cups water
  1 can (6 oz.) tomato paste
  2 dried chili peppers
  ½ cup tomato catsup
  2 tablespoons sugar
  2 teaspoons Worcestershire
  2 teaspoons chili powder
     Juice 2 lemons
  ¼ cup wine vinegar
  2½ teaspoons salt
  ¼ teaspoon cayenne
  ¼ teaspoon Tabasco
  2 teaspoons freshly ground black pepper
  1 large onion, chopped
  1 clove garlic, chopped
  2 bay leaves
  ½ pound butter
  2 teaspoons dry mustard

Combine all ingredients and let simmer over low flame in covered pan for about 30 minutes. Strain through coarse sieve. This sauce can be kept several months in the refrigerator.

◆ Basic Beef Sauce

2 cups tomato juice
1 teaspoon mustard
1 tablespoon sugar
3 tablespoons vinegar
2 teaspoons horseradish
1 tablespoon Worcestershire
¼ cup grated onion
1 clove garlic, minced
¼ cup catsup
½ cup butter or margarine
    Few drops of Tabasco
¾ teaspoon salt
½ teaspoon paprika
½ teaspoon freshly ground pepper

Simmer all ingredients for 30 minutes. For a different flavor, substitute meat stock for the tomato juice, or use half and half.

◆ Roasting Sauce

¼ pound butter
1 cup vinegar
½ teaspoon dry mustard
1 tablespoon chopped onions
2 tablespoons Worcestershire
1 tablespoon chili sauce
1 teaspoon lemon juice
2 lemon slices
1 teaspoon brown sugar
½ pod red pepper, ground

Mix all ingredients together; put over low fire until the butter melts, then set where it will keep warm. Makes about 1½ cups.

◆ Porterhouse Steak Sauce

½ cup olive oil
3 tablespoons wine vinegar
½ tablespoon garlic salt
1 tablespoon paprika
1 teaspoon monosodium glutamate

Paint surfaces of steaks ½ hour before cooking and again just before putting them on the fire. This amount is sufficient for 4 good-sized porterhouse steaks.

◆ All-Purpose Barbecue Sauce

We'd say this is one of the subtlest sauces we've ever used for barbecuing. It has a choice overtone, and it keeps things delectably moist. We suggest it for any meat or fish that needs or deserves any special "saucing." It does not smother a meat (it's all soluble, no solids); it coaxes out the best of its flavor.

¼ cup salad oil
¼ cup bourbon
2 tablespoons soy
1 teaspoon Worcestershire
1 teaspoon garlic powder
    Freshly ground black pepper to taste

Blend all ingredients well. Pour over meat or fish and marinate in refrigerator (turn when you think of it). Marinate roasts for 24 to 48 hours; steaks, 4 hours; salmon or fowl, 2 hours. Also use as a basting sauce during broiling or roasting.

◆ Marinade for Broiling

In addition to exceptional penetration of its own flavors, this marinade seems to have some tenderizing effect on steak. Try it, too, for spareribs, pork or lamb chops, short ribs.

1 tablespoon dry mustard
1 cup water
3 cups soy
3 cloves garlic (about the size of the
    end of your thumb)
6 tablespoons brown sugar
4 tablespoons sherry or bourbon

Mix mustard gradually with 1 cup water to form a paste, then add to soy. Thinly slice garlic or compress it in a garlic press; add it—juice, pulp, and all—to soy. Add sugar and the sherry or bourbon. The entire sauce should be kept at room temperature. The meat should be marinated in this sauce at room temperature from 1 to 2 hours, depending on how thoroughly the chef wishes to have this sauce permeate the meat. Makes approximately 1¼ quarts marinade.

◆ Sandwich Sauce

This sauce is not for basting, but is served over barbecued meats and in sandwiches.

- 1 clove of garlic, minced
- 1 whole onion, minced
- 2 tablespoons oil
- 2 teaspoons chili powder
- 1 teaspoon dry mustard
- 2 bay leaves
- ¼ teaspoon marjoram
- 1 can (1 lb. 13 oz.) tomatoes with purée, sieved
- ¼ cup vinegar
- ½ teaspoon celery salt

Cook the garlic and onion in oil about 5 minutes. Add the rest of the ingredients and simmer gently, stirring frequently, about 40 minutes or until mixture reaches desired thickness. Remove the bay leaves. It's ready for use or can be sealed in jars. If the sauce is heated before serving, the flavors of the meat and sauce are blended better. Makes about 2 cups.

◆ Hamburger Sauce

- ¼ pound butter, melted
- ½ cup olive oil
- ½ cup catsup
- 1 teaspoon prepared mustard
  Dash of Worcestershire
  Grated onion or garlic as desired
  Juice of ½ lemon
  Salt and freshly ground pepper

Shake well. Use either as a marinade or a basting sauce for steaks or hamburgers. Enough for 6.

◆ Simple Steak Sauce

- 1 cup olive oil
- 1 cup wine or wine vinegar
- 2 good-sized onions, grated or minced
  Garlic slices to suit taste
- 1 tablespoon salt
- 1 teaspoon freshly ground pepper

Mix the oil and vinegar, then add the onion, garlic, salt and pepper. Pour into a pint fruit jar and stir until salt is dissolved. Let the mixture stand overnight, then stir well just before using.

◆ Sauce for Steaks or Chops

- ½ cup peanut oil
- ¼ cup wine vinegar
- 1 or 2 tablespoons horse-radish, freshly ground
- 1 cup hot water
- 2 tablespoons Worcestershire
- 2 tablespoons grated onion juice and pulp
- 2 tablespoons chili sauce
- 1 large clove garlic, grated or crushed
- 1 tablespoon each of brown sugar, salt, dry mustard, paprika, black pepper
  Generous sprigs each of fresh rosemary, fresh sage, fresh thyme, parsley

Simmer all ingredients together for about 15 minutes. Cool. Brush over patties while broiling; brush over both sides of chops or steak an hour before cooking. This sauce will keep satisfactorily for 2 weeks in the refrigerator.

◆ Salsa (Steak Sandwich Sauce)

- 4 large onions
- 6 tomatoes
- 2 cans (4 oz. each) green chilis, seeded
  Salt
  Freshly ground pepper
- 2 tablespoons wine vinegar
- ¼ cup olive oil

Mince onions, tomatoes, and green chili. Season with salt and pepper, add vinegar and olive oil. Let stand 2 hours before using.

◆ Kebab Sauce

1 can (10½ oz.) condensed tomato soup
Oil or shortening
1 teaspoon dry mustard
1 teaspoon sugar (brown or granulated)
1 teaspoon salt
2 teaspoons chili powder
3 to 4 tablespoons wine or vinegar
Worcestershire
Paprika
Pepper
1 onion, chopped fine
1 large clove garlic, chopped fine
Pinch rosemary leaves
1 tablespoon liquid smoke

Empty contents of can of tomato soup into a saucepan; fill can about three-fourths full of water, and add enough shortening or oil to bring water to top of the can; pour into saucepan. Add mustard, sugar, salt, chili powder, and wine or vinegar; Worcestershire, paprika, and pepper to taste; chopped onion, chopped garlic, mashed well with a tiny bit of shortening; rosemary leaves, and liquid smoke.

Heat to boiling and cook for about 5 minutes, or until all ingredients are well blended. Makes about 2¾ cups of sauce. May be made in quantity and stored in the refrigerator.

◆ Mellow Barbecue Sauce

Applesauce is the base of this unusual barbecue sauce that requires no cooking and little of your time.

½ cup red wine vinegar
1 clove garlic, minced or mashed
1 sprig fresh rosemary, crushed
    (¼ teaspoon dried)
1 can (1 lb.) apple sauce (2 cups)
1 bottle (14 oz.) chili sauce
1 teaspoon salt
½ teaspoon pepper
1 tablespoon Worcestershire

In a large mixing bowl, combine vinegar, garlic, rosemary, apple sauce, chili sauce, salt, pepper, and Worcestershire. Set bowl in a warm place so ingredients can mellow for an hour or so. Baste beef, pork, chicken, or turkey generously with sauce as it cooks. Makes about 4 cups.

◆ Savory Raisin Baste

This full-flavored, moderately thick baste becomes a crusty glaze on the meat, fruity and slightly sweet-and-sour in flavor. It's especially good on rare beef steak. You can substitute a dry table wine for the bouillon, if you prefer.

½ cup raisins (or cooked prunes, pitted)
¼ cup chopped onion
1 small clove garlic, minced or mashed
½ cup each catsup and bouillon
3 tablespoons salad oil
2 tablespoons wine vinegar
1 tablespoon brown sugar
1 teaspoon prepared mustard
1 teaspoon liquid smoke
½ teaspoon salt
⅛ teaspoon dried dill weed

Purée raisins (or chop very fine). Combine with remaining ingredients. Simmer 10 to 15 minutes. Makes about 1¾ cups.

◆ Smoky Peach or Apricot Baste

If you use peaches for this baste, try a dash of allspice to bring out the peach flavor. Try the baste first on lamb, but you may also like it on pork or chicken.

1 can (about 9 oz.) peaches or apricots, undrained (or use about ½ cup peeled and sliced, ripe fresh fruit mashed with 3 tablespoons sugar)
¼ cup catsup
3 tablespoons lemon juice
2 tablespoons salad oil or melted butter
½ teaspoon liquid smoke
½ teaspoon salt
⅛ teaspoon grated lemon peel

Purée fruits. Combine with remaining ingredients. Simmer 10 to 15 minutes. Makes about 1½ cups.

◆ Honey-Mint Sauce for Lamb

Our testers found this sauce a brand new taste experience. Their reaction was generally favorable, although some liked it considerably better than others. There's no harm in adding a bit more vinegar if you don't like a meat sauce quite this sweet.

    ½ cup water
    1 tablespoon vinegar
    1 cup honey
    ¼ cup chopped fresh mint

Heat water and vinegar together. Add honey, stir well, and then add mint. Cook over a slow fire for 5 minutes. If you don't want a strong sauce, you can strain out the mint as soon as you are through cooking.

This sauce can be used to baste lamb while it is being barbecued over charcoal, or it can be served over the meat at table. For serving over the meat, you can make it more attractive by straining out the cooked mint and adding 1 to 3 teaspoons chopped fresh mint. Makes about 1½ cups sauce.

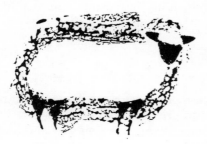

◆ Basic Lamb Sauce

    ¾ cup sherry
    1 slice lemon
    1 sprig parsley, minced
    2 tablespoons olive oil
    1 teaspoon grated onion
    1 teaspoon salt
    ½ teaspoon pepper
    1 sprig each fresh rosemary and oregano,
        minced, or ½ teaspoon each dried
        herbs

Let stand for several hours to blend.

◆ Lamb Shish Kebab Sauce

    1 can (6 oz.) tomato paste
    ½ cup olive oil
    1 cup honey
    1 cup dry white table wine
    2 cloves garlic, crushed
    ½ teaspoon each crushed rosemary
        and oregano
    1 teaspoon salt

Mix all ingredients. Thread squares of lamb (cut from shoulder or leg) on skewers, pour over sauce, and let stand a few minutes before cooking. (You can marinate lamb in your favorite wine-and-oil marinade first and use 1 cup of the marinade instead of the dry white wine.) Barbecue about 20 minutes, basting often with sauce during the process. Sauce is ample for about 3½ pounds of meat on 7 large skewers.

◆ Herb Sauce for Lamb

    1 small onion or half a large one
    3 cloves garlic
    2 sprigs rosemary
    12 fresh mint leaves
    ¼ cup vinegar
    ½ cup water

Chop the onion and garlic fine and add the rosemary and mint leaves which have been crushed or chopped. Then add the vinegar and water and let the mixture stand overnight.

When ready to barbecue steaks or chops, brush them thoroughly with the sauce, using a bunch of mint leaves for a brush. As the meat cooks, baste occasionally with more of the liquid. If still more sauce is desired, pass a cruet of it when serving.

◆ Marinade and Basting Sauce for Lamb

    1 cup olive oil
    ½ cup red wine vinegar (flavored with garlic or eschalot, if desired)
    1 teaspoon thyme
    1 teaspoon monosodium glutamate
    1 teaspoon mint (fresh or dried)
    1 teaspoon freshly ground pepper
    ½ teaspoon salt
    ½ teaspoon paprika

Mix all ingredients. Marinate lamb for at least 2 hours before barbecuing. Baste frequently with sauce while cooking in a Chinese smoke oven or broiling over charcoal. Makes enough sauce for about 6 chops or a 3 to 5-pound roast.

◆ Ham Sauce

    ½ teaspoon black pepper
    ½ teaspoon salt
    1 teaspoon dry mustard
    1 tablespoon sugar
    ½ cup vinegar
    1 egg

Mix dry ingredients, add vinegar and slightly beaten egg. Heat until egg is set, stirring constantly, but do not boil. When slightly thickened, add:

    ½ cup catsup
    ½ cup tart jelly (grape or currant)

Stir until jelly has melted. If the sauce curdles, strain but never boil.

◆ Basic Pork Sauce

    1½ cups tomato sauce
    ½ cup water
    ⅓ cup vinegar
    ⅓ cup brown sugar
    2 tablespoons butter or margarine
    1 teaspoon smoked salt
    1 teaspoon ginger
    ½ teaspoon paprika
    1 small onion, minced

Simmer all ingredients for 30 minutes.

◆ Southern Barbecue Sauce

    1 quart cider vinegar
    5 tablespoons Worcestershire
    2 tablespoons A-1 sauce
    2 teaspoons salt
    1 tablespoon sugar
    6 whole mint leaves
    ¼ teaspoon paprika
    4 shakes Tabasco
    ½ teaspoon black pepper
    1½ tablespoons mixed whole pickling spices
    1 bouillon cube
    3 large slices unpeeled orange
    2 large slices unpeeled lemon
    1 cup water
    1 tablespoon catsup
    Sweet basil and oregano to taste

Combine all ingredients. Put on the stove in an enamel or glass container, and simmer until the orange and lemon peel are pretty well cooked. Use this sauce on either pork or lamb. Excellent for basting spareribs.

◆ Purple Plum Baste

Use either fresh plums or canned purple plums for this baste for chicken or pork. If you use canned plums, simply pit and purée. If you use fresh plums, cook 8 to 10 plums with ½ cup water and ⅓ cup sugar until tender, then purée.

    1 can (1 lb.) purple plums with syrup (or cooked fresh plums) puréed
    ¼ cup lemon juice or vinegar
    2 tablespoons each chopped onions, brown sugar, and salad oil or melted butter
    ½ teaspoon salt

Combine all ingredients; simmer 10 to 15 minutes. Makes about 2 cups sauce.

◆ Sauce for Grilled Chicken

This sauce for chicken cooked over charcoal is also good when the broiling is done in the kitchen range. Slice 2 large onions and wilt them in 2 tablespoons butter. Add 1 cup chicken gravy (canned may be used), 2 tablespoons tarragon vinegar, and ½ teaspoon sugar. Simmer for 20 minutes, adding water if too thick. Strain and season to taste with salt and pepper.

◆ Simple Sauce for Chicken

Let chicken stand for 2 or 3 hours at room temperature in a mixture of:

2 parts olive oil
1 part wine vinegar
1 medium-sized onion, minced
1 clove garlic, minced
  Salt and pepper
  Generous pinch each of tarragon, thyme, and chopped parsley

Use same mixture to baste chicken during cooking.

◆ Duck Sauce

½ cube butter or margarine
2 tablespoons olive oil
2 large onions, chopped
2 cloves garlic
1 large green pepper, chopped
½ cup celery, chopped
  Juice and chopped peel of ½ lemon
1 sprig fresh rosemary
6 sage leaves
½ teaspoon monosodium glutamate
1 pint white or red wine

Melt the butter in frying pan with olive oil, then add all the remaining ingredients except the wine. Sauté until mixture is soft and the onions a golden brown. Just before serving the ducks, add the wine to the mixture, and bring to a boil. Pour over the ducks and serve.

◆ Poultry Marinade

This marinade will flavor 8 fryer halves (1¾ to 2½ pounds) or cut-up young turkeys.

2 to 3 cloves garlic
8 heaping teaspoons quick-cure salt (obtainable in rural localities)
1 level teaspoon each of thyme, celery salt, black pepper
2 heaping teaspoons dry mustard
½ teaspoon each of poultry seasoning, fresh grated ginger root, monosodium glutamate
¾ cup sauterne
1 cup red wine vinegar
  Olive oil

Mince garlic, put in bowl, add salt and crush together. Add other spices, then wine and vinegar. Do not add oil until ready to cook. Stir thoroughly until salt is dissolved, or shake well in covered jar.

Put liquid in large bowl, dip each piece of fowl into it, place fowl in baking dish or flat pan, skin side down. Stir balance of marinade and pour over fowl. Let stand 2 to 3 hours, then turn fowl over and let stand again for 2 to 3 hours.

When ready to barbecue, pour marinade off fowl. Add olive oil to marinade in an amount equal to about ¼ the volume of marinade remaining. Stir thoroughly, brush each piece of fowl with mixture before placing on grill. Paint again each time fowl is turned.

VARIATION:

A simplified version of this sauce is used to flavor steaks.

8 teaspoons quick-cure salt
1 teaspoon black pepper
¾ cup sauterne
1 cup red wine vinegar
½ teaspoon monosodium glutamate
  Olive oil

Mix ingredients together, and soak steaks for 2 to 3 hours. Remove steaks from marinade, add olive oil equal to about ¼ the volume and baste steaks while grilling.

◆ Chicken or Turkey Wine Sauce

1 cup white table wine
¼ cup olive oil
2 tablespoons butter or margarine
1 medium-sized onion, minced
1 clove garlic, crushed
1 teaspoon salt
¼ teaspoon paprika
2 teaspoons fresh rosemary, minced
1 teaspoon parsley, minced
Freshly ground pepper

Simmer all ingredients for 15 minutes. Use as basting sauce.

◆ Golden Papaya Baste

The golden color of papaya coats chicken (or pork) with its own color. In places where the baste caramelizes, the papaya flavor becomes even richer.

1 can (9 oz.) undrained sliced papaya, puréed (or use mashed fresh fruit with 3 tablespoons sugar)
2 tablespoons each white wine vinegar, Sherry or fruit juice, and salad oil or melted butter
1 tablespoon honey
½ teaspoon salt
¼ teaspoon powdered ginger or curry

Combine all ingredients. Simmer 10 to 15 minutes. Makes about 1¼ cups.

◆ Marinade for Poultry or Game

1 part Italian Vermouth
1 part olive oil

Combine wine and olive oil, mixing well. Mix thoroughly each time you baste.

◆ Rosy Cranberry Baste

Cranberries give a unique flavor to pork, chicken, or turkey. The chopped onion is optional.

1 can (7 oz.) jellied cranberry sauce
⅔ cup white or Rosé dinner wine, or chicken stock
2 tablespoons chopped onion (optional)
2 tablespoons each honey and salad oil or melted butter
1 tablespoon wine vinegar
2 teaspoons cornstarch
½ teaspoon salt

Simmer all ingredients together 10 to 15 minutes. Makes about 1¾ cups.

◆ Cooked Marinade for Game

Use this marinade when there is not time for long marinating. When it is poured hot over the meat, it hastens the flavoring and tenderizing process.

4 bay leaves
½ teaspoon thyme (or 4 sprigs fresh thyme)
4 whole cloves
6 whole allspice
1 clove garlic (optional)
6 whole peppercorns
1 onion, sliced
2 sprigs parsley, chopped
2 cups red table wine
1½ oz. brandy

Bruise in a mortar bay leaves, thyme, cloves, allspice, garlic, and peppercorns. Add onion, parsley, wine, and brandy. Bring to a boil and pour over the meat. Marinate from 4 to 24 hours, turning occasionally. Makes about 1 pint of marinade.

◆ Marinade for Game

Try this excellent recipe if you want to disguise the gamy flavor of venison. Marinate small pieces of meat for 24 hours, larger pieces for 2 or 3 days.

    1 bottle (⅘ quart) red wine (preferably a Burgundy or Pinot Noir)
   ¼ cup red wine vinegar
    2 large carrots, sliced
    2 large onions, sliced
    6 shallots, chopped (optional)
   ½ teaspoon each whole peppercorns, whole cloves, juniper berries, and thyme
    1 tablespoon salt
    3 or 4 sprigs parsley
    1 bay leaf

Combine all ingredients. Pour over the meat, cover with foil, and keep cool. Turn meat several times. (If the marinade completely covers the meat, turning is not necessary.) Some cooks pour a little oil on the top of the marinade to seal out the air. Makes about 1 quart marinade.

◆ Venison Sauce

Chop the following fresh herbs: 1 teaspoon each of marjoram, rosemary, sage, thyme. Add:

    1 pint salad oil
   ⅔ pint wine vinegar
    2 tablespoons Worcestershire
   ⅓ cup parsley
    Garlic (let your conscience be your guide, but plenty)

Mix thoroughly, adding salt and pepper to taste, and let the mixture stand overnight. Dip the venison chops or steaks in the sauce and broil, turning once or twice, until medium done.

◆ Soy Marinade for Fish

Marinate fish for 4 to 5 hours in a mixture of equal parts of soy sauce and water, with crushed garlic to taste. Garlic and soy sauce make a combination used frequently by the Japanese in their fish cookery. For added piquancy squeeze a little lemon or lime over the fish while they're cooking.

◆ Fish Sauce

    2 cups meat or chicken stock
    1 tablespoon soy
    1 tablespoon lemon juice
    1 tablespoon Worcestershire
   ¼ cup catsup
    1 teaspoon paprika

Simmer all ingredients for 30 minutes. Pour over fish before serving.

◆ Fish Marinade

   ¼ cup soy
   ¼ cup bourbon or ½ cup sherry wine
    1 clove garlic, crushed
   ¼ cup salad oil (use less oil if your fish is a fat one)
   ½ teaspoon monosodium glutamate

Combine soy, bourbon or sherry, well crushed garlic, olive oil, and monosodium glutamate. Let mixture stand to blend flavors.

◆ Sweet-Sour Pineapple Baste

Brush this over swordfish as it quickly grills over the barbecue coals. Or try it on oven-grilled bass to add moistness and richness. Try it on chicken, too.

    1 can (8½ oz.) crushed pineapple, undrained
   ¾ cup chicken broth or white dinner wine
    3 tablespoons white wine vinegar
    2 tablespoons salad oil
    1 tablespoon soy
    1 tablespoon each chopped onion and brown sugar
    1 teaspoon lemon juice
   ½ teaspoon garlic salt

Combine all ingredients. Simmer 10 to 15 minutes. Makes about 1⅔ cups.

BARBECUE ACCOMPANIMENTS

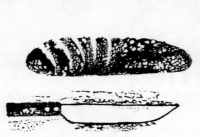

◆ Barbecue Accompaniments

The *pièce de résistance* of your barbecue meal will, of course, be the meat, fowl, or fish that you lift piping hot from the grill, the spit, or the coals. Generally your guests will have watched with growing appetites as this main dish sizzled away on the barbecue. The side dishes that you serve with this flavorsome main course should not in any way detract from it; yet they should be sufficient to satisfy the hearty appetites that go with outdoor dining.

Principal things to consider in planning your menu are (1) that the accompaniments can be prepared ahead of time or can be cooked right on the barbecue, and (2) that they will hold up well while the main course is being cooked and served. Your choice might include a casserole that can be prepared in the kitchen before your guests arrive and can be kept warm at the edge of the fire. Most barbecue menus include a salad. This, too, can be prepared in advance; the dressing can be added at the last minute.

Cold vegetable dishes, relishes, and fruit platters are good choices. There are many skillet dishes that you can cook right on the grill and, like the casserole, they can be kept warm near the fire until serving time.

The recipes included in this chapter were selected primarily because of the ease with which they can be prepared and served. Whatever your choice of accompaniments may be, remember to keep them simple so that you, too, can enjoy the barbecuing of the main course.

CASSEROLES

If you plan to serve a casserole, select one that is light and not too filling so that there will be no chance of its competing with the main course. If you are serving barbecued meat, you will probably want to select a casserole that does not have meat as one of its principal ingredients.

◆ Orange Potatoes

This is a Sicilian way to prepare potatoes that are to be served with game. Peel and boil 2 pounds potatoes in salted water until tender. Drain, shake over heat for a few minutes to dry, then mash. Add ¼ cup melted butter and

¼ cup orange juice. Whip until light, then pile in a casserole and sprinkle top with the grated rind of an orange. Dot with butter and brown in the oven or under the broiler. Makes 4 to 6 servings.

◆ Macaroni Bake

      2 cups shell macaroni
      1 cup cottage cheese
      1 cup commercial sour cream
      1 clove garlic, minced
      1 medium-sized onion, minced
      2 tablespoons Worcestershire
      1 tablespoon chili sauce
      2 drops Tabasco
        Salt and pepper to taste
        Grated Parmesan cheese

Cook macaroni in boiling salted water until just tender. Drain, and rinse with cold water. Place in bowl and combine with cottage cheese, sour cream, garlic, onion, Worcestershire, chili sauce, Tabasco, salt and pepper. Turn into a greased casserole and bake at 350° for about 45 minutes. Sprinkle with cheese, then return to the oven for a few minutes before serving. Makes 6 servings.

◆ Macaroni and Cheese

      1½ cups elbow macaroni, uncooked
       ¼ cup butter
      1½ cups American cheese, cubed
      1½ tablespoons onion, chopped
      1½ tablespoons parsley, chopped fine
      1½ tablespoons pimiento, chopped fine
       1 teaspoon salt
       ⅛ teaspon pepper
       ½ teaspoon paprika
       2 eggs
       2 cups milk

Cook the macaroni in boiling salted water for 15 minutes. Drain and pour cold water through it. Put it in a buttered baking dish. Add the butter, cubed cheese, chopped onion, parsley, pimiento, and seasonings to the macaroni. Beat the eggs slightly and add milk to them. Pour over the macaroni and cheese and bake, uncovered, in a moderately slow oven (325°) for 50 minutes. Makes 6 servings.

◆ Noodles Alfredo

      1 pound narrow noodles or fettucini
      ½ cup (¼ pound) butter
      ⅓ cup grated Parmesan cheese
      ⅓ cup grated Swiss cheese
      ½ cup hot heavy cream

Cook the noodles in boiling salted water until barely tender. Drain and dress immediately with the butter, which has been melted and is still very hot, and the Parmesan and Swiss cheeses. Mix with a fork and spoon, lifting the noodles high so that the steam will escape. When each noodle is well coated with cheese place in casserole, pour heated cream over the noodles, mix lightly, and serve at once. Makes 6 servings.

◆ Noodles Romanoff

In this ideal accompaniment for barbecued meat, the sour cream really asserts itself and gives the noodles character.

      1 package (8 oz.) egg noodles
      1 cup large curd cottage cheese
      1 small clove garlic, minced or mashed
      1 teaspoon Worcestershire
      1 cup (½ pint) commercial sour cream
      ¼ cup grated onion
      ¼ teaspoon Tabasco
      ½ cup grated processed Cheddar cheese

Cook the noodles until just tender in boiling salted water. Combine drained noodles, cottage cheese, garlic, Worcestershire, sour cream, grated onion, and Tabasco. If you like a very colorful casserole, add some chopped pimiento or green pepper. Turn into a buttered casserole; sprinkle grated cheese over the top. Bake in a moderate oven (350°) for 25 minutes, or until heated through. Makes 8 servings.

◆ Hungarian Rice

   4 cups finely chopped cabbage
   1 tablespoon salt
   6 tablespoons butter or margarine
   1 tablespoon sugar
   1 cup raisins
   1 cup rice
1½ cups boiling chicken stock
   2 eggs, beaten
 ¾ cup light cream
   1 teaspoon paprika
     Salt and pepper to taste

Sprinkle cabbage with salt and let stand about 20 minutes. Squeeze out liquid. Simmer cabbage until golden in butter along with sugar and raisins, stirring occasionally. Meanwhile, add rice to boiling chicken stock. Cover, and cook slowly until liquid is absorbed. Combine with cabbage mixture, eggs, cream, paprika, salt, and pepper. Pour into a casserole and bake in a slow oven (300°) for 30 minutes. Makes 5 or 6 servings.

◆ Italian Spinach Rice

This spinach and rice dish tastes best at room temperature, so there's no problem of keeping it hot out-of-doors. Try it, too, with chard or asparagus instead of spinach.

   2 eggs
   1 cup cooked rice
1½ cups chopped cooked spinach (well
     drained)
 ½ cup shredded sharp Cheddar cheese
   4 tablespoons (¼ cup) salad oil
 ½ teaspoon salt
     Pepper
 ¼ teaspoon each crumbled dried
     marjoram and basil

Beat eggs slightly; combine with rice, spinach, cheese, salad oil, salt, pepper to taste, marjoram, and basil; mix well. Spoon into a greased 9 by 5-inch loaf pan. Bake in a moderate oven (350°) for 30 minutes, or until firm. Cut in squares or slices. Makes 6 servings.

◆ Oriental Green Rice

   3 tablespoons butter
 ⅛ teaspoon curry powder
   3 cups cooked rice
 ⅓ cup finely chopped parsley
   1 teaspoon salt
 ¼ cup finely chopped peanuts or toasted
     almonds

Melt butter, add curry powder, and blend. Combine with rice. Season with parsley, salt, and chopped peanuts. Place in casserole or baking pan. Heat 15 to 20 minutes before serving. Makes 6 servings.

◆ Mushroom-Rice Bake

This easy-to-make casserole starts with uncooked rice, canned soups, and mushrooms. If you use packaged precooked rice, baking time is about 30 minutes.

   4 tablespoons butter or margarine
 ¾ cup uncooked rice
   1 can (4 oz.) whole mushroom caps
   2 tablespoons chopped onion
   1 can (10½ oz.) chicken gumbo soup
   1 can (10½ oz.) chicken-with-rice soup

In a 2-quart casserole, melt the butter; stir in rice. In a pan combine the mushrooms (including mushroom liquid), onion, soups. Heat, then pour over rice in casserole; stir until blended. Cover and bake in a moderate oven (350°) for 45 minutes to 1 hour, or until tender. Makes 4 to 6 servings.

◆ Green Pepper-Cheese Casserole

     Butter or margarine
   6 large green peppers
   3 cups cooked rice
   2 cups chopped or grated Cheddar cheese
     Salt and pepper to taste

Grease an 8 to 10-inch baking casserole with butter or margarine. Cut green peppers in half, remove seeds, rinse, and steam until tender.

Put a layer of rice in the bottom of the casserole, then a layer of steamed green pepper, then a layer of cheese, and so on. If the rice seems dry, as day-old cooked rice sometimes does, dot the rice layers with butter. Finish off with a layer of cheese. Place in oven, preheated to 350° (moderate), and bake 30 to 40 minutes. Makes 6 servings.

◆ Cheese and Hominy Casserole

Chopped green chili peppers add spiciness to the ground hominy in this casserole.

    3 medium-sized onions
    2 cans (1 lb. each) hominy
    2 cans (4 oz. each) green chili peppers
    1 clove garlic, minced or mashed
    4 cups (1 lb.) grated Cheddar cheese

Put onions and hominy through food chopper, using medium blade, and mix together. Remove seeds and chop chili peppers; mix with garlic. In a greased, 9-inch, round casserole, arrange alternate layers of the hominy and onions, chili peppers and garlic, and cheese, ending with the cheese. Bake in a moderate oven (350°) for 45 minutes. Makes 6 to 8 servings.

◆ Green Beans Supreme

The simplicity of this dish, made from three canned items, makes it suitable for spur-of-the-moment entertaining. You may substitute 2 packages of partially cooked frozen green beans for the canned ones.

    1 can (1 lb.) green beans, drained
    1 can (10½ oz.) mushroom soup
    ¼ teaspoon oregano (optional)
    1 can (3½ oz.) French-fried onions

Mix the green beans, undiluted mushroom soup, and oregano in a 9-inch square or round baking dish. Bake in a moderate oven (350°) for 15 minutes. Sprinkle with French-fried onions, and continue baking for 5 more minutes.

◆ Curried Lima Casserole

    2 packages (10 oz. each) frozen baby
        lima beans
    1 can (10½ oz.) cream of mushroom
        soup
    1 cup chili sauce
    2 tablespoons maple syrup
    2 teaspoons curry powder
    2 tablespoons brown sugar

Cook the lima beans 10 minutes in 1 cup unsalted water. Stir in all the above ingredients and pour into casserole. Bake uncovered for 30 minutes at 350°. Makes 6 servings.

◆ Three-Bean Casserole

    1 large onion, finely chopped
    1 clove garlic, mashed or minced
    3 tablespoons bacon drippings
    2 packages (10 oz. each) frozen lima
        beans
    1 can (1 lb.) tomato-style baked beans
    1 can (1 lb.) red kidney beans
    ½ cup catsup
    ¼ cup (4 tablespoons) water
    3 tablespoons vinegar
    1 tablespoon brown sugar
    1 teaspoon dry mustard
    1 teaspoon salt
    ¼ teaspoon pepper

In a large, heavy frying pan, sauté onion and garlic in bacon drippings until golden brown. While onion is cooking, cook limas in boiling salted water 16 to 18 minutes, or until tender; drain and add to sautéed onion, along with baked beans, kidney beans, catsup, water, vinegar, brown sugar, mustard, salt, and pepper. Heat mixture, then turn into a 2-quart casserole. Bake in a moderate oven (350°) for 30 minutes. Makes 6 to 8 servings.

◆ Smoky Beans

For quick baked beans, season canned baked beans with a small amount of liquid smoke, then place in a bean pot with a good-sized onion buried in the center. Strip bacon across the top. Bake in a moderately hot oven (375°) for about 45 minutes.

◆ Baked Onions with Almonds

Onions, either raw or cooked, are well suited to barbecue menus. This onion dish goes well with any type of meat. Almonds are an excellent texture contrast. Or you can substitute filberts as the nut meats.

      6 large onions
     ½ teaspoon salt
      1 can (10½ oz.) cream of mushroom
          soup
      1 cup milk
     ½ teaspoon salt
     ¼ teaspoon freshly ground pepper
     ¼ teaspoon paprika
      2 cups chopped almond meats

Peel onions, quarter, and cook in a small amount of boiling water with the ½ teaspoon salt until almost tender; drain. Mix together mushroom soup, milk, ½ teaspoon salt, pepper, and paprika; pour over the cooked onions. Turn half of the onions and sauce into a round, 9-inch casserole and sprinkle with 1 cup of nut meats; cover with the remaining onions and sprinkle the top with the remaining cup of nut meats. Bake in a hot oven (400°) for 20 minutes, then place under the broiler to brown the top lightly (about 2 minutes). Makes 6 generous servings.

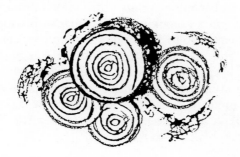

◆ Onions au Gratin

In this case, the "gratin" means, as it so often does in France, browned crumbs of bread rather than of cheese. Peel and cook 4 pounds onions until tender. Drain and chop; mix with 5 chopped hard-cooked eggs, 2 cups of Béchamel or cream sauce, and salt, pepper, and tarragon to taste. Pour into an 8-inch-square baking dish, sprinkle with 1 cup of dried bread crumbs which have been mixed with 3 tablespoons melted butter. Bake in a moderately hot oven (375°) until browned. Makes 8 to 10 servings.

◆ Corn Pudding

This corn pudding made with freshly grated corn and cornmeal is similar to a meatless tamale pie. Because this dish takes the place of both vegetable and rice or potatoes, it needs only an accompaniment of meat from the barbecue.

      2 eggs
   1¼ cups milk
   2½ cups grated raw corn
      1 cup chopped tomatoes
      1 small onion, finely chopped
      1 green pepper, seeded and chopped
      1 can (4 oz.) pimientos, chopped
      1 cup pitted ripe olives
      1 teaspoon salt
     ¼ teaspoon each pepper, paprika, and
          chili powder
      1 cup yellow cornmeal
     ½ cup (¼ pound) butter or margarine

Beat eggs slightly; stir in milk, corn, tomatoes, onion, green pepper, pimientos, olives, salt, pepper, paprika, and chili powder. Add cornmeal and stir until well mixed. Melt butter; stir into cornmeal mixture. Turn into a greased 2-quart casserole. Bake in a moderately slow oven (325°) for 1 hour, or until firm. Makes 6 servings.

Ranchers' Spoon Bread

The Italian cook discovered long ago that cooked ground corn is an excellent accompaniment to chicken. Use either regular cornmeal or coarsely ground Italian-style *polenta* in this recipe.

  2¼ cups milk
  ¾ cup yellow cornmeal or polenta
  ¼ cup sugar
  ½ teaspoon salt
  ½ cup (¼ pound) butter or margarine
  3 eggs, separated

Heat milk just to boiling; stirring constantly, add cornmeal gradually and cook until cornmeal begins to thicken. Add sugar and salt, and stirring occasionally, cook until cornmeal is thick. Remove from heat and stir in butter. Beat egg yolks slightly; stir in a little of the cornmeal mixture. Add the egg yolks to hot cornmeal and mix well. Beat egg whites until stiff; fold into cornmeal mixture.

Turn into a greased 1½-quart casserole. Bake in a moderately hot oven (375°) for 35 minutes, or until a knife inserted in the center comes out clean. Serve with butter or gravy. Makes 6 servings.

Baked Zucchini Casserole

  2 pounds zucchini
  ½ teaspoon salt
  2 medium-sized onions, minced
  1 clove garlic, minced or mashed
  1 tablespoon butter or margarine
  3 slices fresh bread, cut in small cubes
  2 tablespoons minced parsley
  1 cup (¼ lb.) grated Cheddar cheese
  4 eggs
  ½ teaspoon Worcestershire
      Dash of Tabasco
  1 teaspoon salt
  ½ teaspoon each pepper and paprika

Remove ends of zucchini, and cook in a small amount of water with the ½ teaspoon of salt until tender. Drain and mash zucchini to medium smoothness. Sauté onion and garlic in the butter, and add to zucchini along with cubed bread, minced parsley, cheese, well-beaten eggs, and seasonings. Mix well and spoon into a well-buttered baking dish. Set in a pan of hot water and bake in a moderate oven (350°) for 30 minutes, or until firm. Makes 6 to 8 servings.

SKILLET FARE

Many barbecue chefs have learned that it is a simple matter to cook a rice or vegetable dish right on the grill while the meat is barbecuing. Advance preparations can be done in the kitchen, and the dish can then be set over low coals to bubble away until serving time.

Hominy Rio Grande

  1 onion, minced
  2 tablespoons salad oil
  1 pound fresh tomatoes, chopped, or
      1 can (1 lb.) solid pack tomatoes
  ¼ teaspoon chili powder
  1 teaspoon salt
  1 teaspoon sugar
  1 cup uncooked hominy grits (cook ahead of time in salted water) or
      1 large can (1 lb. 13 oz.) hominy
  1 cup grated sharp cheese

Brown onion lightly in oil. Add tomatoes, chili powder, salt, and sugar. Cover and cook slowly on top of barbecue until most of liquid has cooked down. Add cooked hominy grits. Mix in cheese and stir until melted. Remove from heat and serve at once. Makes 4 to 6 servings.

◆ Golden Toasted Rice

> 1 cup uncooked rice
> 2 tablespoons butter or margarine
> 1 can (11 oz.) consommé
> ½ cup water
> 3 or 4 green onions
> 1 to 3 tablespoons soy

Toast the rice by spreading the grains in a heavy pan and heating in a moderate oven (350°) until lightly browned.

Melt butter in a heavy pan with a tight-fitting cover; add rice and cook it slightly, stirring constantly. Pour in hot consommé and water, stir once, cover, and turn heat to the lowest possible point. Let rice steam for 25 minutes.

Stir in finely sliced green onions and tops and the soy. Remove from heat, put on the cover again, and let stand a few minutes to blend the flavors and partially cook the onion. Makes 4 servings.

◆ Pilaff

Pilaff makes an excellent rice accompaniment for shish kebab and may be eaten with or without the sauce. If you wish, you can use regular or quick-cooking cracked wheat instead of rice. Many people feel that rice is best with fowl and wheat with meats, but there is no rule.

BROTH FOR PILAFF

For 6 to 8 persons make 1 quart of broth. Cover with water the lamb bones and trimmings left over after making shish kebab. Season with vegetables and herbs. After the broth cooks down, strain before using in the pilaff.

PREPARATION OF PILAFF

> 2 cups uncooked rice or cracked wheat (do not wash)
> 1 cup uncooked fine noodles
> 4 tablespoons butter
> 4 cups boiling broth

Use long-grained white rice. Buy barley noodles from an Armenian or Italian store. If you can't get them, use the thinnest egg noodles obtainable and crush them until they are all broken into small pieces about ½ inch long or less.

Brown the noodles in the butter until tan, pour in the rice, and mix well. The rice should not fry but should merely become covered with the butter. Pour over it the boiling broth, cover, and allow to simmer slowly without stirring for 20 minutes or until all broth has simmered away. It can be reheated by adding a little water and steaming for a short time. Makes 6 to 8 servings.

◆ Brown Rice Pilaff

Fry 1 cup of uncooked brown rice in 3 tablespoons of oil in a large skillet. Stir it constantly until it turns a golden brown. Then season it and pour on enough soup stock or canned bouillon to cover. (This should take slightly more than 2 cups.) Cover the pan and simmer over a slow fire until all the liquid is absorbed and the rice is almost dry. Then top it with butter and serve. Makes 4 servings.

◆ Risotto à la Ratto

> 1 small yellow onion, chopped
> 2 tablespoons butter or margarine
> 1 cup uncooked white rice
> 4 cups clear chicken broth
> 1 can (4 oz.) button mushrooms
>   Salt to taste
> ½ teaspoon saffron
> ½ cup grated Parmesan-type cheese

Sauté onion in butter until transparent but not brown. Add rice and stir until each grain is coated with the butter. Add 1 cup boiling chicken broth and cook, uncovered, over low fire, stirring frequently, until rice has absorbed liquid. Repeat process with remaining broth, adding 1 cup at a time as rice absorbs it. (This will take about 20 minutes.) Add mushrooms and salt, then stir in saffron which has been dissolved in 1 tablespoon hot water or broth. Cook 5 minutes longer. Blend in the grated cheese, and serve at once. Makes 4 servings.

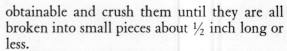

◆ Cowboy Corn

  ¼ pound bacon or salt pork, diced
  2 cans (1 lb. each) whole kernel corn
  1 green pepper, finely chopped
    Onion, celery, garlic, chili powder, and
      pepper to taste

Fry the bacon or salt pork lightly. Drain the juice from the canned corn and save this liquor to use later. Dump the corn into the hot skillet and let it sizzle for two or three minutes before stirring. Drop into this the green pepper (or red pepper if you want it hot) and other seasonings.

When everything is mixed thoroughly, empty the corn liquor into the pan. If this doesn't furnish enough moisture, add fresh or evaporated milk. Let it simmer, with a top on the pan, until liquid substances have almost disappeared. With tortillas replacing silverware, you'll have a real taste treat. Makes 6 servings.

◆ Sautéed Corn

  6 medium-sized ears corn
  3 tablespoons butter or margarine
  ¼ cup (4 tablespoons) light cream
    Salt and pepper

Cut raw corn from the cob. Melt butter in a heavy frying pan; add corn, and stirring constantly, sauté until it begins to brown. Add cream and salt and pepper to taste. Heat thoroughly but do not allow to boil. Makes 4 servings.

◆ Mexican Beans

  2 cups pinto beans
  1½ cloves garlic
  2 medium onions, chopped
  3 green peppers
  2 teaspoons salt
  ½ teaspoon black pepper
  1 tablespoon bacon fat

Wash beans; place in a heavy kettle with water; cover, bring to a boil, and simmer 2 minutes. Remove from heat and let soak 1 hour.

Put fat in skillet; add chopped onion, garlic, peppers, salt and pepper; let cook 5 minutes; then add to beans in pot with enough water to cover. Let boil slowly until thoroughly soft, but not mushy. Add hot water if necessary during the cooking. Warm up or finish cooking on the grill. Makes 6 servings.

◆ Potato Pancakes

  6 medium-sized raw potatoes
  1 onion
  2 eggs, beaten
  2 tablespoons flour
  1 tablespoon milk
  1 teaspoon salt
    Pepper
    Oil or bacon drippings

Grate the potatoes and onion; mix in the eggs, flour, milk, salt, and pepper, and add a little oil or bacon drippings. Shape into flat cakes 2 or 3 inches across, and pan-fry to a golden brown. Makes 6 servings.

◆ Peas and Carrots
a la Nivernaise

  ¼ pound butter
  3 pounds fresh peas, shelled
  12 very small white onions or the white
      bulbs of green onions
    Small, pale inner leaves of 2 bunches of
      Boston or butter lettuce, cut in strips
  6 baby carrots, cut in ½-inch slices
  ½ cup water
  ½ teaspoon sugar
  ½ teaspoon salt
  1 cup light cream

Put butter in a saucepan with the peas, onions, lettuce, carrots, water, sugar, and salt. Cover and cook over low heat for 30 minutes, or until the vegetables are tender. In the meantime, simmer the cream until it is reduced one-half. Arrange the carrots and onions around the edge of a dish, add the cream to the peas and lettuce, and pour in the center of the dish. Makes 6 servings.

◆ Barbecue Style Peas

Here is a method of serving tender young peas that we think will go over well at your next barbecue.

> 2 pounds fresh green peas
> ½ cup boiling water
> ½ teaspoon salt
> ½ teaspoon sugar
> ½ cup (¼ pound) melted butter or margarine

Wash pea pods thoroughly, then place in a saucepan with the water, salt, and sugar. Cover and cook on the grill just until peas are tender, about 10 minutes. (Peas cook in the pod more quickly than when shelled. If overcooked, the pods will open.) Divide the melted butter among 6 tall cordial glasses, or any small slender glasses available. Heat glasses or stand them in hot water until ready to use so that the butter will remain melted.

Pass the cooked unshelled peas in a large bowl, or serve in individual bowls. You dip the pods into the melted butter and then suck the peas into your mouth, much as you eat cocktail tamales. Provide a basket or some container for the discarded pods. Makes 6 servings.

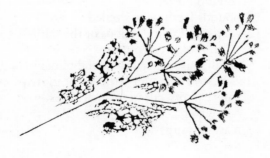

◆ Sautéed Pea Pods

Wash ½ pound of Chinese edible pea pods and break off the stem end. Put 1 tablespoon oil in a small disposable foil pan, add pods, and sauté over the barbecue coals for about 8 minutes, or until crisp-tender, turning occasionally. Makes 2 servings.

◆ Sautéed Carrots Chateau

> 1 tablespoon butter or other shortening
> 2 cups carrots, diced and cooked until tender
> 1½ cups California Tokay or Angelica
> 2 tablespoons lemon juice
> Salt and pepper to taste

Melt butter in frying pan and allow carrots to sauté slowly until slightly browned. Combine wine and lemon juice and pour over carrots. Simmer slowly until candied, and season to taste. Makes 4 servings.

◆ Onions al Greco

> 2 cans (15½ oz. each) small white onions
> 3 tablespoons butter
> 1 cup chicken stock
> 2 tablespoons white wine vinegar
> ½ cup seedless raisins
> 4 tablespoons tomato paste
> 2 tablespoons salad oil
> ½ teaspoon salt
> 2 drops Tabasco
> ¼ teaspoon thyme

Drain onions. Sauté them in butter in a 10-inch frying pan over medium heat for 5 minutes. Combine chicken stock, vinegar, raisins, tomato paste, salad oil, salt, Tabasco, and thyme; pour over the onions. Cover and simmer for 25 to 30 minutes. Serve hot from pan or serving dish. Makes 6 servings.

◆ Chili Fandango

> 2 bell peppers
> ¼ pound sliced bacon, diced
> 1 onion, minced
> 1 clove garlic, minced
> 4 large tomatoes, peeled and diced
> ¼ teaspoon salt

Toast bell peppers over coals until black. Scrape off black skins, and cut each pepper into 3 or 4 pieces. Fry bacon, onion, and garlic together until crisp and brown. Add peppers, tomatoes, and salt. Cook slowly in covered pan for 35 minutes. Makes 6 servings.

◆ Colache

1 pound summer squash
4 ears of corn
3 tomatoes
1 small onion, finely chopped
¼ cup butter
Salt and pepper

Dice or slice squash; cut corn off cob (or use canned). Peel and dice tomatoes (or use canned). Sauté onion in butter, add vegetables. Season to taste. Cover, and cook outside at barbecue for 30 to 35 minutes, while meat is cooking. Stir occasionally so vegetables won't burn. Makes 6 servings.

◆ Garden Bouquet

1 can (1 lb. 13 oz.) tomatoes
1 tablespoon butter ·
Salt and pepper to taste
1 tablespoon sugar
1 cup celery
3 tablespoons parsley (packed)

Heat tomatoes steaming hot, not boiling. Add butter, salt, pepper, and sugar. Last, add the celery, chopped fine, and chopped parsley. Serve at once. Makes 4 servings.

◆ Zucchini Skillet Stew

¼ cup butter or salad oil
1½ pounds zucchini, cut in 1-inch pieces
3 green peppers, cut in pieces ¾ inch square
2 large onions, sliced into rings ¼ inch thick
1 can (1 lb.) stewed tomatoes
Salt and pepper

Heat butter or salad oil in large frying pan. Add zucchini, green peppers, and onions. Sauté over medium heat about 15 minutes, stirring. Add tomatoes. Cover and simmer, stirring occasionally, about 15 minutes or until vegetables are tender. Add salt and pepper to taste. Makes 6 servings.

◆ Tomatoes and Peppers

Wash bell peppers (allow 2 or 3 per person) and soak in ice water for an hour; then dice in about inch squares, discarding the coarse membrane and seeds. Cook in several tablespoons of hot olive oil until soft and slightly browned. Pour off all excess oil and add as much peeled and chopped tomatoes as there are peppers. Season with salt and pepper. Push to back of grill and cook slowly for 20 to 30 minutes. Serve as a side dish with barbecued meats.

SALADS

The best possible complement to barbecued meat is a crisp, cool salad, skillfully torn and tossed, deftly seasoned. The dressing may be varied by the addition of such seasonings as toasted sesame seeds, anchovy paste, or minced herbs. Fruits and vegetables, either raw or cooked, may be tossed into the salad to add color and texture. The list is endless—tomatoes, sweet onion, green pepper, radishes, diced avocado, and cucumbers are some of the most common additions. Some more unusual ones you may wish to try are raw or slightly cooked asparagus tips, sliced raw or cooked mushrooms, artichoke hearts, grated raw beets, hearts of palm, seedless grapes, or sliced apple.

◆ Tomato and Herb Salad

Slice firm tomatoes into medium-thick slices and spread on a large platter. Anoint with a few drops of olive oil and wine vinegar, then sprinkle thickly with chopped herbs—parsley, chives, tarragon, basil, dill, and any others of your choice. Chill thoroughly. This salad can be made well in advance of the barbecue. Store in refrigerator.

◆ Barbecue Salad Bowl

Paste salads take many forms, but we think this is a most unusual one. If you're fond of raisins, include them for the sweetness they add to the rather tart salad combination.

    1 small can (2 oz.) stuffed green olives
    1 cup mayonnaise
    ¼ cup wine vinegar
    2 teaspoons sugar
    1 teaspoon chili powder
      Pinch of cayenne
    ½ teaspoon salt
    ¼ teaspoon pepper
    ½ package (14-oz. size) shell macaroni,
        cooked and drained
    1 can (1 lb.) garbanzos
    1 can (6 or 7 oz.) flaked tuna
    ½ cup raisins (optional)
    1 dill pickle, chopped
    6 green onions, sliced
    ½ cup chopped parsley
    1 clove garlic, minced or mashed
      Crisp greens
    2 tablespoons capers

Drain liquid from olives (retain olives for use later), and combine with mayonnaise, vinegar, sugar, chili powder, cayenne, salt, and pepper. Toss dressing with macaroni, garbanzos, tuna, raisins, pickle, onions, parsley, and garlic. Heap into a salad bowl lined with crisp greens; garnish with halved stuffed olives and capers. Makes 8 servings.

◆ Tossed Cauliflower Salad

    1 medium-sized head of cauliflower
    ½ cup French dressing
    1 small avocado
    ½ cup sliced stuffed green olives
    3 tomatoes, cut in eighths
    ½ cup Roquefort cheese, crumbled
      Crisp greens

Separate cauliflower into flowerets; cover with ice water and chill 1 hour; drain. Chop cauliflower coarsely; pour French dressing and let stand 2 hours. Just before serving, dice avocado and add to salad along with olives, tomatoes, and cheese. Toss lightly; serve on crisp greens. Makes 8 servings.

◆ Mixed Vegetable Salad

    3 large bunches romaine
    6 large heads lettuce
    1 large bunch celery, sliced
    2 packages (10 oz.) frozen peas, cooked
        and chilled
    1 bunch carrots, shredded
    1 bunch radishes, sliced, or 4 tomatoes,
        cut in wedges
    1 pint French dressing

Tear romaine and lettuce into pieces; add celery, peas, carrots, and radishes. Toss with dressing before serving. Makes 24 servings.

◆ Cabbage Salad for a Crowd

     6 firm cabbages, shredded
     6 medium onions, shredded
    16 carrots (approximately), shredded
     1 teaspoon celery seed
     1 jar (8 oz.) sweet pickle relish
       French dressing
       Mayonnaise
       Salt and garlic salt to taste
       Chopped ripe olives, parsley, and
          paprika for garnish

Mix vegetables, celery seed, and relish thoroughly, and marinate in French dressing for about 30 minutes. Drain and add mayonnaise to your liking, then season with salt and garlic salt to taste. Arrange in large bowl and garnish with chopped ripe olives, parsley, and paprika. Makes about 30 servings.

◆ Mix-Your-Own Salad

Provide a small salad bowl for each guest. Also set out assorted salad ingredients: greens, including romaine, cress, raw spinach, and lettuce; some cheeses, perhaps, blue, jack, and Cheddar; and some cold meats such as tongue, ham, and turkey. Hard-cooked eggs, capers, croutons, pickles, olives, anchovies, tuna, and sardines are optional. Onions and garlic are a must, and a variety of salad dressings, as well as oil and vinegar, will be needed. And for creative salad makers, provide an assortment of fresh or dried herbs.

◆ Bean and Celery Salad

This hearty salad—a mixture of kidney beans, celery, and olives—is good with a barbecue dinner.

    1 medium can (1 lb.) kidney beans
    2 cups sliced celery
    1 small onion, finely chopped
    2 tablespoons sliced stuffed olives
    ½ teaspoon salt
      Freshly ground pepper to taste
    3 tablespoons mayonnaise
    2 tablespoons evaporated milk
    1 teaspoon tarragon vinegar
    1 teaspoon sugar
      Dash each salt, garlic salt, and paprika
    1 hard-cooked egg

Drain juice from beans and rinse them with cold water. Toss beans lightly with celery, onion, stuffed olives, salt, and pepper to taste. Chill.

When ready to serve the salad, mix together mayonnaise, milk, vinegar, sugar, salt, garlic salt, and paprika. Pour over beans, fold together, and garnish with the hard-cooked egg you have sliced or chopped. Makes 4 to 6 servings.

RELISHES AND SIDE DISHES

Relishes are the taste-tantalizing side dishes that perk up any meal and add color and interest to the barbecue table. The central idea is variety—in color, texture, and flavor. And, of course, the relishes that you serve must complement the dishes that comprise the main part of the meal.

◆ Caraway-Garlic Pickled Beets

    24 small young beets
     2 teaspoons salt
     6 cups water
     4 cups cider vinegar
    1½ cups brown sugar, firmly packed
     2 teaspoons whole caraway seeds
     8 cloves garlic, cut in half

Scrub and trim beets, leaving on part of stem and all of root; then cook, covered, in boiling salted water for 45 minutes, or until tender. Cool beets in liquid; peel and cut into lengths the size of matchsticks. Return beet strips to pan with 4 cups of the cooking liquid; pour in vinegar, and add brown sugar, stirring until dissolved. Season with caraway seeds and garlic. Bring mixture to a full boil, simmer for 2 minutes, then dip out beets with slotted spoon and pack into sterilized jars, making certain to include 2 pieces of garlic and some caraway seeds in each jar. Boil liquid, then pour over beets; seal jars. Makes 4 pints.

The flavor improves as you let these tiny beets marinate in the caraway seed-garlic mixture. Toss the beets in a salad for a blaze of color, or serve with cuts of lamb or beef.

◆ Barbecue Potato Chips

To heat potato chips pile them in a wire popcorn popper and shake on garlic salt. Shake popper gently over the grill until the potato chips are hot and crisp. Then sprinkle with grated Parmesan cheese.

◆ Pickled Onion Relish

The mild-flavored, yellow-skinned sweet Spanish onion is your best choice for this relish. When the red Bermudas are in season, you might select them because of their bright color and mild flavor.

    4 large onions, thinly sliced
    ½ cup water
    1 cup vinegar
    1 tablespoon sugar
    ¼ cup (4 tablespoons) mayonnaise
    1½ teaspoons celery seed
    Salt

Place sliced onions in a shallow dish. Pour over the water and vinegar and sprinkle with the sugar; cover and chill for 4 hours. When you are ready to serve, drain the onions and mix together lightly with the mayonnaise, celery seed, and salt to taste. Makes 6 servings.

◆ Green Tomato Barbecue Relish

    2 cups ground green tomatoes (approximately 4 to 5)
    2 cups ground peeled cucumbers (approximately 2 medium-sized)
    2 cups ground onions (approximately 4 medium-sized)
    3 medium-sized tart apples, peeled and ground
    1 green pepper, seeded and ground
    2 small sweet red peppers, seeded and ground
    1 quart (4 cups) water
    1½ tablespoons salt
    2 cups sugar
    2 cups cider vinegar
    1 tablespoon mustard seed
    6 tablespoons flour
    1 tablespoon dry mustard
    ¼ teaspoon turmeric

Mix together in a large kettle the prepared green tomatoes, cucumbers, onions, apples, green pepper, red peppers, water, and salt. Let stand for 24 hours; drain. Add sugar, 1½ cups of the vinegar, and mustard seed; bring to a boil. Make a paste of flour, dry mustard, and turmeric with the remaining ½ cup vinegar, and stir into boiling mixture. Stirring occasionally, simmer for 1½ hours. Pour into hot sterilized jars and seal immediately. Makes 4 pints.

◆ Savory Butters

It is a good idea to make up several jars of flavorful butters and store them in the freezer, ready to serve with broiled steaks, hamburgers, fish, roast corn, potatoes, onions.

PARSLEY-LEMON BUTTER, called *maitre d'hotel* in *haute cuisine,* is butter creamed with finely minced parsley and lemon juice. It does wonderful things for hamburgers, is almost a must with fish, and is good with steaks, chops, and liver.

GREEN BUTTER, or *beurre vert,* is butter creamed with pounded or extra well-minced parsley, chives, and sometimes other herbs. It is good with oysters roasted in the shell, and with broiled fish and charcoal-roasted lamb.

ANCHOVY BUTTER, which is butter mixed with anchovy paste, is extra good with broiled chops and steak, though it's good with fish, too. Try it with a roast of veal for a taste sensation.

HERB BUTTER lets you play your own tune. Cream butter with any herb or combination of herbs you choose, but remember not to overdo it. The fine herbs (*fines herbes*) are always safe: parsley, chives, tarragon, and sometimes chervil. To these may be added marjoram or thyme. This butter is used successfully for broiled chicken or turkey, and is good with roasted potatoes. Rosemary butter is nice with·lamb chops, or with steak or fish. And oregano butter is delicious with corn or broiled tomatoes.

BERCY BUTTER, made with chopped shallots or green onions, is delightful on French bread and on corn. It's also good on steaks, chops, and broiled lobsters.

CHILI BUTTER, made with chili powder, butter, and a drop of wine vinegar, seems to go particularly well with thick charcoal-broiled pork chops, or with roast corn or hamburgers.

GARLIC BUTTER is so well known it is almost superfluous to mention it, but we do want to remind you that it has other uses than a spread for bread. Try it with London Broil (broiled flank steak), grilled kidneys, or hamburgers. Try it on baked potatoes, too.

BREADS

Hot buttered French bread—with or without garlic—is a reliable stand-by for outdoor meals. For variety, however, you may wish to dress up your French bread in one of the ways described here. Rolls, rye, nut, and fruit breads are also delicious accompaniments to an outdoor meal.

◆ Grilled French Bread

Cut sour French bread in half lengthwise and toast over the hot embers. Melt butter in shallow pan and dip the toasted bread into it.

VARIATION FOR GARLIC EATERS
Mince garlic and work into soft butter—spread on toasted French bread.

◆ Rye Bread with Eschalots

    2 bunches eschalots, or 1 bunch green
       onions and 1 bunch chives
    1 loaf rye bread (about 20 thin slices)
    ¼ pound butter or margarine

Chop eschalots fine. Spread rye bread generously with butter that has been well creamed first. Then sprinkle each slice with the chopped eschalots and pile bread back in loaf form.

Wrap first in wax paper, then in aluminum foil, and steam in oven at 275° for about 1½ hours—a little longer or shorter time will not matter. Serve very hot.

◆ Venetian Loaf

This treatment gives French bread a distinctly Italian flavor.

    1 long loaf French Bread
    ½ cup softened butter or margarine
    ½ cup grated Parmesan cheese
    2 tablespoons olive oil
    ½ cup finely chopped parsley
    1 clove garlic, finely chopped
    ½ teaspoon sweet basil
       Salt to taste

Slash loaf of French bread crosswise in thick slices, cutting down to but not through the bottom crust. Blend butter and remaining ingredients together; spread between slices of bread. Wrap loaf in waxed paper or aluminum foil. Bake in a moderately hot oven (375°) for 15 to 20 minutes or until piping hot.

◆ French Bread Monterey

Parmesan cheese, mayonnaise, and onion make a really robust loaf.

    1 long loaf French bread
       Softened butter or margarine
    1 cup mayonnaise
    ½ cup grated Parmesan cheese
    ½ cup ground or finely chopped onion
    ½ teaspoon Worcestershire
       Paprika

Cut loaf of French bread lengthwise in halves. Spread cut surfaces with butter. Place in oven to heat through. Meantime, mix all remaining ingredients except paprika; spread mixture on the hot bread; dust with paprika. Broil slowly until delicately browned. Cut crosswise.

◆ Hot Herb Bread

The bread is sourdough French, split the long way and toasted. For 2 big loaves, cream ½ pound butter, ¾ cup each minced chives and parsley, and ¼ cup minced sweet basil. Spread the bread while it is hot. Cut in 2-inch pieces. Makes 12 servings.

◆ Crusty Rolls with Lemon-Parsley Butter

¼ pound softened butter or margarine
1 tablespoon lemon juice
2 tablespoons finely chopped parsley
6 large French rolls

Blend together the butter, lemon juice, and parsley. Split rolls in half lengthwise and spread each half with the butter mixture. Place the halves together again and wrap each roll individually in aluminum foil. Place on the barbecue grill for 10 to 15 minutes, or until hot; turn once or twice. Or place in a moderately hot oven (375°) for 15 minutes.

◆ Pastel De Elote

This can be served as a bread in lieu of the usual garlic bread at barbecues. You may make it in advance and reheat before serving.

½ pound butter or margarine
1 cup sugar
4 eggs
1 can (4 oz.) green chili peppers
1 can (1 lb.) cream style golden bantam corn
½ cup grated jack cheese
½ cup grated Tillamook cheese
¼ teaspoon salt
1 cup flour
1 cup yellow cornmeal
4 teaspoons baking powder

Cream butter and add sugar. Add eggs, one at a time, mixing in well. Chop peppers and add. Add corn and mix well. Add cheeses and pinch of salt. Sift flour and then measure; sift corn-meal and then measure; sift both together with baking powder and add to previous mixture. Pour into greased and floured glass baking dish (8 by 12 by 2 inches). Preheat oven at 350°. Reduce heat to 300° and bake for one hour. Makes 10 servings.

◆ Toasted Herb Roll in Loaf

1 loaf unsliced milk bread
¾ cup butter
¼ teaspoon salt
¼ teaspoon paprika
¼ teaspoon savory
½ teaspoon thyme
Cayenne
Other herbs as desired

Remove crusts from bread and slice through center lengthwise; then cut crosswise into about 2-inch squares—but not quite through. Spread with above mixture; tie loaf together and let stand. Heat in a slow oven (300°) 30 minutes or until it is warmed through. (Serve with *extra* paper napkins.)

◆ Corn Barbecue Rolls

2 cups flour
¾ teaspoon salt
4 teaspoons baking powder
4 tablespoons shortening
1 egg, beaten
⅔ to 1 cup milk
1 can (12 oz.) whole kernel corn
Melted butter
Paprika

Mix the dry ingredients and work in shortening. Add beaten egg and milk; mix to a soft dough. Place on a floured board, roll to ½-inch thickness, spread with drained corn, and brush over with melted butter.

Roll as for jelly roll and cut with a sharp knife into ½ to 1-inch slices. Place the slices, cut side down, on a cooky sheet, and dust with paprika. Bake in a 425° oven for about 15 minutes. Serve with country gravy, or simply as a bread with lots of butter. Makes 6 to 8 rolls.

◆ Photo Guide to Barbecuing

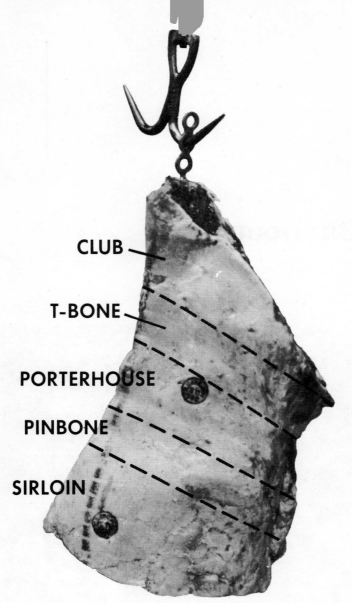

CLUB

T-BONE

PORTERHOUSE

PINBONE

SIRLOIN

LOIN OF BEEF is most tender and most expensive of major beef cuts. From it are taken the five steaks pictured on these two pages: sirloin, pinbone, porterhouse, T-bone, and club. Steaks shown were cut 1½ inches thick—the size most cooks prefer for grilling.

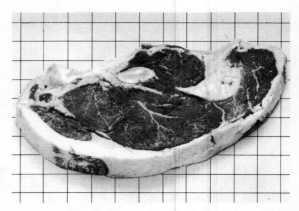

SIRLOIN is family-size steak. It includes a fairly large section of tenderloin, a large section of loin, and a small amount of bone. It is sometimes boned to make New York steaks and choice *filet mignon*.

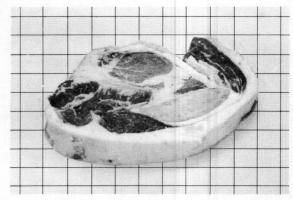

PINBONE has largest tenderloin, but it also has largest amount of bone so costs less per pound. It is sometimes called a hip steak because of the oval-shaped pin (or hip) bone in it.

PORTERHOUSE is a choice steak because it contains a good-sized tenderloin. It is sometimes sold as T-bone —only difference between it and the usual T-bone is that tenderloin is larger.

SEVENTEEN STEAKS above were cut from the loin pictured on the opposite page. From left to right are: sirloin, pinbone, porterhouse, T-bone, club. Weights range from 3 lbs. 15¼ oz. for the sirloin in left foreground to 1 lb. 2 oz. for the small club steak in the right foreground. Each steak was cut 1½ inches thick.

T-BONE steaks from the second third of short loin are named for the shape of the bone. As each steak is removed from the loin, the tenderloin (the meat below the bone) gets smaller until it almost disappears.

CLUB steaks, which have little or no tenderloin, make up the balance of the short loin. This is an individual steak unless cut very thick. If the tail is left on, it is called a short-cut steak.

131

STEAK ON THE COALS (recipe on page 22) is dramatic way to impress your guests! Most of the time, you'll place your steak carefully, but for occasional startling effect, just walk up and throw it on the fire.

Steak does not burn if fire is right—2 to 3 inches of glowing coals with minimum of ash on top. Bed of coals should be big enough so steak can go on new area when it is turned to cook the second side.

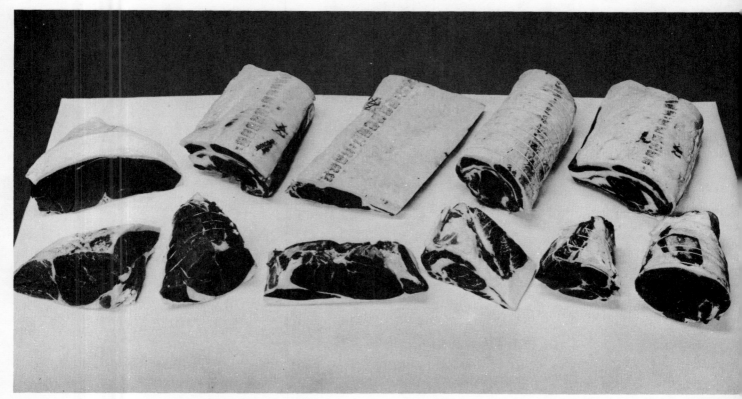

ELEVEN BEEF ROASTS that you can roast on a spit or in a Chinese oven. From left to right: (top row) top round, Spencer, New York strip, rolled rib, standing rib; (bottom row) rump, sirloin tip, top sirloin, mar-ket ("eye" of the rib), double tenderloin, and cross rib. Cost varies widely—lowest for rump and cross rib, highest for tenderloin and New York strip. Price depends on quality, amount of fat and bone, tenderness.

TERIYAKI-FLAVORED flank steak strips in basket holder broil quickly over very hot coals; steaks turn crisp brown on the outside but remain juicy pink inside. See pages 24-25 for Beef Teriyaki recipe.

ECONOMICAL CHUCK STEAK, treated with meat tenderizer, grills to perfection. Turn with tongs or use wide spatula to avoid loss of juices. Tenderest chuck steak is first one cut from area next to rib section.

GARLIC STEAKS, each within a pastry crust, brown and cook on the grill (recipe, page 23). Vegetables keep warm in skillet over the same glowing coals.

TO MAKE STEAK TURNOVERS shown at left, place steak on half of thin pastry oval, moisten pastry edges, fold dough over steak, seal edges. Prick top with fork.

BEEF TERIYAKI (page 24) may be sliced in strips, to be eaten with chopsticks in Oriental fashion, or it may be left whole for fork eating. Use a boneless cut, or bone meat into serving-size pieces before you broil it.

134

1. STARTING THE FIRE. "Kindle can" is 2-pound coffee can with top and bottom removed. Use beer can opener to bend down legs (see page 10).

2. STOKING THE FIRE. Kindle can has been removed with tongs. Put more coals around edge of pilot fire, but not on top. Wait 15 minutes longer before cooking.

3. GETTING READY TO COOK. Rake bed of coals flat, put grill in place, grease grill with piece of fat or brush with oil or melted fat so meat won't stick.

4. FIRE FIGHTING. Lettuce leaf is useful for dousing flame. Other possibilities are water pistol, syringe, sprinkler. Raise grill if it is too close to fire.

PHOTO GUIDE TO BARBECUING **135**

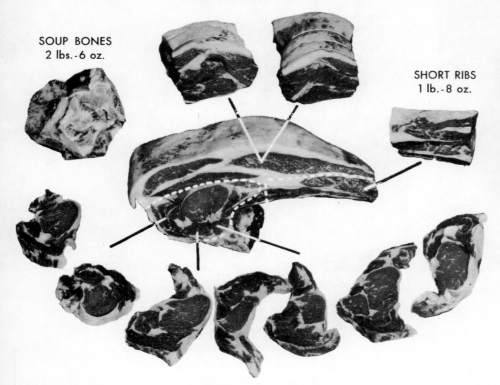

SOUP BONES
2 lbs.-6 oz.

2 POT ROASTS - 4 lbs.-12 oz.

SHORT RIBS
1 lb.-8 oz.

7 MARKET STEAKS - 3 lbs.

SHORT RIBS can be skewered or cooked right on the grill. This is a self-basting cut of meat because it has streaks of fat running through it.

RIB ROAST PLAN NUMBER 1. Seven delicious market steaks, 1 long-rolled pot roast or two small ones, short ribs, and a variety of meaty soup bones were cut from a 10-inch rib roast weighing 13 lbs. 4 oz.

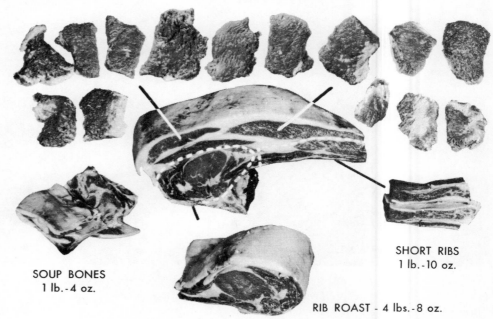

CUBE STEAKS - 3 lbs.-6 oz.

SHORT RIBS
1 lb.-10 oz.

SOUP BONES
1 lb.-4 oz.

RIB ROAST - 4 lbs.-8 oz.

RIB ROAST PLAN NUMBER 2. A good-sized rib roast which includes only tender "eye" meat, 14 cube steaks, meaty short ribs, and soup bones were cut from 2-rib, full-length standing rib roast weighing 12 lbs.

1. CHUCK ROAST (see Chuck Roast Teriyaki, page 28) is flavorful and inexpensive meat for barbecuing. Trim away all bone and fat, then tie as shown below.

2. TWO ROASTS shown at left produced these individual pieces of lean, boneless beef. Save the trimmings, too; they can be used to make a good, rich soup stock.

3. REASSEMBLE BEEF. Tie pieces with heavy cord at 1-inch intervals. Roast has no bone or gristle to hold it together, so must depend on strength of cord.

4. READY FOR MARINATING in teriyaki sauce. Two roasts weighing a total of 7½ pounds produced exactly 4½ pounds of boneless meat, enough to serve 8.

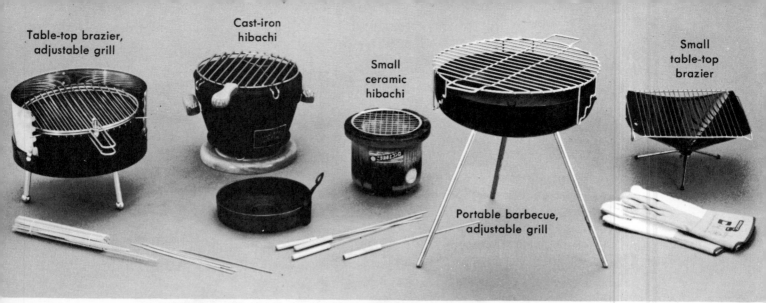

Table-top brazier, adjustable grill

Cast-iron hibachi

Small ceramic hibachi

Portable barbecue, adjustable grill

Small table-top brazier

MINIATURE BARBECUES shown above and opposite include American-made braziers and a bucket-style cooker as well as Japanese hibachis. Grill sizes vary from about 5 inches in diameter on the smallest hibachi to 16 inches on the largest portable brazier shown. Many braziers are designed so grill may be raised or lowered. Hibachis do not have adjustable grills; they are heavier, but hold the heat longer.

IN THE LIVING ROOM, small ceramic hibachis are used in more formal setting. Guests select and grill their own appetizers—tiny kebabs on bamboo skewers.

ON A PICNIC, miniature barbecue is used to cook bouillabaisse. The sauce can be made at home and reheated, fresh fish and shellfish added on the spot.

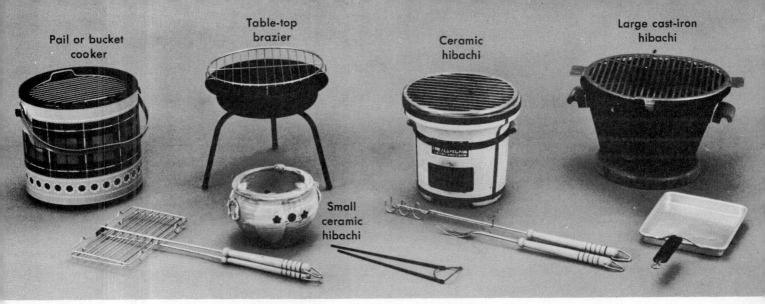

Pail or bucket cooker

Table-top brazier

Ceramic hibachi

Large cast-iron hibachi

Small ceramic hibachi

ACCESSORIES shown in front of miniature barbecues include (starting from left on opposite page): small bamboo skewers for grilling appetizers; sukiyaki pan with removable handle; metal skewers with wooden handles to grill dinner-sized kebabs; heavy gloves; hinged wire toaster; metal chopsticks (use as you would tongs for moving charcoal, hot coals); long-handled forks; rectangular skillet.

GROUND STEAK AND BANANAS have been grilled on a miniature barbecue inside fireplace. Barbecue is moved out onto raised hearth where meal is served.

SUKIYAKI in the park or your own backyard is easy to cook on a quick-heating miniature barbecue. Transport vegetables in a plastic bag to keep them crisp.

139

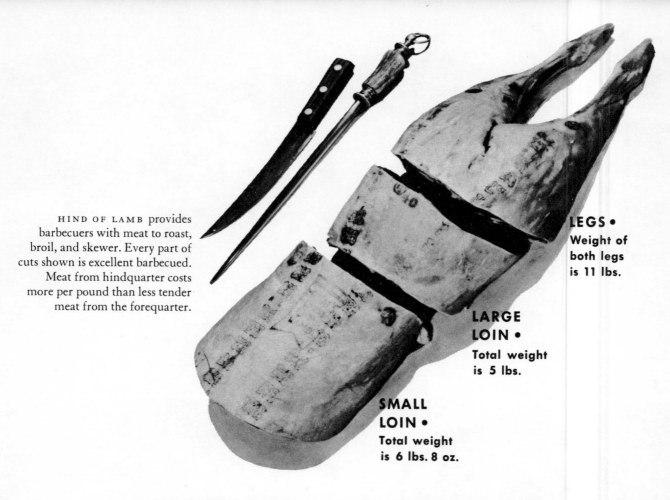

HIND OF LAMB provides barbecuers with meat to roast, broil, and skewer. Every part of cuts shown is excellent barbecued. Meat from hindquarter costs more per pound than less tender meat from the forequarter.

LEGS •
Weight of both legs is 11 lbs.

LARGE LOIN •
Total weight is 5 lbs.

SMALL LOIN •
Total weight is 6 lbs. 8 oz.

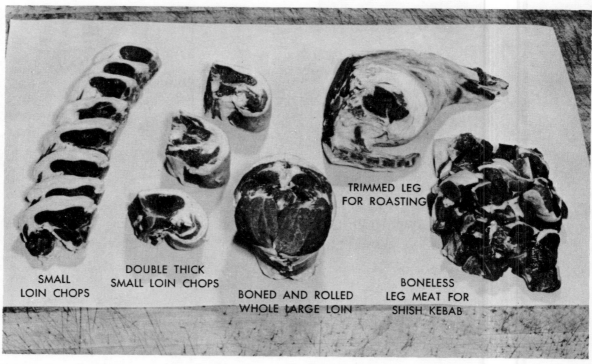

SMALL LOIN CHOPS

DOUBLE THICK SMALL LOIN CHOPS

BONED AND ROLLED WHOLE LARGE LOIN

TRIMMED LEG FOR ROASTING

BONELESS LEG MEAT FOR SHISH KEBAB

CUTS FROM HIND OF LAMB pictured at top of page: eight 1-inch-thick loin chops, weighing about 6¼ ounces each; double-thick, individual lamb chop roasts, weighing almost a pound apiece; whole large loin, boned and rolled; leg trimmed for roasting; meat from other leg cut into squares for skewering.

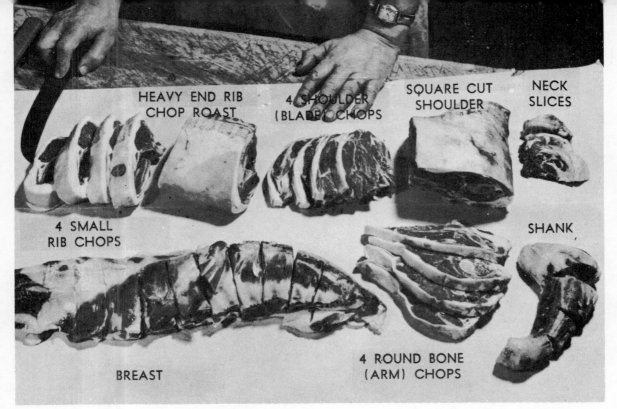

HEAVY END RIB
CHOP ROAST

4 SHOULDER
(BLADE) CHOPS

SQUARE CUT
SHOULDER

NECK
SLICES

4 SMALL
RIB CHOPS

SHANK

BREAST

4 ROUND BONE
(ARM) CHOPS

FOREQUARTER OF LAMB has been cut in one of several ways suitable for the barbecue. From a forequarter weighing 12 to 15 pounds, a family of two can get 7 hearty meals with plenty of extra meaty chops, breast of lamb for guests. Rib rack and shoulder pieces could have been left uncut to be roasted on the spit.

LARGE LEG OF LAMB, weighing 7½ pounds, is cut into 11 steaks about ¾ inch thick for individual servings (see recipe for Barbecued Lamb Steaks, page 35).

BONED LEG OF LAMB is skewered before barbecuing to keep it flat during cooking and make it easy to turn over. Recipe is given on page 34.

141

1. BONED LAMB ROAST (page 34) gets added flavor from bacon rolls inserted in meat. Bacon slices are sprinkled with onion and herbs, rolled, cut in half.

2. INSERT BACON ROLLS in cut side of roast. Make three or four deep incisions in the thickest parts of the meat; insert bacon roll well down into meat.

3. BRING CORNERS of boned roast into center, overlapping them and holding them firmly in place with skewers. Make compact piece with no exposed ends.

4. CARVING THE BONED ROAST is easy. Here it is done at table near barbecue and served directly onto each plate. A 6 to 7-pound leg will serve 8 to 10.

LAMB STEAKS, cut from leg of lamb (see photo, page 141), cook over medium coals. Baste steaks with garlic sauce, using rosemary twigs for baster.

PEKING LAMB (page 36) grills on brazier with sheet of expanded steel on top to keep small pieces from falling into fire; guests watch and turn own pieces.

PORK CUTS for barbecuing: (back row) fresh ham, loin, spareribs; (front row) shoulder, loin chops, sausage, smoked ham steak. Leg, shoulder, and loin take slow roasting to cook properly. Parboil the sausage before grilling. The ham steak, right foreground, can be grilled right over the coals.

SPLIT BROILERS, grilled over glowing coals, are served here with corn (cooked over the same fire) and sliced tomatoes with Roquefort dressing. Baste broilers often while they are cooking.

CHARCOAL-BROILED DUCKLING, brushed with honey and soy, is a special barbecue treat. Here it is served with an exotic rice casserole—cooked rice tossed with raisins, slivered toasted almonds, and sliced pimientos.

1. TO BONE TURKEY HALF (recipe on page 42), first cut through joint to remove drumstick. Next remove flat wing with wing tip, cutting through joint.

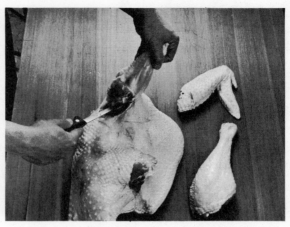

2. REMOVE WING DRUM by cutting through joint where upper section of wing joins body. Cut away as little of the breast meat as possible.

3. USING SHORT-BLADED, sharp-pointed knife, start at back bone to cut meat from carcass. Use thumb to ease out meat from concave sections of back.

4. TO FREE upper thigh bone from carcass, grasp, lift, and twist until it snaps. Sever joint (leave bone in) and continue to strip meat from rib cage.

5. TURN TURKEY over. Lift feather-shaped piece, called fillet, from breast. Pull upper thigh bone through to back side, remove bone from meat.

6. SCORE DRUMSTICK and wing drum—4 lengthwise slashes in each. Marinate, then arrange meat on grill, cut side down. Put dark meat over highest heat.

145

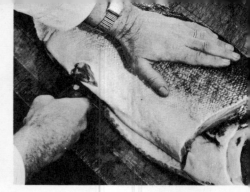

1. TO FILLET SALMON, first scale fish, then remove head, fins except near head; cut to bone behind this fin.

2. HOLD KNIFE flat; cut between bones and flesh—use a long, thin, well-sharpened knife for this job.

3. CONTINUE cutting down the backbone of the fish to the tail, keeping close to the layer of bone as you cut.

4. CAREFULLY lift the top fillet off the fish carcass and set it aside. Turn the salmon to the other side.

BARBECUED SALMON (page 48) is served buffet-style on the patio. You can have the fish filleted at the market where you buy it, or if you have caught your own fish, fillet it yourself as shown on this page.

5. CUT straight to the bone (behind the head); then cut a second fillet the same as the first one.

146

SALMON FILLETS barbecue under hood shaped of foil. They need not be turned, but baste frequently with lemon butter sauce (page 48).

FISH FILLETS and steaks can be broiled on hardware cloth so meat does not fall apart or stick to grill.

FOR A BEACH PICNIC, two whole rockfish cook over low-burning coals in hibachi. Fish is turned just once; the cooked side is kept warm by a loose wrapping of foil.

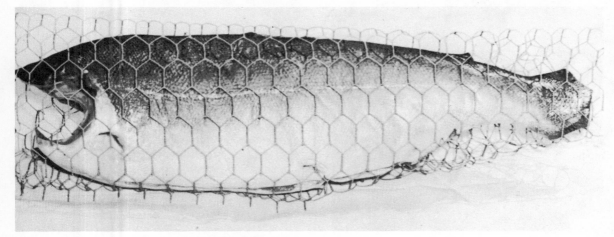

WHOLE FISH is wrapped in a chicken wire shield to keep the meat from falling off the bones during cooking. Fish such as salmon, bass, small tuna may be cooked in this way.

147

WILD BOAR, weighing 150 pounds, is shown in photo at left as it cooks on spit over temporary firepit of concrete block, and above as it is dressed for final display before guests. See page 77 for details on how it was barbecued.

SPIT-ROASTED PORK is the *pièce de résistance* of Hawaiian party. At left, it is impressive as it is removed from the spit. Above, sliced and ready to serve, it presents a beautiful picture. Sweet potatoes in orange baskets, hot from the oven, surround the meat slices. They are given a flower garnish of white marguerites stuck on toothpicks. Recipe for spit-roasted pork is given on page 76.

1. TO PREPARE boned turkey roll for spit roasting, insert meat thermometer into center of roll; do not touch end to spit. With thin wire, fasten to meat, spit.

2. BONED TURKEY ROLL roasts and browns evenly over a low bed of coals. Meat thermometer is most satisfactory way to test when meat is done.

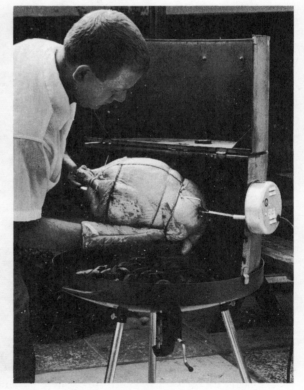

SQUABS roast to perfection on rotating spit. With toothpicks, fasten half slice of bacon over each breast.

TWO LEGS OF LAMB cook on revolving spit while foil-wrapped corn roasts on rack set on upright firebricks.

TO BALANCE TURKEY on spit, insert spit in front of tail and run it diagonally through the breastbone.

PHOTO GUIDE TO BARBECUING **149**

1. TO BONE TURKEY, cut down backbone, using short-bladed knife. Work down side, cutting flesh from bone.

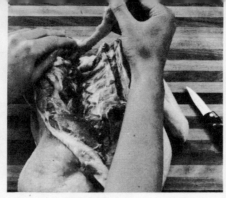

2. SLIP KNIFE along each side of projecting breast bone to cut it free. Bend backbone until it snaps at joint; remove.

3. CONTINUE DOWN one side to center of breast, cracking thigh and wing joints to sever them. Repeat on other side.

SPIT-BARBECUE the stuffed, boned turkey over moderately hot coals (see page 78). A 10-pound hen turkey, an ideal size for boning and spit-cooking, will cook in approximately 2 hours.

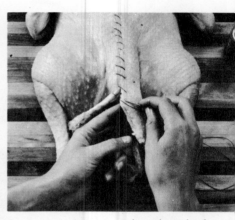

4. STITCH FLESH together along backbone, using heavy thread; stuff with a stuffing that is particularly dry.

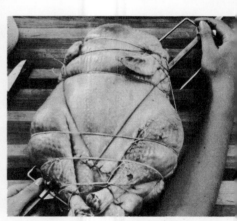

5. TRUSS BIRD with double thickness of cord. Skewer on diagonal, spitting from under thigh through opposite wing.

PIPING HOT appetizers on sticks: at top, tiny meat balls, banana; below left, bacon, pineapple, banana; right, chicken liver, bacon, mushroom.

LARGE chopping board is convenient for cutting and assembling ingredients. Shown here: roast pork, pineapple, apple; beef, pineapple, banana, papaya.

APPETIZERS designed to broil at the last minute, after being assembled earlier. Shown are: shrimp, mushroom, green pepper; frankfurter, onion, mushroom.

TO BROIL on table-top barbecue: beef, tomato, celery, green pepper; chicken, water chestnut, mushroom. See page 58 for more about combinations shown.

151

TO PREPARE VEGETABLES for skewer cooking: cut onions and unpeeled tomatoes in quarters lengthwise. Split green peppers, remove seeds, stems, and cut into eighths. Pull stems from mushroom caps.

TO RUFFLE ROUND STEAK STRIPS, start with trimmed piece of meat 1 to 1½ inches thick. Cut into thin slices across grain of the meat. Thread several strips onto skewer, dip them in soy, then grill.

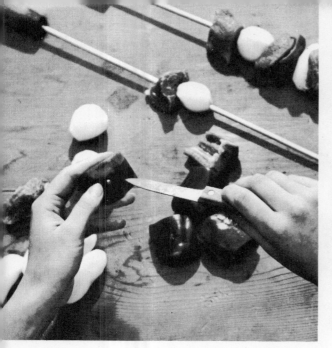

GREEN PEPPERS for shish kebab are less likely to split and fall off the skewer if you cut out a small crater at each end to act as a "pilot hole" for the skewer. This is true for other crisp vegetables, too.

GRILL LOADED SKEWERS over low coals, basting often with a marinade to suit the food. Pictured here are two of the many possible combinations: raw prawns and pork sausage, left; lamb shish kebab, right.

HERE ARE JUST A FEW of the skewer combinations that can be assembled from raw materials shown in upper half of photograph. See page 57 for descriptions of these nine skewer combinations and the three sauces used for marinating and basting.

153

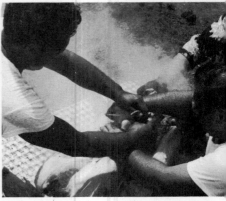

1. HAWAIIAN LUAU (page 86) featured two 130-pound pigs cooked in pit. Here, volcanic rock heats over oak fire. Fire burned for 2½ hours.

2. HOT ROCKS were shoved into leg pockets, body cavity. Have branch of wet leaves to knock out any fat fire that might flare up.

3. LEGS tied together with cords in order to hold rocks in place. Chicken wire frame brought up around pig, firmly fastened with baling wire.

4. WET TI LEAVES, tied in bundles of 10 to 15, were thrown over hot rocks in pit. Pigs, lowered on leaves, were covered with more wet leaves to give added flavor and moisture during cooking.

5. SMASHED BANANA STALKS cover leaves. These were followed by a thick coating of wet breadfruit leaves. (Corn husks, cauliflower leaves may be used instead of the banana stalks and cauliflower leaves.)

6. WET GUNNYSACKS went over heaped-up mound of leaves to protect the pigs from dirt covering, which will be added next, and to help keep any of the steam from escaping from the pit.

7. DIRT was shoveled over the sacks, starting at the outer rim first. Whole mound was sprinkled with water in order to compact the dirt and seal in all of the heat, steam, and flavor.

1. PIT-ROASTED BEEF to serve 250. Fire started at 6:30 A.M., burned 6 hours, used ½ cord of oak. Pit is 4 by 7 by 3½ feet deep, bottom covered with brick. Twenty 6 to 10-pound rolls of beef were cooked.

2. EACH ROLL gets ¼ cup of this seasoning: 1 pound each garlic and onion salt, large bottle chili powder, small can of dry mustard, ½ package poultry seasoning, ½ small can pepper, 2 tablespoons sugar.

3. FINAL ADDITIONS to each roll: 2 tablespoons of Kitchen Bouquet, 2 teaspoons salt, 2 twigs rosemary, 2 bay leaves. Rolls are then wrapped in 2-foot square of parchment paper, previously soaked in water.

4. PARCHMENT-WRAPPED rolls are then put in burlap bags, pre-soaked in water, tied with baling wire—tightened with pliers. Ready to go on the fire, rolls are wet with hose—but not soaked.

5. MEAT GOES ON COALS at 12:15 P.M. to cook for 5 hours. It must go on fast so sacks don't burn (these may be used over and over). Packages are covered with short pieces of corrugated, galvanized iron.

6. DIRT is shoveled on fast to a depth of about 1 foot. One man stays in pit to stamp down dirt (wears heavy shoes, jacket to protect arms). At 5:10 P.M., dirt is removed and rolls of meat are taken out.

155

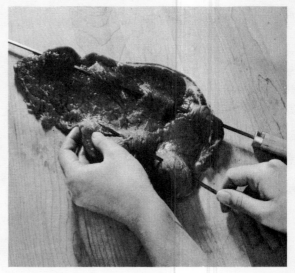

SKEWERED BEEF CHUNKS (page 63). To slice cooked chunks, put point of skewer down on board, slide chunks to tip and slice down across the grain.

SKEWERED ROUND STEAK (page 62). Weave two skewers about 1 to 1½ inches in from side edges of meat. Leave 1½ inches between each "stitch."

HIND OF LAMB, secured on tepee arrangement of poles, roasts over medium fire. Burgundy wine baste enhances flavor of lamb. Thermometer inserted in leg or loin shows when meat is ready to eat. The fire under the lamb is arranged in a triangle; center area is clear. Three logs border the coals. (Recipe page 91).

FILLETS of large fish may be cooked this way. Secure fillets between cross sticks held between two poles. Wire poles together tightly. Baste fish often.

STEAK ON A PLANK (page 90), braced upright before fire, slowly browns and cooks from one side only. The bottom side is seared first in hinged grill.

OAK BARREL COOKER has notched crosspieces to hold rods from which meat is suspended. Hooks of heavy-gauge steel wire have an added loop for finger hold.

MORE ELABORATE VERSION of barrel cooker, this one has a copper lining and an electric spit attachment. Handle operates winch to adjust fire pan inside oven.

157

ECONOMICAL SMOKE OVEN is made from portable oven with bottom removed. Oven is set on clay flue tile. To control heat, simply stack bricks at opening.

ALL IMPORTANT PRINCIPLES of Chinese oven are followed in this version. Food can be hung from hooks at top or placed on a metal grill inside the door.

IMPROVISED TENT of aluminum foil can substitute for a hood on conventional barbecue. Throw green wood, twigs, sawdust on coals to create smoke.

COMMERCIAL SMOKE COOKERS are clean and shiny, convenient to use. Most models are equipped with rubber-tired wheels. Many have spit attachment.

◆ Index

160

Photographs in this book are by the following photographers: Ernest Braun,
Clyde Childress, Glenn Christiansen, Robert Cox, Richard Dawson, Ken Patton,
Blair Stapp, Darrow Watt, R. Wenkam.